The
Gallup
Poll

Public Opinion 1986

Other Gallup Poll Publications Available from Scholarly Resources

The Gallup Poll: Public Opinion Annual Series

1985 (ISBN 0-8420-2249-X)	*1980* (ISBN 0-8420-2181-7)
1984 (ISBN 0-8420-2234-1)	*1979* (ISBN 0-8420-2170-1)
1983 (ISBN 0-8420-2220-1)	*1978* (ISBN 0-8420-2159-0)
1982 (ISBN 0-8420-2214-7)	*1972–77* (ISBN 0-8420-2129-9, 2 vols.)
1981 (ISBN 0-8420-2200-7)	*1935–71* (ISBN 0-394-47270-5, 3 vols.)

International Polls

The International Gallup Polls: Public Opinion, 1979
ISBN 0-8420-2180-9 (1981)

The International Gallup Polls: Public Opinion, 1978
ISBN 0-8420-2162-0 (1980)

The Gallup International Public Opinion Polls:
France, 1939, 1944–1975
2 volumes ISBN 0-394-40998-1 (1976)

The Gallup International Public Opinion Polls:
Great Britain, 1937–1975
2 volumes ISBN 0-394-40992-2 (1976)

The Gallup Poll

Public Opinion 1986

George Gallup, Jr.

SR *Scholarly Resources Inc.*
Wilmington, Delaware

ACKNOWLEDGMENTS

The preparation of this volume has involved the entire staff of the Gallup Poll, and their contributions are gratefully acknowledged. I particularly wish to thank James Shriver III, editor of the Gallup Poll, and Professor Fred L. Israel of the City College of New York, who was the principal coordinator.

G.G., Jr.

The paper used in this publication meets the minimum requirements of the American National Standard for permanence of paper for printed library materials, Z39.48, 1984.

© 1987 Scholarly Resources Inc.
All rights reserved
First published 1987
Printed in the United States of America

Scholarly Resources Inc.
104 Greenhill Avenue
Wilmington, DE 19805-1897

Library of Congress Catalog Card Number: 79-56557
International Standard Serial Number: 0195-962X
International Standard Book Number: 0-8420-2274-0

CONTENTS

DESIGN OF THE SAMPLE

The design of the sample used in the Gallup Poll is that of a replicated probability sample down to the block level in the case of urban areas and to segments of townships in the case of rural areas.

After stratifying the nation geographically and by size of community in order to insure conformity of the sample with the latest available estimates by the Census Bureau of the distribution of the adult population, about 350 different sampling locations or areas are selected on a strictly random basis. The interviewers have no choice whatsoever concerning the part of the city or county in which they conduct their interviews.

Interviewers are given maps of the area to which they are assigned, with a starting point indicated, and are required to follow a specified direction. At each occupied dwelling unit, interviewers are instructed to select respondents by following a prescribed systematic method. This procedure is followed until the assigned number of interviews is completed. The standard sample size for most Gallup Polls is 1500 interviews. This is augmented in specific instances where greater survey accuracy is considered desirable.

Since this sampling procedure is designed to produce a sample that approximates the adult civilian population (18 and older) living in private households in the United States (that is, excluding those in prisons and hospitals, hotels, religious institutions, and on military reservations), the survey results can be applied to this population for the purpose of projecting percentages into numbers of people. The manner in which the sample is drawn also produces a sample that approximates the population of private households in the United States. Therefore, survey results also can be projected in terms of numbers of households when appropriate.

SAMPLING TOLERANCES

It should be remembered that all sample surveys are subject to sampling error; that is, the extent to which the results may differ from what would be obtained if the whole population surveyed had been interviewed. The size of such a sampling error depends largely on the number of interviews. Increasing the sample size lessens the magnitude of possible error and vice versa.

The following tables may be used in estimating sampling error. The computed allowances (the standard deviation) have taken into account the effect of the sample design upon sampling error. They may be interpreted as indicating the range (plus or minus the figure shown) within which the results of repeated samplings in the same time period could be expected to vary, 95 percent of the time (or at a confidence level of .5), assuming the same sampling procedure, the same interviewers, and the same questionnaire.

Table A shows how much allowance should be made for the sampling error of a percentage. The table would be used in the following manner: Say a reported percentage is 33 for a group that includes 1500 respondents. Go to the row "percentage near 30" in the table and then to the column headed "1500." The number at this point is three, which means that the 33 percent obtained in the sample is subject to a sampling error of plus or minus 3 points. Another way of saying it is that very probably (95 chances out of 100) the average of repeated samplings would be somewhere between 30 and 36, with the most likely figure being the 33 obtained.

In comparing survey results in two subsamples, such as men and woman, the question arises as to how large must a difference between them be before one can be reasonably sure that it reflects a statistically significant difference. In Table B and C, the number of points that must be allowed for, in such comparisons, is indicated.

For percentages near 20 or 80, use Table B; for those near 50, Table C. For percentages in between, the error to be allowed for is between that shown in the two tables.

Here is an example of how the tables should be used: Say 50 percent of men and 40 percent of women respond the same way to a question—a difference of 10 percentage points. Can it be said with any assurance that the ten-point difference reflects a significant difference between men and women on the question? (Samples, unless otherwise noted, contain approximately 750 men and 750 women.)

Because the percentages are near 50, consult Table C. Since the two samples are about 750 persons each, look for the place in the table where the column and row labeled "750" converge. The number six appears there. This means the allowance for error should be 6 points, and the conclusion that the percentage among men is somewhere between 4 and 16 points higher than the percentage among women would be wrong only about 5 percent of the time. In other words, there is a considerable likelihood that a difference exists in the direction observed and that it amounts to at least 4 percentage points.

If, in another case, male responses amount to 22 percent, and female to 24 percent, consult Table B because these percentages are near 20. The column and row labeled "750" converge on the number five. Obviously, then, the two-point difference is inconclusive.

TABLE A

Recommended Allowance for Sampling Error of a Percentage

In Percentage Points
(at 95 in 100 confidence level)*
Size of the Sample

	3000	1500	1000	750	600	400	200	100
Percentages near 10	2	2	2	3	4	4	5	7
Percentages near 20	2	3	3	4	4	5	7	9
Percentages near 30	2	3	4	4	4	6	8	10
Percentages near 40	3	3	4	4	5	6	9	11
Percentages near 50	3	3	4	4	5	6	9	11
Percentages near 60	3	3	4	4	5	6	9	11
Percentages near 70	2	3	4	4	4	6	8	10
Percentages near 80	2	3	3	4	4	5	7	9
Percentages near 90	2	2	2	3	4	4	5	7

*The chances are 95 in 100 that the sampling error is not larger than the figures shown.

TABLE B

Recommended Allowance for Sampling Error of the Difference Between Two Subsamples

In Percentage Points
(at 95 in 100 confidence level)*

Percentages near 20 or percentages near 80

Size of the Sample	1500	750	600	400	200
1500	3				
750	4	5			
600	5	6	6		
400	6	7	7	7	
200	8	8	8	9	10

TABLE C

Percentages near 50

Size of the Sample	1500	750	600	400	200
1500	4				
750	5	6			
600	6	8	8		
400	7	8	8	9	
200	10	10	11	11	13

*The chances are 95 in 100 that the sampling error is not larger than the figures shown.

RECORD OF
GALLUP POLL ACCURACY

Year	Gallup Final Survey*		Election Result*	
1984	59.0%	Reagan	59.2%	Reagan
1982	55.0	Democratic	55.8	Democratic
1980	47.0	Reagan	50.8	Reagan
1978	55.0	Democratic	54.0	Democratic
1976	48.0	Carter	50.0	Carter
1974	60.0	Democratic	58.9	Democratic
1972	62.0	Nixon	61.8	Nixon
1970	53.0	Democratic	54.3	Democratic
1968	43.0	Nixon	43.5	Nixon
1966	52.5	Democratic	51.9	Democratic
1964	64.0	Johnson	61.3	Johnson
1962	55.5	Democratic	52.7	Democratic
1960	51.0	Kennedy	50.1	Kennedy
1958	57.0	Democratic	56.5	Democratic
1956	59.5	Eisenhower	57.8	Eisenhower
1954	51.5	Democratic	52.7	Democratic
1952	51.0	Eisenhower	55.4	Eisenhower
1950	51.0	Democratic	50.3	Democratic
1948	44.5	Truman	49.9	Truman
1946	58.0	Republican	54.3	Republican
1944	51.5	Roosevelt	53.3**	Roosevelt
1942	52.0	Democratic	48.0	Democratic
1940	52.0	Roosevelt	55.0	Roosevelt
1938	54.0	Democratic	50.8	Democratic
1936	55.7	Roosevelt	62.5	Roosevelt

*The figure shown is the winner's percentage of the Democratic-Republican vote except in the elections of 1948, 1968, and 1976. Because the Thurmond and Wallace voters in 1948 were largely split-offs from the normally Democratic vote, they were made a part of the final Gallup Poll preelection estimate of the division of the vote. In 1968 Wallace's candidacy was supported by such a large minority that he was clearly a major candidate, and the 1968 percentages are based on the total Nixon-Humphrey-Wallace vote. In 1976, because of interest in McCarthy's candidacy and its potential effect on the

Average Deviation for 24
National Elections .... 2.3 percentage points

Average Deviation for 17
National Elections
Since 1950, inclusive .... 1.5 percentage points

Trend in Deviation Reduction

Elections	Average Error
1936–48	4.0
1950–58	1.7
1960–68	1.5
1970–82	1.4
1966–82	1.2
1972–84	1.2

Carter vote, the final Gallup Poll estimate included Carter, Ford, McCarthy, and all other candidates as a group.

**Civilian vote 53.3, Roosevelt soldier vote 0.5 = 53.8% Roosevelt. Gallup final survey based on civilian vote.

CHRONOLOGY

The chronology is provided to enable the reader to relate poll results to specific events, or series of events, that may have influenced public opinion.

1985

December 1   The unemployment rate continued to hold steady in November, standing at 6.9%.

December 3   President Ronald Reagan, adhering to his free-trade philosophy, vetoes a bill that would have limited American imports of textiles and shoes.

December 4   The president names Vice Admiral John Poindexter as his national security adviser.

December 5   The Dow Jones Industrial Average climbs past 1,500 for the first time in history.

December 12   President Reagan signs a bill mandating a balanced budget.

December 19   Senator Edward Kennedy says he will not seek the Democratic nomination for president in 1988.

December 27   Terrorists kill twenty civilians at airports in Rome and Vienna.

1986

January 2   President Reagan accuses the Soviet Union and Cuba of sponsoring terrorism and drug trafficking in Latin America.

January 8   The Dow Jones Industrial Average falls a record of 39.10 points.

January 20	For the first time the United States officially observes Martin Luther King Day.
January 22	The Commerce Department reports that, after inflation, the gross national product has increased by 2.3% in 1985, representing a sharp decline from the 6.6% advance in 1984.
January 28	The U.S. space shuttle *Challenger* explodes shortly after lift-off from Cape Canaveral. All seven crew members die instantly.
January 29	Jonas Savimbi, leader of the rebel forces opposing the Communist-supported government of Angola, meets with President Reagan to seek American financial assistance.
February 7	The Labor Department reports that the nation's unemployment rate fell to 6.6% in January, the lowest level since March 1980.
February 10	President Reagan renews his efforts on behalf of the *contras* fighting against the Sandinista government of Nicaragua. He asks Congress for $100 million in military and humanitarian aid.
February 19	The Senate ratifies a UN treaty outlawing genocide.
February 24	President Reagan proposes to eliminate U.S. and Soviet medium-range missiles within three years.
February 25	Corazon Aquino is sworn in as president of the Philippines after Ferdinand Marcos fled into exile in Hawaii, ending his twenty-year rule.
March 1	The president's Commission on Organized Crime issues reports on criminal involvement in narcotics and labor unions. According to the commission, drug trafficking is "the most serious problem presented by organized crime."
March 4	The commission estimates that 20 million Americans smoke marijuana at least once a month, 500,000 are heroin users, and 5 to 6 million use cocaine in a month's time.
	South Africa lifts the state of emergency it had imposed on many black areas in July 1985.
March 20	The Dow Jones Industrial Average closes above 1,800 for the first time.

March 24	U.S.-Libyan relations further deteriorate after President Reagan challenges Libya's claim to sovereignty over the Gulf of Sidra.
April 5	A bomb explodes in a discotheque frequented by U.S. military personnel in Germany. American officials blame Libya.
April 15	U.S. warplanes strike targets in Libya.
April 17	The Commerce Department reports that real (after inflation) growth in the economy was 3.2% during the first quarter of 1986.
April 18	The Federal Reserve Board reduces from 7% to 6.5% the interest charged to member financial institutions, leaving the discount rate at its lowest level since 1978.
	The U.S. space program suffers another setback when a Titan rocket carrying a secret military payload blows up five minutes after takeoff from Vandenberg Air Force Base in California.
April 29	The most serious accident in the history of nuclear energy occurs at the Soviet Chernobyl power plant in the Ukraine. While official reports of casualties are initially low, experts on radiation sickness expect the death toll to rise steadily.
May 2	Prices paid by consumers and producers continued their almost unprecedented decline in April.
May 4–6	Leaders of the world's major industrial democracies meet in Tokyo to discuss the threat posed by international terrorism.
May 5	The Commerce Department reported that personal income rose 5.3% in 1985; per capita income was highest in Alaska and lowest in Mississippi.
May 13	Reagan administration officials quarrel with Mexican political leaders over whether the Mexican government is involved in drug trafficking.
May 23	The United States and Great Britain veto a UN resolution calling for stiff economic sanctions against South Africa.
June 3	Former Governor of Delaware Pierre (Pete) du Pont announces that he will be a candidate for the 1988 Republican presidential nomination.

June 4	Jonathan Pollard, a former U.S. Navy intelligence analyst, pleads guilty to spying on behalf of Israel.
June 12	U.S. health officials say that deaths from Acquired Immune Deficiency Syndrome (AIDS) will increase rapidly over the next five years.
June 17	President Reagan announces that Warren Burger, chief justice of the United States for seventeen years, is retiring and nominates Associate Justice William Rehnquist to replace him. Court of Appeals Judge Antonin Scalia will succeed Rehnquist.
June 19	Len Bias, an all-American basketball player at the University of Maryland, dies of a cocaine overdose.
July 1	According to Commerce Department figures, the four-year economic boom is slowing down.
July 4	In a four-day extravaganza that attracted millions of observers, the United States celebrates the 100th birthday of the Statue of Liberty.
July 9	The final report of the attorney general's Commission on Pornography calls for public authorities at all levels to take action against the pornography industry. The commission claims that the laws on obscenity are being poorly enforced.
July 14	The U.S. government steps up its war on cocaine production by sending American army personnel into Bolivia.
July 15	The LTV Corporation, the second largest steel company in the United States, files for bankruptcy.
July 19	Caroline Kennedy, daughter of former President John F. Kennedy, marries Edwin Schlossberg.
July 23	Prince Andrew, second son of Queen Elizabeth II, marries Sarah Ferguson, as an estimated 300 million watch the televised ceremony.
August 1	The United States says it will subsidize American wheat exports to the Soviet Union.
August 6	President Reagan reaffirms his support for the Strategic Defense Initiative ("Star Wars").

August 23	Gennadi Zakharov, a Soviet employee of the United Nations, is arrested in New York on espionage charges.
August 30	Nicholas Daniloff, a correspondent for *U.S. News & World Report,* is arrested in Moscow on espionage charges.
September 11	The Dow Jones Industrial Average falls 86.61 points.
September 12	Zakharov and Daniloff are freed from prison in the custody of their embassies.
September 17	The Senate confirms Rehnquist as the sixteenth chief justice and Scalia as an associate justice.
October 11–12	President Reagan and Soviet leader Mikhail Gorbachev meet in Reykjavík, Iceland, to discuss arms control issues. Gorbachev calls for a limitation on the development of "Star Wars," a proposal Reagan refuses to consider.
October 20	The United States expels fifty-five Soviet diplomats.
October 22	The Soviet Union expels five American diplomats and withdraws all 260 Soviet employees of the U.S. mission in the USSR.
	The economy grew at an annual rate of 2.4% during the third quarter of 1986, while inflation rose to 2.5% from 1.7%, mainly because of higher food prices.
	President Reagan signs the new tax revision bill.
October 27	The United States pays less than one-half of its yearly payment to the United Nations.
	President Reagan signs a comprehensive $1.7-billion antidrug bill into law and proclaims a "drug-free generation."
October 28	The New York Mets defeat the Boston Red Sox to win the World Series.
October 30	The nation's trade deficit narowed in September for the second straight month. The amount by which imports exceeded exports shrank by $760 million to $12.56 billion, a modest improvement but considerably better than most economists had expected.

November 2	The Islamic Holy War organizations free an American hostage, David Jacobsen, after holding him for nearly eighteen months.
November 4	In the congressional elections, the Democrats retain control of the House of Representatives and win a 55-to-45 margin in the Senate.
November 6	President Reagan vetoes legislation to strengthen the Clean Water Act, saying it is too expensive. The legislation was passed without dissent by both houses of Congress.
	The president signs a landmark immigration bill prohibiting employers from hiring illegal aliens and offering legal status to many illegal aliens already in the United States.
	The General Motors Corporation announces that it will close eleven plants in the United States, affecting 29,000 employees, or 5% of GM's work force.
	The United States sends military spare parts to Iran as part of a secret operation intended to gain the release of American hostages in Lebanon.
	The United States and the Soviet Union fail to agree on arms control in two days of talks in Vienna.
November 13	The country's Roman Catholic bishops adopt a pastoral letter declaring that current levels of poverty in the United States are "a social and moral scandal," and the government must do more to create jobs and help the poor.
	President Reagan, under intense domestic and international criticism, defends his "secret diplomatic initiative to Iran" and vigorously denies that the United States seeks to exchange weapons for American hostages in Lebanon.
November 25	The president admits not having been in full control of his administration's Iranian policy, and the White House reports that, as a consequence, up to $30 million intended to pay for American arms has been secretly diverted to rebel forces in Nicaragua.
December 1	President Reagan announces that, if the Justice Department recommends it, he will appoint a special prosecutor to investigate the diversion of millions of dollars to Nicaraguan rebels

from U.S. arms deals with Iran. At the same time, he ordered the National Security Council staff not to conduct diplomatic, military, or intelligence operations until a three-member review board examines the operations of the council.

Overall public approval rating of President Reagan plunges to 46%, from 67% one month ago, amid deep concern over his administration's arms deal with Iran and the funneling of funds to Nicaraguan rebels. This decline represents the sharpest one-month drop ever recorded by a public opinion poll in measuring the approval of presidential job performance, according to Andrew Kohut, president of the Gallup Organization.

December 15   Output of the nation's factories, mines, and utilities jumped 6/10 of 1% in November, the biggest increase since April.

Developing Nations

	Better	Worse	Same	Don't know
Peru	66%	2%	25%	7%
Argentina	57	16	19	7
Brazil	54	25	17	4
South Korea	50	15	30	5
India	46	22	22	10
Uruguay	45	33	**	2
Bolivia	40	37	19	4
South Africa (whites only)† ..	40	41	13	7
Chile	29	35	31	5
Costa Rica	29	20	25	26
Colombia	25	58	13	4
Turkey	24	41	16	19
Philippines	24	33	42	1
Mexico	21	64	11	4
Average	39	32	22	7

JANUARY 2
PREDICTIONS FOR 1986

Interviewing Date: 11/11–18/85
Special Telephone Survey

So far as you are concerned, do you think that 1986 will be better or worse than 1985?

Better 65%
Worse 20
Same (volunteered) 9
Don't know 6

Selected National Trend

	Better	Worse	Same	Don't know
1985	61%	20%	12%	6%
1984	70	15	7	8
1983	50	32	10	8
1982	41	44	11	4
1980	31	56	*	13
1979	33	55	*	12
1978	45	30	18	7
1972	57	22	*	21
1960	56	7	28	9

*"Same" responses were recorded with "don't know."

The following figures are the current survey results for member organizations of the Gallup International Research Institutes, grouped by developing and industrial nations and ranked from most to least optimistic:*

*Interviews were conducted in these nations during the last weeks of 1985. Some totals do not add to 100% because of rounding.
**Less than 1%
†The figures for black women are: "better," 14%; "worse," 53%; "same," 15%; "don't know," 18%.

Industrial Nations

	Better	Worse	Same	Don't know
United States	65%	20%	9%	6%
Canada	53	16	26	6
Australia	52	24	18	6
Sweden	43	12	42	3
Italy	41	31	25	3
Iceland	38	3	57	2
Great Britain	37	30	25	8
Ireland	36	34	25	5
Luxembourg	35	16	45	4
Norway	34	8	50	7
Netherlands	33	16	46	5
Spain	33	25	28	14
Denmark	32	11	51	6
Switzerland	32	9	53	6

West Germany	27	11	56	6
Greece	26	45	19	10
France	26	21	45	8
Portugal	25	29	22	24
Belgium	22	32	41	5
Finland	20	22	56	2
Japan	18	8	47	27
Austria	17	18	58	7
Average	34	20	38	8

Note: Of the people of the industrialized nations surveyed in a recent study by Gallup International Research Institutes (GIRI), Americans are found to be the most optimistic about the coming year. As many as two in three (65%) expect 1986 to be still better than 1985 in terms of their own personal lives, while 20% say worse and 9% foresee little change. Optimism in the United States is due in considerable measure to the public's bullish views about the economy, with 49% in a Gallup survey saying they anticipate their financial situation to be better one year from now, compared to 12% who think it will be worse and 32% who predict little change.

Among Americans, the high point in the twenty-five-year trend was recorded at the start of 1984 when 70% predicted an improvement that year in their personal lives. The low point was recorded at the beginning of 1979 when only one-third (33%) said they anticipated a better year.

The next most optimistic among the citizens of the industrial nations are the Canadians (53% say 1986 will be a better year than 1985) and the Australians (52%). Least optimistic among this group are the Japanese (18%) and the Austrians (17%).

Among citizens of the developing nations surveyed, the Peruvians (66%) and the Argentinians (57%) are found to be the most optimistic about the coming year, while least optimistic are the Mexicans (21%) and citizens of the Philippines (24%) and Turkey (24%).

Gallup-affiliated organizations were in operation in half a dozen countries before the start of World War II, beginning with the U.S. Gallup Poll in 1935 and the British Institute of Public Opinion/Gallup Poll in 1938. GIRI was formally founded in May of 1947 with eleven member organizations. Today, GIRI consists of thirty-nine affiliate members which conduct research in eighty-six nations on six continents, serving a wide range of clients including multinational corporations, national governments, universities, foundations, and international institutions.

JANUARY 5
WAR AND PEACE

Interviewing Date: 11/11–18/85 (U.S. only)*
Special Telephone Survey

Asked by Gallup-affiliated organizations in thirty-five nations: I'd like your opinion of the chances of a world war breaking out in the next ten years. If 10 means it is absolutely certain that a world war will break out and 0 means that there is no chance of a world war breaking out, where on this scale of 10 to 0 would you rate the chances of a world war breaking out in the next ten years?

	50-50 chance or greater
Colombia	52%
Chile	45
Mexico	42
United States	42
Australia	38
Uruguay	38
Philippines	37
Brazil	34
Costa Rica	34
South Africa (whites only)**	34
Bolivia	32
Portugal	30
Peru	29
Canada	28
France	26
Ireland	25
Switzerland	25
Argentina	24
Spain	23
Norway	21
South Korea	21
West Germany	20

Italy 19
Netherlands 19
Belgium 18
India 18
Japan 18
Great Britain 18
Denmark 17
Luxembourg 17
Sweden 16
Turkey 15
Iceland 14
Greece 13
Finland 11
    Average 26

*Interviews in other nations were conducted during the last weeks of 1985.
**The figure for black women is 49%.

Asked by Gallup-affiliated organizations in thirty-six nations: Do you think that 1986 will be a peaceful year more or less free of international dispute, a troubled year with much international discord, or remain the same?

	Peaceful	Troubled	Remain the same	Don't know*
South Africa (whites only)**	8%	56%	28%	8%
Colombia	19	55	23	3
Chile	16	52	28	4
Luxembourg	9	52	34	5
Mexico	8	51	40	1
Great Britain	7	50	38	5
Bolivia	13	44	37	6
Ireland	16	44	34	6
Netherlands	8	43	44	5
Uruguay	18	42	34	6
South Korea	14	42	13	31
Turkey	16	41	17	26
Australia	9	41	44	6
Greece	10	40	35	15
Italy	16	40	39	5
Switzerland	19	39	34	6
Peru	14	38	44	4
Spain	17	38	18	17
Brazil	31	37	28	4
Denmark	6	36	48	10
Belgium	9	35	50	6
France	8	35	49	8
Portugal	22	35	24	19
United States	12	31	51	6
Philippines	24	30	44	2
Canada	11	30	51	8
Argentina	34	29	30	7
West Germany	17	29	45	9
India	34	29	26	11
Finland	23	25	45	7
Japan	6	24	42	28
Norway	11	23	58	8
Costa Rica	28	22	33	17
Austria	16	21	53	10
Sweden	14	18	64	4
Iceland	34	10	53	3
Average	16	37	38	9

*Some totals do not add to 100% due to rounding.
**The figures for black women are: "peaceful," 11%; "troubled," 48%; "remain the same," 20%; "don't know," 21%.

Note: Many Americans and other people around the globe predict international discord during 1986 and see the possibility of a world war during the next decade, as determined by a thirty-six-nation survey carried out by Gallup International Research Institutes.

Although 1985 was the year of the summit meeting between President Ronald Reagan and Soviet leader Mikhail Gorbachev—and what some observers believe to be the beginning of a new phase in the relationship of the two superpowers since World War II—the outlook of Americans and the people of other nations at the start of 1986 is no more optimistic than it was at the beginning of last year. Specifically, the proportions of citizens who see a troubled year ahead or predict a world war within the next ten years (where comparisons with last year's survey are available) show little change.

While there have been reopened arms control talks, negotiations on Afghanistan, discussions about the Middle East situation, and a step-up in cultural and scientific exchanges, many people surveyed are adopting a wait-and-see attitude about whether the apparent thaw in relations between the two superpowers will lead to substantial progress in key areas. Undoubtedly contributing to the gloomy outlook of some Americans and others surveyed have been the worsening race relations in South Africa, where more than 1,000 blacks have been killed by police in the past six months.

Americans are found to be among the most pessimistic in their long-range views on the prospects of war, with four in ten (42%) holding the opinion that the chances of a war breaking out in the next ten years are 50-50 or greater. Their pessimism is matched by the Mexicans and is exceeded by the people of Chile (45%) and Colombia (52%). Optimism runs highest among the Finns, with only 11% saying that the chances of an all-out war in the next decade are 50-50 or better, and among the residents of Greece (13%), Iceland (14%), and Turkey (15%).

Three in ten Americans (31%) interviewed in this survey predict that 1986 will be a troubled year with much international discord, while 51% say the situation will remain much the same as in 1985; only 12% think that the next twelve months will be peaceful. The views of Americans are at about midpoint among the peoples surveyed in thirty-six nations. Most pessimistic are South African whites, with 56% predicting a year of discord, followed by the Colombians (55%). At the other end of the scale are the citizens of Iceland, with only 10% foreseeing international trouble in the coming year, and the Swedes (18%).

JANUARY 9
STRIKES AND INDUSTRIAL DISPUTES

Interviewing Date: 11/11–18/85 (U.S. only)*
Special Telephone Survey

> *Asked by Gallup-affiliated organizations in thirty-six nations: So far as you are concerned, do you think that in 1986 strikes and industrial disputes in this country will increase, decrease, or remain the same?*

United States Only

Increase	33%
Decrease	16
Remain the same	44
No opinion	7

Selected National Trend

	Increase	Decrease	Remain the same	No opinion
1985	32%	20%	38%	10%
1984	38	18	35	9
1983	34	22	33	11
1982	44	21	29	6
1981	33	16	42	9

*Interviews in other nations were conducted during the last weeks of 1985.

The following predictions are ranked from most to least pessimistic:*

Industrialized Nations	Increase	Decrease	Remain the same	No opinion
Greece	51%	10%	24%	15%
Ireland	45	16	34	5
Australia	44	11	38	7
Austria	43	10	46	1
France	41	10	41	8
Italy	41	21	32	6
Finland	40	5	50	5
Great Britain	36	24	35	5
Sweden	36	9	53	3
Netherlands	35	14	43	8
Switzerland	35	21	35	9
Canada	33	16	44	7
United States	33	16	44	7
Spain	32	18	32	18
West Germany	30	13	50	7
Belgium	28	16	51	5
Norway	27	7	57	9
Luxembourg	26	9	59	6
Portugal	26	20	26	28
Denmark	25	16	49	10

			Remain	No
			the	
	Iceland	24	31	42	3

Iceland   24   31   42   3
Japan   11   12   41   36
  Average   32   15   42   11

*Some totals do not add to 100% due to rounding.

Developing Nations	Increase	Decrease	Remain the same	No opinion
Mexico	67%	9%	21%	3%
Colombia	62	9	25	4
South Africa (whites only)*	57	14	22	7
Chile	52	11	33	4
Brazil	44	19	33	4
Philippines	44	18	37	1
Turkey	39	10	25	26
South Korea	38	18	14	30
Uruguay	36	30	25	9
Bolivia	32	35	28	5
India	30	35	27	9
Argentina	28	37	27	7
Peru	23	46	28	3
Costa Rica	19	30	26	25
Average	41	22	27	10

*The figures for black women are: "increase," 50%; "decrease," 17%: "remain the same," 13%; "no opinion," 20%.

Note: One-third (33%) of Americans predicts an increase in strikes and industrial disputes during 1986, while 16% foresee a decrease and 44% little change. Most pessimistic are blacks, with 49% anticipating labor unrest in the coming year. The labor outlook of Americans today closely parallels that of one year ago when 32% predicted strikes and industrial disputes during 1985, 20% saw a decrease, and 38% believed that there would be little change.

The expectations of U.S. citizens are similar to the average of persons in thirty-six nations recently interviewed by Gallup International Research Institutes: 36% predict an increase in strikes and industrial disputes, 18% a decrease, and 36% see little change.

Citizens of the fourteen developing nations surveyed tend to be somewhat more pessimistic than those of the industrialized nations, where the Greeks (51%) and the Irish (45%) anticipate the greatest incidence of industrial strife. Among the developing countries, pessimism runs highest in Mexico (67% predict 1986 will be a year of strikes and industrial disputes), Colombia (62%), and South Africa (whites only, 57%).

JANUARY 12
PRESIDENT REAGAN

Interviewing Date: 12/6–9/85
Survey #260-G

Do you approve or disapprove of the way Ronald Reagan is handling his job as president?

Approve 63%
Disapprove 29
No opinion 8

Selected National Trend

1985	Approve	Disapprove	No opinion
November 11–18	65%	24%	11%
November 1–4	62	28	10
October 11–14	63	29	8
September 13–16	60	30	10
August 13–15	65	26	9
July 12–15	63	28	9
June 7–10	58	32	10
May 17–20	55	37	8
April 12–15	52	37	11
March 8–11	56	37	7
February 15–18	60	31	9
January 25–28	64	28	8
January 11–14	62	29	9

The following table compares Reagan's first and final 1985 job performance ratings with those of his predecessors during the first year of their second or elective term:

Presidential Performance Ratings

Incumbent	Year-Month	Approve	Dis-approve	No opinion
Reagan	1985–Jan.	62%	29%	9%
	–Dec.	63	29	8
Nixon	1973–Jan.	51	37	12
	–Dec.	29	60	11
Johnson	1965–Jan.	71	15	14
	–Dec.	63	26	11
Eisenhower	1957–Jan.	73	14	13
	–Oct.	57	27	16
Truman	1949–Jan.	69	17	14
	–Sept.	51	31	18

Interviewing Date: 11/11–18/85
Special Telephone Survey

Asked of the 89% who said they either approved or disapproved of Reagan's job performance: How strongly would you say you approve/disapprove—very strongly, or not so strongly?

Approve 65%
    Very strongly 40
    Not so strongly 23
    No opinion 2
Disapprove 24
    Not so strongly 8
    Very strongly 16
    No opinion .... *
No opinion 11

By Sex

Male

Approve 68%
    Very strongly 44
    Not so strongly 22
    No opinion 2
Disapprove 24
    Not so strongly 8
    Very strongly 16
    No opinion .... *
No opinion 8

Female

Approve 64%
    Very strongly 36
    Not so strongly 26
    No opinion 2
Disapprove 23
    Not so strongly 7
    Very strongly 16
    No opinion .... *
No opinion 13

By Ethnic Background

White

Approve 70%
    Very strongly 43
    Not so strongly 24
    No opinion 3
Disapprove 20
    Not so strongly 7
    Very strongly 13
    No opinion .... *
No opinion 10

Nonwhite

Approve 38%
    Very strongly 15
    Not so strongly 23
    No opinion .... *
Disapprove 49
    Not so strongly 7
    Very strongly 41
    No opinion 1
No opinion 13

Black

Approve 29%
    Very strongly 8
    Not so strongly 21
    No opinion .... *

Disapprove 59
  Not so strongly 9
  Very strongly 49
  No opinion 1
No opinion 12

By Education

College Graduate

Approve 71%
  Very strongly 37
  Not so strongly 29
  No opinion 5
Disapprove 21
  Not so strongly 6
  Very strongly 15
  No opinion . . . . *
No opinion 8

College Incomplete

Approve 70%
  Very strongly 42
  Not so strongly 26
  No opinion 2
Disapprove 20
  Not so strongly 7
  Very strongly 13
  No opinion . . . . *
No opinion 10

High-School Graduate

Approve 69%
  Very strongly 48
  Not so strongly 19
  No opinion 2
Disapprove 22
  Not so strongly 8
  Very strongly 14
  No opinion . . . . *
No opinion 9

Less Than High-School Graduate

Approve 50%
  Very strongly 27
  Not so strongly 23
  No opinion . . . . *

Disapprove 33
  Not so strongly 10
  Very strongly 23
  No opinion . . . . *
No opinion 17

By Region

East

Approve 69%
  Very strongly 39
  Not so strongly 27
  No opinion 3
Disapprove 21
  Not so strongly 6
  Very strongly 14
  No opinion 1
No opinion 10

Midwest

Approve 62%
  Very strongly 38
  Not so strongly 21
  No opinion 3
Disapprove 30
  Not so strongly 11
  Very strongly 19
  No opinion . . . . *
No opinion 8

South

Approve 66%
  Very strongly 45
  Not so strongly 19
  No opinion 2
Disapprove 22
  Not so strongly 5
  Very strongly 17
  No opinion . . . . *
No opinion 12

West

Approve 66%
  Very strongly 37
  Not so strongly 28
  No opinion 1

Disapprove 22
    Not so strongly 8
    Very strongly 14
    No opinion . . . . *
No opinion 12

By Age
18–29 Years

Approve 73%
    Very strongly 39
    Not so strongly 31
    No opinion 3
Disapprove 19
    Not so strongly 7
    Very strongly 12
    No opinion . . . . *
No opinion 8

30–49 Years

Approve 68%
    Very strongly 41
    Not so strongly 25
    No opinion 2
Disapprove 21
    Not so strongly 7
    Very strongly 14
    No opinion . . . . *
No opinion 11

50 Years and Over

Approve 58%
    Very strongly 40
    Not so strongly 17
    No opinion 1
Disapprove 29
    Not so strongly 9
    Very strongly 20
    No opinion . . . . *
No opinion 13

By Politics
Republicans

Approve 90%
    Very strongly 67
    Not so strongly 20
    No opinion 3

Disapprove 5
    Not so strongly 2
    Very strongly 3
    No opinion . . . . *
No opinion 5

Democrats

Approve 41%
    Very strongly 17
    Not so strongly 22
    No opinion 2
Disapprove 46
    Not so strongly 13
    Very strongly 33
    No opinion . . . . *
No opinion 13

Independents

Approve 66%
    Very strongly 35
    Not so strongly 29
    No opinion 2
Disapprove 20
    Not so strongly 7
    Very strongly 13
    No opinion . . . . *
No opinion 14

*Less than 1%

Selected National Trend
(Reagan Performance Ratings)*

	Approve		Disapprove	
		Moder-		Moder-
	Strongly	ately	Strongly	ately
1984				
June–July . . .	29%	24%	24%	13%
January	31	24	26	11
1983				
September . . .	22	25	28	15
June	21	26	29	15
January	17	18	19	37
1982				
October	23	19	14	33
March	24	22	29	16

1981

November ...	25	24	24	16
July	33	27	17	12
March	35	25	15	9

*"No opinion" has been omitted.

Apart from whether you approve or disapprove of the way Ronald Reagan is handling his job, what do you think of Reagan as a person? Would you say you approve or disapprove of him?

Approve 81%
Disapprove 10
No opinion 9

Selected National Trend

	Approve	Dis-approve	No opinion
August 1983	67%	21%	12%
April–May 1982	69	19	12
November 1981	73	17	10
July 1981	78	13	9

Note: President Ronald Reagan completed his fifth year in office with the endorsement of more than six in ten Americans, matching his public support at the beginning of the year. In so doing, he avoided a fate that befell his reelected postwar predecessors and those beginning their first elective terms, each of whom ended the year with diminished public confidence. In the Gallup Poll's final 1985 assessment, 63% approved of Reagan's job performance, while 29% disapproved and 8% had no opinion. In the year's first measurement, he received a 62% approval rating with 29% disapproving.

The president's December performance rating not only matches that accorded him last January but also is statistically indistinguishable from the 65% approval scores recorded in August shortly after his cancer operation and in mid-November on the eve of his summit meeting in Geneva with Soviet leader Mikhail Gorbachev. Reagan received his lowest 1985 rating in April when 52% approved and 37% disapproved of the way he was carrying out his presidential duties. That period was marked by sharp congressional debate over funding for the MX missile, aid for the Nicaraguan *contras*, and the foreign trade deficit.

Another measure of President Reagan's high current standing with the American people is the strength of their approval of his job performance. In mid-November, when 65% offered a positive evaluation of Reagan's stewardship, 40% said they approved very strongly, while 25% expressed moderate approval. On the negative side, 8% moderately disapproved and 16% disapproved strongly. The 40% approval figure is the highest recorded since the president took office in 1981.

Aside from the strong confidence they currently have in Reagan's handling of his presidential duties, Americans also hold a high regard for him as a person. In a November poll, 81% expressed personal approval of Reagan while only 10% disagreed. This level of popularity, corroborated in a smaller mid-December survey, is the highest measure of personal esteem recorded in surveys taken throughout Reagan's five-year tenure.

The extent of the president's personal popularity is attested to by the fact that 69% of Democrats and 81% of independents, in addition to 95% of his fellow Republicans, approve of him as a person. Also, 56% of persons who disapprove of his performance in office nonetheless said they like Reagan, the man.

JANUARY 16
RELIGION

Interviewing Date: Five Selected Weeks During 1985
Various Surveys

How important would you say religion is in your life—very important, fairly important, or not very important?

Very important 55%
Fairly important 31
Not very important 13

	Very important	Fairly important	Not very important
1984	56%	30%	13%
1983	56	30	13
1982	56	30	13
1981	56	29	14
1980	55	31	13
1978	52	32	14
1965	70	22	7
1952	75	20	5

*"No opinion" has been omitted. Some totals do not add to 100% due to rounding.

Interviewing Date: 11/11–18/85
Special Telephone Survey

Do you believe that religion can answer all or most of today's problems, or that religion is largely old-fashioned and out of date?

Can answer today's problems 58%
Old-fashioned/out of date 24
No opinion 18

By Sex

Male

Can answer today's problems 50%
Old-fashioned/out of date 32
No opinion 18

Female

Can answer today's problems 65%
Old-fashioned/out of date 18
No opinion 17

By Ethnic Background

White

Can answer today's problems 57%
Old-fashioned/out of date 25
No opinion 18

Nonwhite

Can answer today's problems 66%
Old-fashioned/out of date 16
No opinion 18

Black

Can answer today's problems 72%
Old-fashioned/out of date 12
No opinion 16

By Education

College Graduate

Can answer today's problems 47%
Old-fashioned/out of date 33
No opinion 20

College Incomplete

Can answer today's problems 57%
Old-fashioned/out of date 25
No opinion 18

High-School Graduate

Can answer today's problems 61%
Old-fashioned/out of date 25
No opinion 14

Less Than High-School Graduate

Can answer today's problems 65%
Old-fashioned/out of date 15
No opinion 20

By Region

East

Can answer today's problems 50%
Old-fashioned/out of date 35
No opinion 15

Midwest

Can answer today's problems 63%
Old-fashioned/out of date 23
No opinion 14

South

Can answer today's problems	67%
Old-fashioned/out of date	17
No opinion	16

West

Can answer today's problems	49%
Old-fashioned/out of date	24
No opinion	27

By Age
18–24 Years

Can answer today's problems	50%
Old-fashioned/out of date	36
No opinion	14

25–29 Years

Can answer today's problems	54%
Old-fashioned/out of date	24
No opinion	22

30–49 Years

Can answer today's problems	57%
Old-fashioned/out of date	27
No opinion	16

50–64 Years

Can answer today's problems	64%
Old-fashioned/out of date	19
No opinion	17

65 Years and Over

Can answer today's problems	65%
Old-fashioned/out of date	14
No opinion	21

By Income
$25,000 and Over

Can answer today's problems	53%
Old-fashioned/out of date	30
No opinion	17

Under $25,000

Can answer today's problems	63%
Old-fashioned/out of date	19
No opinion	18

By Religion
Protestants

Can answer today's problems	67%
Old-fashioned/out of date	18
No opinion	15

Catholics

Can answer today's problems	50%
Old-fashioned/out of date	34
No opinion	16

Selected National Trend

	Can answer today's problems	Old-fashioned/ out of date	No opinion
1985	61%	22%	17%
1984	56	21	23
1982	60	22	18
1981	65	15	20
1974	62	20	18
1957	81	7	12

At the present time, do you think religion as a whole is increasing its influence on American life, or losing its influence?

Increasing influence	45%
Losing influence	41
Same (volunteered)	7
Don't know	7

By Sex
Male

Increasing influence	40%
Losing influence	42
Same (volunteered)	10
Don't know	8

Female

Increasing influence 50%
Losing influence 39
Same (volunteered) 4
Don't know 7

By Ethnic Background

White

Increasing influence 45%
Losing influence 42
Same (volunteered) 5
Don't know 8

Nonwhite

Increasing influence 48%
Losing influence 33
Same (volunteered) 14
Don't know 5

Black

Increasing influence 50%
Losing influence 32
Same (volunteered) 12
Don't know 6

By Education

College Graduate

Increasing influence 46%
Losing influence 42
Same (volunteered) 6
Don't know 6

College Incomplete

Increasing influence 47%
Losing influence 40
Same (volunteered) 6
Don't know 7

High-School Graduate

Increasing influence 49%
Losing influence 39
Same (volunteered) 6
Don't know 6

Less Than High-School Graduate

Increasing influence 37%
Losing influence 44
Same (volunteered) 8
Don't know 11

By Region

East

Increasing influence 46%
Losing influence 44
Same (volunteered) 4
Don't know 6

Midwest

Increasing influence 42%
Losing influence 44
Same (volunteered) 6
Don't know 8

South

Increasing influence 47%
Losing influence 37
Same (volunteered) 7
Don't know 9

West

Increasing influence 46%
Losing influence 39
Same (volunteered) 8
Don't know 7

By Age

18–24 Years

Increasing influence 43%
Losing influence 46
Same (volunteered) 7
Don't know 4

25–29 Years

Increasing influence 48%
Losing influence 44
Same (volunteered) 2
Don't know 6

30–49 Years

Increasing influence 50%
Losing influence 36
Same (volunteered) 6
Don't know 8

50–64 Years

Increasing influence 42%
Losing influence 44
Same (volunteered) 7
Don't know 7

65 Years and Over

Increasing influence 39%
Losing influence 40
Same (volunteered) 10
Don't know 11

By Income
$25,000 and Over

Increasing influence 50%
Losing influence 41
Same (volunteered) 5
Don't know 4

Under $25,000

Increasing influence 43%
Losing influence 41
Same (volunteered) 8
Don't know 8

By Religion
Protestants

Increasing influence 47%
Losing influence 38
Same (volunteered) 8
Don't know 7

Catholics

Increasing influence 44%
Losing influence 46
Same (volunteered) 4
Don't know 6

Selected National Trend

	Increasing influence	Losing influence	Same; don't know
1985	48%	39%	13%
1984	42	39	19
1983	44	42	14
1981	38	46	16
1980	35	46	19
1978	37	48	15
1977	36	45	19
1976	44	45	11
1975	39	51	10
1974	31	56	13
1970	14	75	11
1969	14	70	16
1968	18	67	15
1967	23	57	20
1965	33	45	22
1962	45	31	24
1957	69	14	17

Note: Despite the new interest of Americans in religion and the spiritual life—evidenced by book sales, the popularity of college courses on religion, and a growth in Bible study groups—little change has occurred in recent years in the importance people place on religion in their lives, their perceptions of the impact of religion on society, and church membership and attendance. The latest series of Gallup surveys on the importance of religion, based on interviews with 7,649 adults in 1985, shows 55% saying religion is very important in their lives, statistically the same as in six previous studies conducted since 1958.

Little change has occurred in Americans' perceptions of the impact of religion on society:

1) The 1985 surveys found 58% believing religion can answer all or most of today's problems, similar to the findings of five earlier surveys conducted since 1974.

2) In a recent Gallup Poll, 45% said religion is increasing its influence on American life, statistically close to the results of surveys taken since 1983.

3) Finally, annual Gallup audits have found little recent change in the proportions who say they are church members and who attend church weekly. In the 1985 audits, 71% reported being

members and 42% attended church in a typical week.

JANUARY 19
VIEWS OF 65-AND-OLDER AGE GROUP

Interviewing Date: July–December 1985
Various Surveys

Do you approve or disapprove of the way Ronald Reagan is handling his job as president?

	65 and older	Under 65
Approve	60%	62%
Disapprove	30	29
No opinion	10	9

Interviewing Date: 10/11–14/85
Survey #258-G

How closely have you followed the discussions over the administration's so-called Star Wars proposal—that is, its proposal to develop a space-based defense against nuclear attack—very closely, fairly closely, or not at all?

	65 and older	Under 65
Very closely	21%	14%
Fairly closely	42	46
Not at all	32	37
Don't know	5	3

Asked of the aware group: Would you like to see the United States go ahead with the development of such a system, or not?

	65 and older	Under 65
Yes, develop	46%	44%
No, don't develop	22	25
No opinion	32	31

In your opinion, which of the following increases the chances of nuclear war more—a continuation of the nuclear arms buildup here and in the Soviet Union, or the United States falling behind the Soviet Union in nuclear weaponry?

	65 and older	Under 65
Continued arms buildup	27%	34%
United States falling behind	42	46
No opinion	31	20

Interviewing Date: 11/11–18/85
Special Telephone Survey

Do you favor or oppose the death penalty for persons convicted of murder?

	65 and older	Under 65
Favor	75%	75%
Oppose	11	18
No opinion	4	7

Note: Recent Gallup survey results dispel the widely held notion of older Americans as an inactive, disinterested, and poorly informed segment of society. Evidence of the involvement of the 65-and-older age group, which comprises about one-sixth of the adult population, includes the following:

1) One in three (34%) is engaged in charitable or social service activities such as helping the poor, sick, or elderly; the comparable figure among those under 65 is 31%.

2) Older people (80%) are considerably more likely than younger people (69%) to be members of a church or synagogue and to attend services weekly (49% compared to 40%).

3) Persons 65 and older are just as likely as those under 65 to exercise regularly, with 44% in each age group saying they perform some type of daily exercise to keep fit.

4) Older people are more active in the political process. Higher proportions of the 65-and-older group, together with their slightly younger counterparts (50 to 64), are registered to vote and to cast their ballots in national elections than are those under 50.

Although older people generally espouse conservative values on social issues, such as homosexuality, school prayer, and abortion, their views on many contemporary political issues, in both domestic and foreign affairs, frequently parallel those of people under 65.

JANUARY 23
RELIGIOUS PREFERENCE

Interviewing Date: January–December 1985*
Various Surveys

What is your religious preference—Protestant, Roman Catholic, Jewish, Mormon, or an Orthodox church such as the Greek or Russian Orthodox church?

Protestant	57%
Catholic	28
Jewish	2
Mormon (Latter-day Saints)	2
Orthodox church	1
Other	1
None	9

*The 1985 religious preference figures are based on in-person interviews with 18,439 adults 18 and older, conducted in more than 300 scientifically selected localities across the nation. For results based on samples of this size, one can say with 95% confidence that the error attributable to sampling and other random effects could be 1% in either direction.

Selected National Trend*

	Protestant	Catholic	Jewish	Other	None
1985	57%	28%	2%	4%	9%
1984	57	28	2	4	9
1983	56	29	2	4	9
1982	57	29	2	4	8
1981	59	28	2	4	7
1980	61	28	2	2	7
1979	59	29	2	2	8
1977–78	60	29	2	1	8
1976	61	27	2	4	6
1975	62	27	2	4	6
1974	60	27	2	5	6
1972	63	26	2	4	5
1967	67	25	3	3	2
1962	70	23	3	2	2

1957	66	26	3	1	3
1952	67	25	4	1	2
1947	69	20	5	1	6

*Percentages for the Mormon and Orthodox churches have been omitted because of insufficient historical data. Totals for some years do not add to 100% due to rounding.

Selected National Trend

(Preference in Major Protestant Church)

	Baptist	Methodist	Lutheran	Presbyterian	Episcopalian
1985	20%	10%	6%	2%	2%
1984	20	9	7	2	3
1983	21	10	7	3	2
1982	19	10	6	4	2
1981	19	10	6	4	2
1980	19	10	6	4	2
1979	19	11	6	4	2
1977–78	19	11	6	4	2
1976	21	11	7	5	3
1975	20	11	7	5	3
1974	21	14	7	6	3
1969	20	14	7	6	3
1967	21	14	7	6	3

Note: Religious preferences among Americans have shifted dramatically over the last four decades. In thirteen Gallup surveys in 1985, nine in ten adults state a preference, with 57% saying they are Protestant, 28% Catholic, 2% Jewish, and 2% Mormon. Another 2% claim affiliation with an Eastern Orthodox church or other churches. The current findings statistically match those recorded in annual surveys since 1981. However, it should be kept in mind that many of those who state a preference may not be formally affiliated with any religious body.

In 1947, when Gallup first began reporting religious preferences, 69% said they were Protestant, 20% Catholic, and 5% Jewish. The growth in Catholics has been due to such factors as a higher birth rate and the influx of Hispanics in recent years.

Religious Preference

	1985	1947	Percent increase/ decrease
Protestant	57%	69%	−17
Catholic	28	20	+40
Jewish	2	5	−60

One person in eleven (9%) in the 1985 surveys gives no religious preference. This percentage, while on a gradual uptrend from 1972 to 1983, has leveled off in the last three years. The trend in individual Protestant denominational groupings shows that the Baptist group of churches has changed little since this measurement was started in 1967. Declines, however, have occurred among Methodists, Lutherans, Presbyterians, and Episcopalians, although there is some evidence that these declines may be stabilizing.

JANUARY 26
POLITICAL AFFILIATION

Interviewing Date: October–December 1985
Various Surveys*

> In politics, as of today, do you consider yourself a Republican, a Democrat, or an independent?**

Republican 33%
Democrat 40
Independent 27

By Sex
Male

Republican 34%
Democrat 37
Independent 29

*Findings are based on more than 3,900 interviews.
**Those saying they have no party preference, or who named other parties (3% in the latest surveys), are excluded.

Female

Republican 31%
Democrat 44
Independent 25

By Ethnic Background
White

Republican 35%
Democrat 36
Independent 29

Black

Republican 6%
Democrat 81
Independent 13

Hispanic

Republican 23%
Democrat 57
Independent 20

By Education
College Graduate

Republican 40%
Democrat 31
Independent 29

College Incomplete

Republican 39%
Democrat 34
Independent 27

High-School Graduate

Republican 31%
Democrat 41
Independent 28

Less Than High-School Graduate

Republican 23%
Democrat 52
Independent 25

By Region

East

Republican 31%
Democrat 43
Independent 26

Midwest

Republican 34%
Democrat 36
Independent 30

South

Republican 32%
Democrat 43
Independent 25

West

Republican 35%
Democrat 38
Independent 27

By Age

18–29 Years

Republican 35%
Democrat 33
Independent 32

30–49 Years

Republican 30%
Democrat 40
Independent 30

50 Years and Over

Republican 33%
Democrat 46
Independent 21

By Income

$35,000 and Over

Republican 40%
Democrat 30
Independent 30

$15,000–$34,999

Republican 34%
Democrat 40
Independent 26

Under $15,000

Republican 26%
Democrat 49
Independent 25

By Occupation

Professional and Business

Republican 40%
Democrat 32
Independent 28

Other White Collar

Republican 35%
Democrat 37
Independent 28

Blue Collar Workers

Republican 26%
Democrat 44
Independent 30

Skilled Workers Only

Republican 32%
Democrat 36
Independent 32

Unskilled Workers Only

Republican 21%
Democrat 50
Independent 29

By Labor Union Household

Labor Union Members

Republican 25%
Democrat 49
Independent 26

Nonlabor Union Members

Republican 35%
Democrat 38
Independent 27

Selected National Trend

	Republican	Democrat	Independent
1985			
4th Quarter	33%	40%	27%
3d Quarter	32	37	31
2d Quarter	33	38	29
1st Quarter	35	37	28
1984	31	40	29
1982	26	45	29
1980	24	46	30
1976	23	47	30
1972	28	43	29
1968	27	46	27
1964	25	53	22
1960	30	47	23
1954	34	46	20
1950	33	45	22
1946	40	39	21
1937	34	50	16

Note: The early months of 1985 saw the Democratic party's historic advantage over the Republican party virtually disappear, with almost as many voting-age Americans describing themselves as Republicans (35%) as Democrats (37%). As the year wore on, however, the Democratic party regained support, and in the final months 40% said they were Democrats, 33% Republicans, and 27% independents. The 2-percentage point gap in party affiliation observed during the first quarter of 1985 is the closest the two parties have come to numerical parity in almost forty years: in 1946 Republican affiliation was 40%, Democrats 39%, and independents 21%.

The largest Democratic advantage during President Ronald Reagan's tenure occurred during the second quarter of 1983 when the nation was still recovering from the recession. At that time, there were twice as many nominal Democrats (46%) as Republicans (23%). The GOP's competitive position improved steadily from then until the second quarter of 1985 when the gap once more began to widen, culminating in the 7-point disadvantage recorded during the last quarter of 1985.

The first quarter of 1985 also brought the Republican party unaccustomed leadership in key demographic groups. In earlier periods the Republicans could claim small pluralities over the Democrats only among college graduates and persons from households in which the chief wage earner was employed in business or the professions.

By early 1985 the GOP also led among whites, 18 to 29 year olds, persons who attended but did not graduate from college, those with family incomes of $20,000 or more per year, and midwesterners. In addition, the two parties were at a virtual standoff, not only nationally and among voters of both sexes but also among high-school graduates, skilled blue collar workers, nonunion households, and westerners. In the latest surveys the GOP has retained an edge only among the college educated, business and professional people, and the affluent. Parity with the Democrats has been lost among women and high-school graduates.

JANUARY 30
ALCOHOLIC BEVERAGES

Interviewing Date: 1984 and 1985
Various Surveys

Do you have occasion to use alcoholic beverages such as liquor, wine, or beer, or are you a total abstainer?

	Those who drink
National	67%

By Age

18–29 years 74%
30–49 years 74
50 years and over 54

Asked of those who drink alcoholic beverages: Do you sometimes drink more than you think you should?

	Yes
National	32%

By Age

18–29 years	43%
30–49 years	33
50 years and over	16

Has drinking ever been a cause of trouble in your family?

	Yes
National	21%

By Age

18–29 years	24%
30–49 years	24
50 years and over	15

Would you favor a national law that would raise the legal drinking age in all states to 21?

	Yes
National	79%

By Age

18–29 years	69%
30–49 years	81
50 years and over	83

Interviewing Date: June 1984
Special Survey*

Asked of those who drink alcoholic beverages: Have you or has anyone else in your immediate family ever driven a car when, in your judgment, that person had had too much to drink to drive safely?

	Yes
National	35%

*This survey was conducted for *Reader's Digest*.

By Age

18–29 years	45%
30–49 years	37
50 years and over	22

Note: Although the national spotlight recently has focused on the drinking problems of teenagers and young adults, Gallup surveys reveal that such problems are common to older Americans as well. Fewer drinkers are found among the 50 and older group (54% as opposed to 74% among 18 to 29 year olds), but the frequency of drinking is as high. A total of 40% of older drinkers, compared to 38% of younger, reported having had a drink within the twenty-four hours prior to the interview. However, a somewhat smaller proportion of older (24%) than younger (37%) consider themselves to be "moderate" or "heavy" drinkers. A sharp variance also is found in the trend in alcohol consumption: only 3% of the older group said their use of alcohol had increased during the last five years, compared to 21% among young adults.

A wide difference in overindulgence was reported, with twice the proportion of young adults (33%) as older adults (16%) saying they sometimes drink more than they think they should. Furthermore, a considerably higher percentage of young adults (24%) than older (15%) expressed that drinking had been a cause of trouble in their families. Nearly half of drinkers under 30 (45%) said they or someone else in their immediate family had driven a car after having had too much to drink. About one-fifth of the 50-and-older group (22%) gave the same response.

Both age groups agree that alcohol abuse is a major national problem, with 78% of the younger group and 82% of the older group expressing this view. The two groups (69% of young adults and 83% of older adults) also overwhelmingly favor a national law that would raise the legal drinking age in all states to 21. Solid majorities, however, reject a return to Prohibition, with 79% of young people opposed, compared to 69% among the older group. One adult in ten said he or she had sought professional or medical counseling to help overcome a drinking problem, with little difference in the proportion in each age group having done so.

FEBRUARY 2
ATTITUDES TOWARD PUBLIC SCHOOLS

Interviewing Date: 5/17–26/85
Special Survey*

Public Grades Public Schools

Students are often given the grades A, B, C, D, and Fail to denote the quality of their work. Suppose the public schools themselves, in this community, were graded in the same way. What grade would you give the public schools here—A, B, C, D, or Fail?

	National	No children in school	Public school parents	Non-public school parents
A	9%	9%	8%	4%
B	34	30	44	29
C	30	30	33	31
D	10	10	9	23
Fail	4	4	4	7
Don't know	13	17	2	6

By Sex
Male

A	8%
B	33
C	32
D	11
Fail	3
Don't know	13

Female

A	10%
B	34
C	29
D	10
Fail	5
Don't know	12

*This survey was conducted by the Gallup Organization for Phi Delta Kappa, a professional education fraternity.

By Ethnic Background
White

A	9%
B	34
C	30
D	10
Fail	4
Don't know	13

Nonwhite

A	7%
B	35
C	32
D	10
Fail	8
Don't know	8

By Education
College

A	9%
B	33
C	29
D	11
Fail	5
Don't know	13

High School

A	8%
B	34
C	32
D	10
Fail	5
Don't know	11

Grade School

A	14%
B	30
C	26
D	8
Fail	4
Don't know	18

By Region

East

A	7%
B	34
C	28
D	12
Fail	5
Don't know	14

Midwest

A	12%
B	38
C	30
D	7
Fail	2
Don't know	11

South

A	9%
B	33
C	28
D	10
Fail	5
Don't know	15

West

A	6%
B	28
C	37
D	13
Fail	6
Don't know	10

By Age

18–29 Years

A	5%
B	27
C	33
D	15
Fail	5
Don't know	15

30–49 Years

A	7%
B	39
C	32
D	9
Fail	5
Don't know	8

50 Years and Over

A	14%
B	32
C	27
D	9
Fail	3
Don't know	15

By Family Income

$40,000 and Over

A	9%
B	39
C	30
D	12
Fail	4
Don't know	6

$30,000–$39,999

A	8%
B	39
C	32
D	7
Fail	4
Don't know	10

$20,000–$29,999

A	8%
B	34
C	34
D	9
Fail	4
Don't know	11

$10,000–$19,999

A 8%
B 32
C 29
D 13
Fail 5
Don't know 13

Under $10,000

A 12%
B 26
C 27
D 10
Fail 4
Don't know 21

By Community Size

One Million and Over

A 8%
B 28
C 29
D 13
Fail 8
Don't know 14

500,000–999,999

A 13%
B 30
C 37
D 10
Fail .... *
Don't know 10

50,000–499,999

A 8%
B 36
C 29
D 11
Fail 3
Don't know 13

2,500–49,999

A 11%
B 41
C 30
D 10
Fail 1
Don't know 7

Under 2,500; Rural

A 10%
B 37
C 32
D 6
Fail 2
Don't know 13

Central City Only

A 6%
B 27
C 33
D 14
Fail 8
Don't know 12

*Less than 1%

Selected National Trend

	A	B	C	D	Fail	Don't know
1984	10%	32%	35%	11%	4%	8%
1983	6	25	32	13	7	17
1982	8	29	33	14	5	11
1981	9	27	34	13	7	10
1980	10	25	29	12	6	18
1979	8	26	30	11	7	18
1978	9	27	30	11	8	15
1977	11	26	28	11	5	19

How about the public schools in the nation as a whole? What grade would you give the public schools nationally—A, B, C, D, or Fail?

	National	No children in school	Public school parents	Non-public school parents
A	3%	4%	4%	1%
B	24	22	28	22
C	43	43	42	47
D	12	11	14	19
Fail	3	3	2	6
Don't know ...	15	17	10	5

Selected National Trend

	A	B	C	D	Fail	Don't know
1984	2%	23%	49%	11%	4%	11%
1983	2	17	38	16	6	21
1982	2	20	44	15	4	15
1981	2	18	43	15	6	16

Public School Parents Grade Public Schools

Asked of those who have children attending public schools: Using the A, B, C, D, and Fail scale again, what grade would you give the school your oldest child attends?

A 23%
B 48
C 19
D 5
Fail 2
Don't know 3

By Education
College

A 22%
B 54
C 15
D 3
Fail 1
Don't know 5

High School

A 23%
B 44
C 22
D 7
Fail 3
Don't know 1

By Occupation
White Collar

A 26%
B 56
C 9
D 4
Fail 2
Don't know 3

Blue Collar

A 23%
B 41
C 25
D 7
Fail 2
Don't know 2

By School Oldest Child Attends
High School

A 24%
B 45
C 22
D 7
Fail 1
Don't know 1

Grade School

A 23%
B 52
C 18
D 4
Fail 3
Don't know .... *

By Oldest Child's Class Standing
Above Average

A 33%
B 51
C 13
D 2
Fail 1
Don't know .... *

A	13%
B	47
C	28
D	9
Fail	3
Don't know	*

*Less than 1%

Public Grades Teachers in Local Public Schools

Now, what grade would you give the teachers in the public schools in this community?

	National	No children in school	Public school parents	Non-public school parents
A	12%	13%	12%	8%
B	37	34	46	33
C	26	24	31	29
D	7	7	5	15
Fail	3	3	4	4
Don't know	15	19	2	11

Selected National Trend

	A	B	C	D	Fail	Don't know
1984	13%	37%	31%	7%	3%	9%
1981	11	28	31	9	6	15

Now, what grade would you give the principals and administrators in the public schools in this community?

	National	No children in school	Public school parents	Non-public school parents
A	14%	14%	16%	6%
B	34	21	40	32
C	25	23	27	31
D	9	9	10	19
Fail	4	4	4	5
Don't know	14	19	3	7

Selected National Trend

	A	B	C	D	Fail	Don't know
1984	13%	34%	29%	8%	5%	11%
1981	10	26	28	12	9	15

Public School Parents Grade Teachers, Principals, and Administrators in Local Public Schools

Asked of those who have children attending public schools: Using the A, B, C, D, and Fail scale again, what grade would you give the teachers in the school your oldest child attends?

A	22%
B	46
C	21
D	5
Fail	2
Don't know	4

By Education
College

A	24%
B	48
C	17
D	4
Fail	1
Don't know	6

High School

A	18%
B	46
C	25
D	5
Fail	3
Don't know	3

By Occupation
White Collar

A	21%
B	53
C	17
D	2
Fail	1
Don't know	6

Blue Collar

A	24%
B	40
C	25
D	6
Fail	3
Don't know	2

By School Oldest Child Attends

High School

A	16%
B	46
C	26
D	7
Fail	3
Don't know	2

Grade School

A	25%
B	48
C	20
D	3
Fail	2
Don't know	2

By Oldest Child's Class Standing

Above Average

A	29%
B	51
C	16
D	3
Fail	*
Don't know	1

Average or Below

A	14%
B	42
C	29
D	7
Fail	5
Don't know	3

*Less than 1%

Asked of those who have children attending public schools: Using the A, B, C, D, and Fail scale again, what grade would you give the principals and administrators in the school your oldest child attends?

A	23%
B	46
C	19
D	4
Fail	4
Don't know	4

By Education

College

A	24%
B	41
C	22
D	4
Fail	2
Don't know	7

High School

A	22%
B	49
C	15
D	4
Fail	7
Don't know	3

By Occupation

White Collar

A	27%
B	45
C	14
D	4
Fail	3
Don't know	7

Blue Collar

A	23%
B	43
C	20
D	5
Fail	6
Don't know	3

By School Oldest Child Attends

High School

A	20%
B	48
C	18
D	5
Fail	7
Don't know	2

Grade School

A	25%
B	46
C	20
D	4
Fail	3
Don't know	2

By Oldest Child's Class Standing

Above Average

A	32%
B	45
C	16
D	4
Fail	2
Don't know	1

Average or Below

A	13%
B	49
C	22
D	5
Fail	8
Don't know	3

Teachers' Salaries

Do you think salaries in this community for teachers are too high, too low, or just about right?

	National	No children in school	Public school parents	Non-public school parents
Too high	6%	5%	7%	5%
Too low	33	30	38	42
Just about right	43	44	42	37
No opinion	18	21	13	16

Selected National Trend

	Too high	Too low	Just about right	No opinion
1984	7%	37%	41%	15%
1983	8	35	31	26
1981	10	29	41	20
1969	2	33	43	22

Attitudes Toward Merit Pay Programs

How do you, yourself, feel about the idea of merit pay for teachers? In general, do you favor or oppose it?

	National	No children in school	Public school parents	Non-public school parents
Favor	60%	59%	62%	69%
Oppose	24	23	25	21
No opinion	16	18	13	10

Attitudes Toward Competency Testing of Teachers

Before they are hired by a school district, do you feel all teachers should or should not be required to pass a basic competency test to measure such things as their general knowledge and ability to think?

	National	No children in school	Public school parents	Non-public school parents
Should	89%	88%	89%	92%
Should not	6	6	7	5
Don't know	5	6	4	3

Required Courses for High-School Students

Would you look over this card, which lists high-school subjects. If you were the one to decide, what subjects would you require every high-school student who plans to go on to college to take?

What about those public high-school students who do not plan to go to college when they graduate? Which courses would you require them to take?

| | Should Be Required | |
	For those planning to go to college	For those not planning to go to college
Mathematics	91%	85%
English	88	81
History/U.S. government	76	61
Science	76	51
Computer training	71	57
Business	59	60
Career education	57	57
Foreign language	53	17
Health education	48	43
Physical education	40	40
Vocational training	27	75
Music	24	15
Art	23	15

Selected National Trend

| | Should be required for those planning to go to college | | |
	1984	1983	1981
Mathematics	96%	92%	94%
English	94	88	91
History/U.S. government	84	78	83
Science	84	76	76
Computer training	*	*	*
Business	68	55	60
Career education	*	*	*
Foreign language	57	50	54
Health education	52	43	47
Physical education	43	41	44
Vocational training	37	32	34
Music	22	18	26
Art	24	19	28

| | Should be required for those not planning to go to college | | |
	1984	1983	1981
Mathematics	92%	87%	91%
English	90	83	89
History/U.S. government	71	63	71
Science	61	53	58
Computer training	*	*	*
Business	76	65	75
Career education	*	*	*
Foreign language	19	19	21
Health education	50	42	46
Physical education	44	40	43
Vocational training	83	74	64
Music	18	16	20
Art	18	16	20

*These subjects were not included in earlier surveys.

Sex Education

Do you feel the public high schools should or should not include sex education in their instructional program?

	National	No children in school	Public school parents	Non-public school parents
Should	75%	72%	81%	80%
Should not	19	21	16	15
Don't know	6	7	3	5

Do you feel the public elementary schools should or should not include sex education in grades 4 through 8?

	National	No children in school	Public school parents	Non-public school parents
Should	52%	50%	54%	64%
Should not	43	43	43	31
Don't know	5	7	3	5

Which of the following topics, if any, listed on this card should be included in high school?

	National	No children in school	Public school parents	Non-public school parents
Birth control	85%	85%	83%	88%
Venereal disease	84	85	81	89
Biology of reproduction	82	82	79	90
Premarital sex	62	63	59	69

	National	No children in school	Public school parents	Non-public school parents
Nature of intercourse	61	62	57	73
Abortion	60	61	57	68
Homosexuality	48	48	45	62

Which of the following topics, if any, listed on this card should be included in elementary school?

	National	No children in school	Public school parents	Non-public school parents
Birth control	48%	49%	44%	51%
Venereal disease	49	50	45	60
Biology of reproduction	89	87	91	99
Premarital sex	34	35	28	48
Nature of intercourse	45	48	37	54
Abortion	28	28	26	42
Homosexuality	28	29	22	41

Importance of Extracurricular Activities

I'd like your opinion about extracurricular activities such as the school band, dramatics, sports, and the school newspaper. How important are these to a young person's education—very important, fairly important, not too important, or not at all important?

	National	No children in school	Public school parents	Non-public school parents
Very important	39%	37%	44%	57%
Fairly important	41	43	37	31
Not too important	14	14	16	10
Not at all important	3	3	2	2
No opinion	3	3	1	*

*Less than 1%

Do you feel that high-school students who participate in sports and extracurricular activities should or should not be required to maintain a minimum grade-point average and school attendance record?

	National	No children in school	Public school parents	Non-public school parents
Should	91%	90%	91%	97%
Should not	6	6	7	1
Don't know	3	4	2	2

Attitudes Toward Coeducational Sports

Do you think high-school boys and girls should or should not be allowed to play on the same school teams in the following sports:

	National	No children in school	Public school parents	Non-public school parents
Tennis	85%	84%	87%	89%
Swimming	79	78	80	81
Track	68	67	69	76
Baseball	48	47	49	57
Basketball	40	40	39	48
Football	16	16	14	15
Wrestling	11	12	8	10

*13–18 Year Olds Only**

Tennis	95%
Swimming	88
Track	86
Baseball	49
Basketball	43
Football	21
Wrestling	16

*Findings are from an April 1985 Gallup Youth Survey.

Attitudes Toward Homework

Do you think elementary school children in the public schools here should be assigned more homework or not?

	National	No children in school	Public school parents	Non-public school parents
Should	40%	37%	45%	53%
Should not	38	35	48	22
Don't know	22	28	7	25

Do you think high-school students in the public schools here should be assigned more homework or not?

	National	No children in school	Public school parents	Non-public school parents
Should	47%	46%	49%	60%
Should not	31	29	37	19
Don't know	22	25	14	21

Asked of those who have children attending public schools: Do you require that your oldest child spend a minimum amount of time on homework during the school week?

Yes 61%
No 36
No answer 3

Asked of those who have children attending public schools: Do you place a definite limit on the amount of time your child spends viewing television during the school week?

Yes 49%
No 46
No answer 5

Major Problems Confronting Public Schools

What do you think are the biggest problems with which the public schools in this community must deal?*

	National	No children in school	Public school parents	Non-public school parents
Lack of discipline	25%	23%	25%	43%
Use of drugs	18	18	20	11
Poor curriculum/ poor standards	11	11	11	10
Difficulty getting good teachers	10	10	12	12
Lack of proper financial support	9	9	9	8
Pupils' lack of interest/ truancy	5	6	4	3
Large schools/ overcrowding	5	4	7	7
Integration/ busing	4	5	2	**
Teachers' lack of interest	4	3	6	8
Drinking/ alcoholism	3	3	2	5
Parents' lack of interest/ support	3	3	3	6
Lack of respect for teachers/ other students	3	3	2	1
Mismanagement of funds/ programs	2	2	4	5
Low teacher pay	2	1	2	4
Moral standards	2	2	1	2
Lack of needed teachers	2	1	3	1
Communication problems	2	1	3	1
Crime/vandalism	2	1	2	**
Lack of proper facilities	1	1	1	1
Problems with administration	1	**	1	1
School board policies	1	1	1	**
Government interference/ regulation	1	1	**	1
Teachers' strikes	1	1	**	1
Other problems	9	9	11	7
There are no problems	2	1	4	**
Don't know	14	19	4	4

*Totals add to more than 100% due to multiple responses.
**Less than 1%

Rights and Privileges of Public School Students

Generally speaking, do the local public school students in this community have too many rights and privileges, or not enough?

	National	No children in school	Public school parents	Non-public school parents
Too many	40%	38%	42%	55%
Not enough	12	12	13	5
Just about right (volunteered)	25	23	35	22
No opinion	23	27	10	18

Do you feel that teachers or school authorities should or should not be allowed to open students' lockers or examine personal property if they suspect drugs, liquor, or stolen goods are hidden there?

	National	No children in school	Public school parents	Non-public school parents
Should	78%	76%	84%	89%
Should not	18	19	15	10
Don't know	4	5	1	1

Preferred Solutions to Discipline Problems

Lack of discipline is often cited as a problem confronting the public schools. Please look over this list and tell me which of these possible solutions you think would be most helpful in improving discipline:*

	National	No children in school	Public school parents	Non-public school parents
Classes for teachers on dealing with problem children	64%	62%	67%	73%
Discussion groups with parents of problem children	62	61	66	71
Classes for parents of problem children	50	50	51	59
Suspension of students with extreme behavior problems	46	44	50	50
Classes for students with behavior problems	45	45	43	43
Work-study, half-time programs for problem children	44	44	43	53
Classes for administrators	43	43	43	48
Tougher courts, probation systems, and work programs	42	41	44	52
Curriculum more relevant to students' interests and concerns	32	31	34	31
Alternative schools	21	21	20	25

*Totals add to more than 100% due to multiple responses.

Caring for Preschool and Latchkey Children

A proposal has been made to make child care centers available for all preschool children as part of the public school system. This program would be supported by taxes. Would you favor or oppose such a program in your school district?

	National	No children in school	Public school parents	Nonpublic school parents
Favor	43%	42%	47%	44%
Oppose	45	44	47	50
Don't know	12	14	6	6

A proposal has been made to extend the school day for so-called latchkey children, that is, children whose parents are still at work when the children get home from school. This program would be supported by taxes. Would you favor or oppose such a program in your school district?

	National	No children in school	Public school parents	Nonpublic school parents
Favor	43%	42%	46%	53%
Oppose	46	45	48	41
Don't know	11	13	6	6

Financing Public Schools

Suppose the local public schools said they needed much more money. As you feel at this time, would you vote to raise taxes for this purpose, or would you vote against raising taxes for this purpose?

	National	No children in school	Public school parents	Nonpublic school parents
For raising taxes	38%	35%	46%	37%
Against raising taxes	52	53	47	52
No opinion	10	12	7	11

Selected National Trend

	For tax raise	Against tax raise	No opinion
1984	41%	47%	12%
1983	39	52	9
1981	30	60	10
1972	36	56	8
1971	40	52	8
1970	37	56	7
1969	45	49	6

Support for Special Programs

How do you feel about the spending of public school funds for special instruction and homework programs for students with learning problems? Do you feel that more public school funds should be spent on students with learning problems than on average students, or the same amount?

	National	No children in school	Public school parents	Nonpublic school parents
More spent	51%	52%	50%	49%
Same amount	40	38	44	43
Less spent (volunteered)	2	2	2	1
Don't know	7	8	4	7

How do you feel about the spending of public school funds for special instruction and homework programs for gifted and talented students? Do you feel that more school funds should be spent on gifted and talented students than on average students, or the same amount?

	National	No children in school	Public school parents	Nonpublic school parents
More spent	30%	30%	32%	36%
Same amount	58	58	58	56
Less spent (volunteered)	5	5	5	3
Don't know	7	7	5	5

Private and Church-Related Schools

In recent years the number of nonpublic schools, that is, private and church-related schools, has increased in many parts of the country. In general, do you think this increase in nonpublic schools is a good thing or a bad thing for the nation?

	National	No children in school	Public school parents	Non-public school parents
Good thing	55%	54%	56%	71%
Bad thing	27	27	28	21
No opinion	18	19	16	8

Home Schools

Recently there has been a movement toward home schools, that is, schools where parents keep their children at home and teach the children themselves. In general, do you think this movement is a good thing or a bad thing for the nation?

	National	No children in school	Public school parents	Non-public school parents
Good thing	16%	16%	14%	22%
Bad thing	73	72	75	71
Don't know	11	12	11	7

Do you think that the home schools should or should not be required to meet the same teacher certification standards as the public schools?

	National	No children in school	Public school parents	Non-public school parents
Should	82%	81%	84%	87%
Should not	10	10	11	9
Don't know	8	9	5	4

Support for Vouchers

In some nations the government allots a certain amount of money for each child for his education. The parents can then send the child to any public, parochial, or private school they choose. This is called the voucher system. Would you like to see such an idea adopted in this country?

	National	No children in school	Public school parents	Non-public school parents
Favor	45%	42%	49%	63%
Oppose	40	40	41	32
No opinion	15	18	10	5

Selected National Trend

	Favor	Oppose	No opinion
1983	51%	38%	11%
1981	43	41	16
1971	38	44	18
1970	43	46	11

Importance of College Education

How important is a college education today—very important, fairly important, or not too important?

	National	No children in school	Public school parents	Non-public school parents
Very important	64%	64%	66%	64%
Fairly important	27	27	24	29
Not too important	7	7	9	7
Don't know	2	2	1	*

*Less than 1%

*What do you feel are the chief advantages of a college education, if any?**

Job opportunities/better jobs	52%
Higher income	18
More knowledge	14
Preparation for life	13
Opens doors/provides opportunities	10
Specialized training	10
Maturation	6
Higher social level/status	6
Exposure to new experiences/ideas	6
Teaches person to think/learn	3
No advantages	4
Other/don't know	4
	146%*

*Total adds to more than 100% due to multiple responses.

FEBRUARY 2
PRESIDENT REAGAN

Interviewing Date: 1/10–13/86
Survey #261-G

Do you approve or disapprove of the way Ronald Reagan is handling his job as president?

Approve 64%
Disapprove 27
No opinion 9

Selected National Trend

	Approve	Disapprove	No opinion
1985			
October 11–14	63%	29%	8%
July 12–15	63	28	9
May 17–20	55	37	8
March 8–11	56	37	7
January 11–14	62	29	9

Now let me ask you about some specific foreign and domestic problems. As I read off each problem, would you tell me whether you approve or disapprove of the way President Reagan is handling that problem:

Economic conditions in this country?

Approve 53%
Disapprove 38
No opinion 9

By Sex
Male

Approve 58%
Disapprove 35
No opinion 7

Female

Approve 48%
Disapprove 41
No opinion 11

By Ethnic Background
White

Approve 55%
Disapprove 36
No opinion 9

Nonwhite

Approve 35%
Disapprove 56
No opinion 9

Black

Approve 28%
Disapprove 64
No opinion 8

By Education
College Graduate

Approve 63%
Disapprove 30
No opinion 7

College Incomplete

Approve 56%
Disapprove 37
No opinion 7

High-School Graduate

Approve 56%
Disapprove 36
No opinion 8

Less Than High-School Graduate

Approve 37%
Disapprove 49
No opinion 14

By Region
East

Approve 49%
Disapprove 41
No opinion 10

Midwest

Approve 53%
Disapprove 37
No opinion 10

South

Approve 52%
Disapprove 39
No opinion 9

West

Approve 57%
Disapprove 35
No opinion 8

By Age
18–29 Years

Approve 55%
Disapprove 35
No opinion 10

30–49 Years

Approve 53%
Disapprove 41
No opinion 6

50–64 Years

Approve 51%
Disapprove 38
No opinion 11

65 Years and Over

Approve 49%
Disapprove 37
No opinion 14

By Income
$50,000 and Over

Approve 64%
Disapprove 30
No opinion 6

$35,000–$49,999

Approve 65%
Disapprove 29
No opinion 6

$25,000–$34,999

Approve 61%
Disapprove 32
No opinion 7

$15,000–$24,999

Approve 48%
Disapprove 42
No opinion 10

$10,000–$14,999

Approve 47%
Disapprove 46
No opinion 7

Under $10,000

Approve 39%
Disapprove 45
No opinion 16

By Politics
Republicans

Approve 79%
Disapprove 15
No opinion 6

Democrats

Approve 32%
Disapprove 59
No opinion 9

Independents

Approve 51%
Disapprove 38
No opinion 11

Selected National Trend

	Approve	Disapprove	No opinion
1985			
October 11–14	48%	44%	8%
July 12–15	53	39	8
March 8–11	51	44	5
January 11–14	51	41	8

Foreign policy?

Approve 50%
Disapprove 34
No opinion 16

By Sex
Male

Approve 54%
Disapprove 33
No opinion 13

Female

Approve 45%
Disapprove 36
No opinion 19

By Ethnic Background
White

Approve 53%
Disapprove 32
No opinion 15

Nonwhite

Approve 26%
Disapprove 53
No opinion 21

Black

Approve 23%
Disapprove 55
No opinion 22

By Education
College Graduate

Approve 55%
Disapprove 36
No opinion 9

College Incomplete

Approve 54%
Disapprove 30
No opinion 16

High-School Graduate

Approve 51%
Disapprove 33
No opinion 16

Less Than High-School Graduate

Approve 41%
Disapprove 38
No opinion 21

By Region
East

Approve 46%
Disapprove 32
No opinion 22

Midwest

Approve 50%
Disapprove 37
No opinion 13

South

Approve 51%
Disapprove 35
No opinion 14

West

Approve 52%
Disapprove 34
No opinion 14

By Age
18–29 Years

Approve 46%
Disapprove 37
No opinion 17

30–49 Years

Approve 54%
Disapprove 35
No opinion 11

50 Years and Over

Approve 49%
Disapprove 32
No opinion 19

By Politics
Republicans

Approve 68%
Disapprove 18
No opinion 14

Democrats

Approve 37%
Disapprove 48
No opinion 15

Independents

Approve 47%
Disapprove 36
No opinion 17

Selected National Trend

	Approve	Disapprove	No opinion
1985			
July 12–15	50%	37%	13%
March 8–11	45	39	16
January 11–14	52	33	15

Relations with the Soviet Union?

Approve 65%
Disapprove 22
No opinion 13

By Sex
Male

Approve 69%
Disapprove 20
No opinion 11

Female

Approve 61%
Disapprove 24
No opinion 15

By Ethnic Background
White

Approve 68%
Disapprove 20
No opinion 12

Nonwhite

Approve 41%
Disapprove 39
No opinion 20

Black

Approve 38%
Disapprove 42
No opinion 20

By Education
College Graduate

Approve 72%
Disapprove 20
No opinion 8

College Incomplete

Approve 70%
Disapprove 20
No opinion 10

High-School Graduate

Approve 70%
Disapprove 17
No opinion 13

Less Than High-School Graduate

Approve 49%
Disapprove 31
No opinion 20

By Region
East

Approve 65%
Disapprove 18
No opinion 17

Midwest

Approve 70%
Disapprove 21
No opinion 9

South

Approve 63%
Disapprove 24
No opinion 13

West

Approve 62%
Disapprove 24
No opinion 14

By Age
18–29 Years

Approve 64%
Disapprove 23
No opinion 13

30–49 Years

Approve 65%
Disapprove 24
No opinion 11

50 Years and Over

Approve 65%
Disapprove 19
No opinion 16

By Politics
Republicans

Approve 80%
Disapprove 10
No opinion 10

Democrats

Approve 52%
Disapprove 33
No opinion 15

Independents

Approve 68%
Disapprove 19
No opinion 13

Selected National Trend

	Approve	Disapprove	No opinion
1985			
July 12–15	52%	31%	7%
March 8–11	53	34	13
January 11–14	54	31	15

Situation in the Middle East?

Approve 43%
Disapprove 40
No opinion 17

By Sex
Male

Approve 47%
Disapprove 40
No opinion 13

Female

Approve 39%
Disapprove 40
No opinion 21

By Ethnic Background
White
Approve 46%
Disapprove 38
No opinion 16

Nonwhite
Approve 19%
Disapprove 60
No opinion 21

Black
Approve 16%
Disapprove 65
No opinion 19

By Education
College Graduate
Approve 46%
Disapprove 44
No opinion 10

College Incomplete
Approve 47%
Disapprove 38
No opinion 15

High-School Graduate
Approve 47%
Disapprove 38
No opinion 15

Less Than High-School Graduate
Approve 32%
Disapprove 42
No opinion 26

By Region
East
Approve 37%
Disapprove 44
No opinion 19

Midwest
Approve 42%
Disapprove 43
No opinion 15

South
Approve 44%
Disapprove 38
No opinion 18

West
Approve 49%
Disapprove 35
No opinion 16

By Age
18–29 Years
Approve 41%
Disapprove 42
No opinion 17

30–49 Years
Approve 46%
Disapprove 42
No opinion 12

50 Years and Over
Approve 41%
Disapprove 37
No opinion 22

By Politics
Republicans
Approve 59%
Disapprove 26
No opinion 15

Democrats
Approve 30%
Disapprove 55
No opinion 15

Independents

Approve 42%
Disapprove 39
No opinion 19

Nuclear disarmament negotiations with the Soviet Union?

Approve 57%
Disapprove 27
No opinion 16

By Sex
Male

Approve 63%
Disapprove 26
No opinion 11

Female

Approve 51%
Disapprove 30
No opinion 19

By Ethnic Background
White

Approve 59%
Disapprove 26
No opinion 15

Nonwhite

Approve 40%
Disapprove 43
No opinion 17

Black

Approve 36%
Disapprove 46
No opinion 18

By Education
College Graduate

Approve 62%
Disapprove 29
No opinion 9

College Incomplete

Approve 61%
Disapprove 26
No opinion 13

High-School Graduate

Approve 57%
Disapprove 27
No opinion 16

Less Than High-School Graduate

Approve 49%
Disapprove 30
No opinion 21

By Region
East

Approve 61%
Disapprove 29
No opinion 10

Midwest

Approve 57%
Disapprove 26
No opinion 17

South

Approve 57%
Disapprove 26
No opinion 17

West

Approve 54%
Disapprove 29
No opinion 17

By Age
18–24 Years

Approve 51%
Disapprove 33
No opinion 16

25–29 Years

Approve	54%
Disapprove	34
No opinion	12

30–49 Years

Approve	57%
Disapprove	30
No opinion	13

50–64 Years

Approve	60%
Disapprove	23
No opinion	17

65 Years and Over

Approve	59%
Disapprove	19
No opinion	22

By Politics

Republicans

Approve	73%
Disapprove	14
No opinion	13

Democrats

Approve	47%
Disapprove	38
No opinion	15

Independents

Approve	54%
Disapprove	28
No opinion	18

Selected National Trend

	Approve	Disapprove	No opinion
1985			
July 12–15	49%	33%	18%
March 8–11	49	35	16
January 11–14	52	32	16

Note: The public's assessments of President Ronald Reagan's conduct of relations with the Soviet Union and of the nuclear arms negotiations have improved sharply in recent months. Reagan currently has greater public support on both key dimensions of foreign policy than at any other time during his five-year tenure.

In Gallup's first 1986 assessment, 65% approve of the way the president is handling relations with the USSR, while 57% approve of his nuclear disarmament negotiations. Last July, when the previous measurements were made, 52% gave him a positive rating for his handling of U.S.-Soviet relations, while 49% approved of his efforts in disarmament negotiations. Reagan's highest approval ratings were 58% in March 1981 for his dealings with the Soviets and 52% in January 1985 for his handling of disarmament negotiations.

Despite Reagan's strong gains in public support in these two areas, the president's rating for his overall conduct of foreign policy remains unchanged from last July, with 50% in each survey giving him a positive grade. At least part of this anomaly may be rooted in the lower marks he consistently has received for his achievements in such international trouble spots as the Middle East (43% currently approve), South Africa (33% approved in an October survey), and Nicaragua (25% approved last March).

FEBRUARY 6
DEMOCRATIC PRESIDENTIAL CANDIDATES

Interviewing Date: 1/10–13/86
Survey #261-G

Asked of Democrats and independents: Will you please look over this list and tell me which of these persons, if any, you have heard of?

	Democrats	Independents
Jesse Jackson	91%	91%
Gary Hart	83	84
Lee Iacocca	66	74
Tom Bradley	54	59

Jay Rockefeller	51	50
Mario Cuomo	50	51
Dianne Feinstein	39	46
Bill Bradley	31	38
Charles Robb	31	33
Mark White	24	22
Sam Nunn	20	25
Patricia Schroeder	19	23
Richard Gephardt	15	19
Dale Bumpers	15	20
Bruce Babbitt	14	12
Tony Coelho	8	6
Joseph Biden ....∙	7	9

Also asked of Democrats and independents: Which one would you like to see nominated as the Democratic party's candidate for president in 1988? And who would be your second choice?*

	Democrats	Independents
Hart	47%	35%
Cuomo	22	19
Iacocca	18	18
Jackson	16	10
Bradley (Bill)	8	7
Bradley (Tom)	8	5
Rockefeller	6	4
White	5	4
Feinstein	3	4
Robb	3	5
Nunn	3	2
Gephardt	2	2
Babbitt	1	1
Bumpers	1	1
Biden	1	1
Coelho	1	**
Schroeder	1	2

*First and second choices are combined.
**Less than 1%

Note: Senator Gary Hart of Colorado has moved into a strong early lead for the 1988 Democratic presidential nomination, following the withdrawal of Massachusetts Senator Edward Kennedy. In the latest survey, Hart receives 47% of Democrats' combined first and second place nomination votes,

more than twice as many as runners-up New York Governor Mario Cuomo (22%), businessman Lee Iacocca (18%), or the Reverend Jesse Jackson (16%). However, in a test conducted last June in which Senator Kennedy's name was included, he was the choice of 46% of Democrats to 31% for Senator Hart. Among independents Hart also is the early front-runner, winning 35% of their nomination votes to 19% for Cuomo, 18% for Iacocca, and 10% for Jackson.

Next among the Democratic contenders are New Jersey Senator Bill Bradley and Los Angeles Mayor Tom Bradley (8% each), West Virginia Senator Jay Rockefeller (6%), and Governor Mark White of Texas (5%). None of the nine others on the list receives more than 3% of the Democratic vote.

With more than two years remaining before the Democratic party actually selects its presidential nominee, name recognition plays a vital role in the possible candidates' current standings with the Democratic rank and file. At present the names of only six of the seventeen persons tested are familiar to at least one-half of Democrats and independents.

FEBRUARY 9
PRESIDENTIAL TRIAL HEATS

Interviewing Date: 1/10–13/86
Survey #261-G

Asked of registered voters: Suppose the 1988 presidential election were being held today. If Vice President George Bush were the Republican candidate and Senator Gary Hart were the Democratic candidate, which would you like to see win? [Those who named other candidates or were undecided were then asked: As of today, do you lean more to Bush, the Republican, or to Hart, the Democrat?]

Bush	45%
Hart	47
Other; undecided	8

By Sex

Male

Bush 52%
Hart 40
Other; undecided 8

Female

Bush 39%
Hart 54
Other; undecided 7

By Politics

Republicans

Bush 77%
Hart 19
Other; undecided 4

Democrats

Bush 19%
Hart 74
Other; undecided 7

Independents

Bush 44%
Hart 41
Other; undecided 15

Asked of registered voters: Suppose the 1988 presidential election were being held today. If Vice President George Bush were the Republican candidate and New York Governor Mario Cuomo were the Democratic candidate, which would you like to see win? [Those who named other candidates or were undecided were then asked: As of today, do you lean more to Bush, the Republican, or to Cuomo, the Democrat?]

Bush 54%
Cuomo 34
Other; undecided 12

By Sex

Male

Bush 61%
Cuomo 30
Other; undecided 9

Female

Bush 48%
Cuomo 38
Other; undecided 14

By Politics

Republicans

Bush 84%
Cuomo 10
Other; undecided 6

Democrats

Bush 31%
Cuomo 56
Other; undecided 13

Independents

Bush 50%
Cuomo 31
Other; undecided 19

Note: GOP Vice President George Bush and Democratic Senator Gary Hart would run neck and neck if the 1988 presidential election were held now, according to a recently conducted Gallup test election. Hart currently is the choice of 47% of registered voters nationwide to 45% for Bush, with 8% naming other candidates or undecided. In a similar test election, Bush leads Democratic contender Mario Cuomo by a wide 54%-to-34% margin. Cuomo's conventional Democratic views suggest that he might be a more logical inheritor than Hart of Senator Edward Kennedy's constituency. However, Cuomo currently is not familiar to enough Democrats (only half claim to have heard of him) to make him an effective rival to Bush at this early stage in the election process.

As reported in an earlier survey, Hart is now the Democratic front-runner, winning 47% of the

Democratic nomination votes to 22% for runner-up Cuomo. In a poll taken before he announced that he would not be a candidate, Kennedy was the clear choice for his party's nomination. At that time, Kennedy and Hart were tied for the lead among independents. The current survey shows that, in succeeding to Kennedy's former role as the Democratic favorite, Hart has gained many of Kennedy's political constituents as well.

In test elections last July, Bush held a strong 50%-to-39% advantage over Hart, while Bush and Kennedy were deadlocked with 46% apiece. Both Democrats lost to Bush among Republicans by identical margins. Among independents, the Bush-Kennedy contest ended in a statistical draw, while Bush narrowly defeated Hart.

Hart's comparative weakness among Democrats was the principal ingredient in Kennedy's superior overall showing against Bush. While Kennedy won 78% of Democrats' votes to 16% for Bush, Hart received just 62% to 27% for Bush. In the newest survey, Hart not only fares slightly better against Bush among Republicans and independents but also has substantially more Democratic support than he had last summer.

Although Bush and Hart are statistically tied for the lead among all registered voters, the test election choices of men and women differ markedly. Men vote for Bush over Hart by a 52%-to-40% edge, but Bush is a decided underdog among women, losing to Hart by a 39%-to-54% margin.

The difference goes beyond women's relatively greater tendency to align themselves with the Democratic party. In the survey, 47% of the women voters identify themselves as Democrats, while 34% say they are Republicans. By comparison, 39% of registered men claim affiliation with the Democratic party and 38% with the Republican party.

FEBRUARY 13
FEDERAL BUDGET DEFICIT

Interviewing Date: 1/10–13/86
Survey #261-G

> *At present, the federal budget deficit is running at the rate of about $200 billion per year. Basically, there are only a few ways this deficit can be reduced. Please tell me whether you approve or disapprove of each of the following ways to reduce the deficit:*

Raise income taxes?

Approve 22%
Disapprove 73
No opinion 5

By Politics
Republicans

Approve 25%
Disapprove 69
No opinion 6

Democrats

Approve 21%
Disapprove 74
No opinion 5

Independents

Approve 20%
Disapprove 75
No opinion 5

Selected National Trend

	Approve
April 1985	18%
December 1984	23
January 1983	18

> *Make cuts in government spending for social programs?*

Approve 42%
Disapprove 51
No opinion 7

By Sex
Male

Approve 46%
Disapprove 48
No opinion 6

Female

Approve 39%
Disapprove 54
No opinion 7

By Ethnic Background
White

Approve 44%
Disapprove 49
No opinion 7

Nonwhite

Approve 27%
Disapprove 68
No opinion 5

Black

Approve 24%
Disapprove 70
No opinion 6

By Education
College Graduate

Approve 50%
Disapprove 45
No opinion 5

College Incomplete

Approve 40%
Disapprove 54
No opinion 6

High-School Graduate

Approve 43%
Disapprove 50
No opinion 7

Less Than High-School Graduate

Approve 39%
Disapprove 53
No opinion 8

By Region
East

Approve 38%
Disapprove 55
No opinion 7

Midwest

Approve 43%
Disapprove 51
No opinion 6

South

Approve 46%
Disapprove 46
No opinion 8

West

Approve 42%
Disapprove 53
No opinion 5

By Age
18–29 Years

Approve 36%
Disapprove 58
No opinion 6

30–49 Years

Approve 43%
Disapprove 51
No opinion 6

50 Years and Over

Approve 47%
Disapprove 44
No opinion 9

By Income
$50,000 and Over

Approve 57%
Disapprove 40
No opinion 3

$35,000–$49,999

Approve 40%
Disapprove 49
No opinion 11

$25,000–$34,999

Approve 47%
Disapprove 48
No opinion 5

$15,000–$24,999

Approve 43%
Disapprove 53
No opinion 4

$10,000–$14,999

Approve 39%
Disapprove 53
No opinion 8

Under $10,000

Approve 36%
Disapprove 54
No opinion 10

By Politics
Republicans

Approve 55%
Disapprove 38
No opinion 7

Democrats

Approve 34%
Disapprove 61
No opinion 5

Independents

Approve 41%
Disapprove 51
No opinion 8

Selected National Trend

                                   Approve
April 1985 ....39%
December 1984 41
January 1983 41

Make cuts in defense spending?

Approve 59%
Disapprove 33
No opinion 8

By Politics
Republicans

Approve 46%
Disapprove 47
No opinion 7

Democrats

Approve 68%
Disapprove 26
No opinion 6

Independents

Approve 62%
Disapprove 28
No opinion 10

Selected National Trend

                                   Approve
April 1985 ....66%
December 1984 61
January 1983 57

Make cuts in "entitlement" programs such as Social Security, Medicare, and the like?

Approve 9%
Disapprove 88
No opinion 3

By Sex
Male

Approve 10%
Disapprove 87
No opinion 3

Female

Approve 8%
Disapprove 89
No opinion 3

By Ethnic Background
White

Approve 10%
Disapprove 87
No opinion 3

Nonwhite

Approve 4%
Disapprove 90
No opinion 6

Black

Approve 3%
Disapprove 91
No opinion 6

By Education
College Graduate

Approve 20%
Disapprove 76
No opinion 4

College Incomplete

Approve 8%
Disapprove 90
No opinion 2

High-School Graduate

Approve 7%
Disapprove 90
No opinion 3

Less Than High-School Graduate

Approve 6%
Disapprove 90
No opinion 4

By Region
East

Approve 9%
Disapprove 88
No opinion 3

Midwest

Approve 7%
Disapprove 90
No opinion 3

South

Approve 10%
Disapprove 87
No opinion 3

West

Approve 10%
Disapprove 86
No opinion 4

By Age
18–29 Years

Approve 7%
Disapprove 90
No opinion 3

30–49 Years

Approve 12%
Disapprove 86
No opinion 2

50–64 Years

Approve 10%
Disapprove 87
No opinion 3

65 Years and Over

Approve 6%
Disapprove 88
No opinion 6

By Income

$50,000 and Over

Approve 19%
Disapprove 79
No opinion 2

$35,000–$49,999

Approve 18%
Disapprove 78
No opinion 4

$25,000–$34,999

Approve 9%
Disapprove 88
No opinion 3

$15,000–$24,999

Approve 7%
Disapprove 91
No opinion 2

$10,000–$14,999

Approve 5%
Disapprove 92
No opinion 3

Under $10,000

Approve 4%
Disapprove 90
No opinion 6

By Politics

Republicans

Approve 11%
Disapprove 86
No opinion 3

Democrats

Approve 7%
Disapprove 91
No opinion 2

Independents

Approve 9%
Disapprove 87
No opinion 4

Selected National Trend

	Approve
April 1985	9%
December 1984	11
January 1983	12

Have you heard or read about the Gramm-Rudman-Hollings Act which sets mandatory targets for spending reductions that would cut the federal deficit from about $200 billion at present to zero by 1991?

	Yes
National	47%

Note: In calling for steep cuts in domestic programs, such as education and welfare, and a 6% increase in military spending, the deficit reduction measures proposed in President Ronald Reagan's 1987 budget clearly are not in tune with the priorities of the American people. The public's top concern for reducing the deficit is cutting defense spending, cited by 59% in the latest Gallup Poll. Next are cuts in government spending for social programs (42%), raising income taxes (22%), and reducing "entitlement" benefits such as Social Security and Medicare (9%).

The survey found general agreement on the measures that should be taken to reduce the deficit, with majorities in most major population groups favoring cuts in defense spending. Sharp differences, however, are found along political party lines. Republicans, for example, favor cuts in spending for social programs (55%) to a slightly greater extent than defense cuts (46%). On the other hand, 68% of Democrats favor defense cuts, but only 34% approve of cuts in social programs.

Roughly equal proportions of Republicans (25%) and Democrats (21%) favor raising income taxes to offset the deficit. Cuts in entitlements are not popular with members of either party, with only 11% of Republicans and 7% of Democrats approving. Political independents take positions between those of Republicans and Democrats on three of the four measures.

The latest figures represent some loss of public support for defense cuts since last April when 66% approved. Declines are noted among both Republicans, from 56% to 46% approval, and Democrats, from 76% to 68%, with the views of independents statistically unchanged.

A panel of federal judges recently ruled that a key provision of the Gramm-Rudman-Hollings Act was unconstitutional. However, President Reagan pledged that he would continue to adhere to the act's budget-balancing principle. Also, the panel's ruling did not affect the Gramm-Rudman timetable: the House and Senate still must agree on a 1987 budget resolution by April 15, with a deficit no larger than $144 billion. The constitutional issue will be heard by the Supreme Court this spring.

FEBRUARY 16
MOST IMPORTANT PROBLEM

Interviewing Date: 1/10–13/86
Survey #261-G

What do you think is the most important problem facing this country today?

International tensions; fear of war 30%
Unemployment; recession 18
Budget deficit 11
High cost of living; taxes 8
Poverty; hunger 7
Economy (general) 4
Problems of farmers 4
Moral, religious decline in society 4
Crime 3

Problems of elderly 3
All others 24
No opinion 4
                                      ─────
                                      120%*

*Total adds to more than 100% due to multiple responses.

Selected National Trend

	Oct. 1985	May 1985	Jan. 1985
International tensions; fear of war	20%	23%	27%
Unemployment; recession	24	21	20
Budget deficit	16	6	16
High cost of living; taxes	7	11	12
Poverty; hunger	3	6	6
Economy (general)	4	8	6
Problems of farmers	3	1	2
Moral, religious decline in society	4	6	2
Crime	3	4	4
Problems of elderly	2	2	2
All others	23	28	16
No opinion	4	3	3
	113%*	119%*	116%*

*Total adds to more than 100% due to multiple responses.

All of those who named a problem were then asked: Which political party do you think can do a better job of handling the problem you have just mentioned—the Republican party or the Democratic party?

Republican party 33%
Democratic party 28
No difference (volunteered) 27
No opinion 12

	Oct. 1985	May 1985	Jan. 1985
Republican party ...	32%	37%	39%
Democratic party ...	32	31	29
No difference (volunteered)	23	23	24
No opinion	13	9	8

Note: International tensions are considered the most urgent problem facing the nation, according to the latest Gallup Poll, with three in ten Americans expressing this opinion, up sharply from 20% last October. Chief among the specific concerns cited are the threat of nuclear war and the arms race (11%), terrorism (6%), and the situation in the Middle East (5%).

Unemployment and the fear of recession are named next by 18%, down from 24% in October. The federal budget deficit currently is cited by 11%; public concern over this issue has varied from survey to survey, peaking at 16% last January and October. The high cost of living, currently named by 8%, also continues to trouble many Americans, with others citing poverty and hunger (7%), the economy in general (4%), farmers' economic problems (4%), and a perceived moral and religious decline (4%). Crime and problems of the elderly are mentioned by 3% each.

Major differences about which problems are most urgent are found among the major demographic groups. Unemployment, for example, is considered a much more pressing national priority by blacks (29%), Democrats (23%), and those with family incomes of less than $25,000 (21%) than by whites (16%), Republicans (14%), and those with incomes of $25,000 or more (13%). Similarly, college graduates are more likely to name the budget deficit than are persons whose education did not include a college degree, 18% and 10%, respectively.

Currently, 33% consider the Republican party and 28% the Democratic party as more qualified to cope with the nation's most pressing problems, while 27% think that neither party enjoys an advantage and 12% express no opinion. The latest figures represent a slight gain for the GOP since

last October when equal proportions (32%) named each party as superior in this respect.

After leading the Democrats on this political barometer in early 1981, the Republicans trailed throughout 1982 and 1983, a consequence of the recession. The two parties were neck and neck during 1984, but the GOP regained the lead in early 1985, holding it until the October survey.

FEBRUARY 20
ABORTION

Interviewing Date: 1/10–13/86
Survey #261-G

The U.S. Supreme Court has ruled that a woman may go to a doctor to end pregnancy at any time during the first three months of pregnancy. Do you favor or oppose this ruling?

Favor	45%
Oppose	45
No opinion	10

By Sex
Male

Favor	45%
Oppose	43
No opinion	12

Female

Favor	45%
Oppose	46
No opinion	9

By Ethnic Background
White

Favor	44%
Oppose	45
No opinion	11

Nonwhite

Favor	55%
Oppose	39
No opinion	6

Black

Favor	53%
Oppose	41
No opinion	6

By Education
College Graduate

Favor	59%
Oppose	35
No opinion	6

College Incomplete

Favor	47%
Oppose	43
No opinion	10

High-School Graduate

Favor	43%
Oppose	47
No opinion	10

Less Than High-School Graduate

Favor	36%
Oppose	50
No opinion	14

Grade School

Favor	27%
Oppose	57
No opinion	16

By Region
East

Favor	50%
Oppose	39
No opinion	11

Midwest

Favor	46%
Oppose	46
No opinion	8

South

Favor	36%
Oppose	52
No opinion	12

West

Favor	52%
Oppose	39
No opinion	9

By Age
18–24 Years

Favor	50%
Oppose	39
No opinion	11

25–29 Years

Favor	48%
Oppose	45
No opinion	7

30–49 Years

Favor	49%
Oppose	44
No opinion	7

50–64 Years

Favor	40%
Oppose	49
No opinion	11

65 Years and Over

Favor	34%
Oppose	47
No opinion	19

By Income
$25,000 and Over

Favor	51%
Oppose	42
No opinion	7

Under $25,000

Favor 40%
Oppose 48
No opinion 12

By Politics
Republicans

Favor 42%
Oppose 49
No opinion 9

Democrats

Favor 48%
Oppose 44
No opinion 8

Independents

Favor 45%
Oppose 42
No opinion 13

By Religion
Protestants

Favor 42%
Oppose 50
No opinion 8

Southern Baptists Only

Favor 31%
Oppose 60
No opinion 9

Methodists Only

Favor 53%
Oppose 40
No opinion 7

Catholics

Favor 40%
Oppose 48
No opinion 12

Selected National Trend

	Favor	Oppose	No opinion
1983	50%	43%	7%
1981	45	46	9
1974	47	44	9

Note: The U.S. public is evenly divided, 45% to 45%, between those who favor and those who oppose the 1973 Supreme Court ruling that a woman may go to a doctor to end pregnancy at any time during the first three months. The latest Gallup Poll provides still further evidence that few issues of recent years have so sharply separated Americans. Public opinion also was closely divided in earlier Gallup surveys, although support for the ruling has declined slightly since 1983.

The small changes in opinion that have occurred between surveys are due in considerable measure to the shifting views of men. Women's views today are statistically the same as those recorded in 1983, but among men support for the Court ruling has fallen by 11 percentage points.

The 1973 decision said that the states cannot place restrictions on a woman's right to have an abortion during the first three months of pregnancy. In the second three months the Court ruled that the states still have no authority to prevent abortion, but that they can regulate certain medical aspects involved. Only during the final three months, when medical experts generally agree that the fetus is capable of living outside the womb, can the states impose restrictions on a woman's right to have an abortion.

Analysis by groups shows men and women now holding similar views and little difference between the opinions of Protestants and Catholics. Furthermore, the views of young adults closely parallel those in the next oldest age group (30 to 49), but persons 50 and older tend to oppose the ruling.

Substantial differences are found on the basis of education and Protestant denomination. Six in ten college graduates, compared to 27% of persons with only a grade-school background, favor the Court ruling. Among Southern Baptists, opposition outweighs support by a 2-to-1 ratio, while the views of Methodists lean in the other direction.

Democrats are quite evenly divided on the issue, but Republicans are narrowly opposed.

FEBRUARY 23
PERSONAL FINANCES

Interviewing Date: 1/10–13/86
Survey #261-G

> We are interested in how people's financial situation may have changed. Would you say that you are financially better off now than you were a year ago, or are you financially worse off now?

Better 40%
Worse 30
Same (volunteered) 29
No opinion 1

By Sex
Male

Better 43%
Worse 27
Same (volunteered) 29
No opinion 1

Female

Better 37%
Worse 33
Same (volunteered) 29
No opinion 1

By Ethnic Background
White

Better 42%
Worse 28
Same (volunteered) 30
No opinion . . . . *

Nonwhite

Better 29%
Worse 45
Same (volunteered) 23
No opinion 3

Black

Better 25%
Worse 48
Same (volunteered) 23
No opinion 4

By Education
College Graduate

Better 48%
Worse 21
Same (volunteered) 30
No opinion 1

College Incomplete

Better 48%
Worse 25
Same (volunteered) 27
No opinion . . . . *

High-School Graduate

Better 40%
Worse 33
Same (volunteered) 27
No opinion . . . . *

Less Than High-School Graduate

Better 28%
Worse 36
Same (volunteered) 34
No opinion 2

By Region
East

Better 42%
Worse 27
Same (volunteered) 30
No opinion 1

Midwest

Better 39%
Worse 32
Same (volunteered) 29
No opinion . . . . *

South

Better	37%
Worse	30
Same (volunteered)	33
No opinion	*

West

Better	43%
Worse	33
Same (volunteered)	23
No opinion	1

By Age

18–29 Years

Better	49%
Worse	32
Same (volunteered)	18
No opinion	1

30–49 Years

Better	46%
Worse	30
Same (volunteered)	24
No opinion	*

50 Years and Over

Better	27%
Worse	29
Same (volunteered)	43
No opinion	1

By Family Income

$25,000 and Over

Better	48%
Worse	22
Same (volunteered)	30
No opinion	*

Under $25,000

Better	34%
Worse	36
Same (volunteered)	29
No opinion	1

*Less than 1%

Selected National Trend

	Better	Worse	Same	No opinion
1985				
October	38%	27%	34%	1%
June	43	29	26	2
March	48	25	26	1
1984				
November–December	43	24	32	1
July	40	25	34	1
March	36	26	37	1
1983				
June	28	39	32	1
March	25	46	28	1

Now looking ahead, do you expect that at this time next year you will be financially better off than now, or worse off than now?

Better	53%
Worse	15
Same (volunteered)	25
No opinion	7

Selected National Trend

	Better	Worse	Same	No opinion
1985				
October	49%	12%	32%	7%
June	52	19	19	10
March	57	12	26	5
1984				
November–December	50	17	28	5
July	52	12	28	8
March	54	11	28	7
1983				
June	43	19	28	10
March	45	22	24	9

The following is a demographic profile of "super optimists," those who claim to be better off now than they were one year ago and expect to be still better off next year:

National	31%

By Sex

Male 35%
Female 27

By Ethnic Background

White 32%
Black 20

By Education

College graduate 39%
College incomplete 38
High-school graduate 30
Less than high-school graduate 20

By Age

18–29 years 40%
30–49 years 36
50–64 years 25
65 years and over 10

By Income

$35,000 and over 46%
$15,000–$34,999 31
Under $15,000 20

Note: Americans remain highly optimistic about their financial prospects for 1986, amid falling oil prices and signs of renewed vigor in the nation's economy. In the latest Gallup audit, 40% now see an improvement in their current financial status vis-à-vis one year ago, 30% claim to be worse off, and 29% perceive no change.

In response to another survey question, 53% say they expect to be financially better off one year from now, 15% predict a downturn, and 25% think that their situation will be about the same. These latest figures mark a halt in the gradual downward trend in consumer optimism observed last year. In a March 1985 survey, the public's financial outlook was more bullish than at any other time since 1976, when this measurement first began, with 57% optimistic about their economic future. That figure slipped to 52% in June and to 49% in October.

Currently, about one-third of adult Americans (31%) may be classified as "super optimists." Studies have shown that these people are more likely to be buyers of big-ticket discretionary items, such as houses, cars, and major appliances, and to be heavy users of credit. In the October survey, 28% qualified as super optimists.

FEBRUARY 27
HALLEY'S COMET

Interviewing Date: 1/10–13/86
Survey #261-G

Have you heard or read about Halley's Comet?

	Yes
National	92%

Asked of those who replied in the affirmative: Have you, yourself, seen it either with your own eyes or with the aid of binoculars or a telescope? (Multiple responses were permitted.)

Have seen comet 6%
  With own eyes 2
  Through binoculars/telescope 4
Not sure 1
Aware of; not seen 85
Not aware of 8

By Region
South

Have seen comet 9%
Have not seen; not sure 80
Not aware of 11

Non-South

Have seen comet 4%
Have not seen; not sure 90
Not aware of 6

By Age
18–29 Years

Have seen comet 5%
Have not seen; not sure 89
Not aware of 6

30–49 Years

Have seen comet 9%
Have not seen; not sure 86
Not aware of 5

50 Years and Over

Have seen comet 4%
Have not seen; not sure 85
Not aware of 11

Note: Halley's Comet has been seen every seventy-six years since 240 B.C. It is named after English scientist Edmund Halley, who correctly predicted in 1682 that the comet would reappear in 1758; its next appearance will be in the year 2061. About 10 million American adults (6%) report having seen the comet, with an additional 2 million (1%) claiming they may have seen it but are not sure. Many others undoubtedly have tried but without success. According to astronomers, viewing conditions for Halley's 1985–86 visit were perhaps the worst in the past 2,000 years.

An impressive 92% of adults have heard or read about Halley's Comet. Awareness is highest among the college educated (99%) and lowest among those whose formal education ended before high-school graduation. Yet, even among this group, more than three-quarters (79%) have heard or read about it.

The comet first became visible to amateur observers with binoculars and small telescopes in early November 1985. By mid-December it was occasionally visible to the naked eye throughout most of the United States. During late autumn the comet swung around the far side of the sun. Because the sun had now come between the earth and the comet, daytime glare made it difficult to see. Of the estimated 10 million adults who report having seen Halley's Comet, nearly one-half have observed it through binoculars, one-third with the naked eye, and almost as many through a telescope.

MARCH 2
DEATH PENALTY

Interviewing Date: 1/10–13/86
Survey #261-G

Do you favor or oppose the death penalty for persons convicted of murder?

Favor 70%
Oppose 22
No opinion 8

By Sex
Male

Favor 74%
Oppose 19
No opinion 7

Female

Favor 67%
Oppose 24
No opinion 9

By Ethnic Background
White

Favor 73%
Oppose 19
No opinion 8

Nonwhite

Favor 50%
Oppose 41
No opinion 9

Black

Favor 47%
Oppose 43
No opinion 10

By Education
College Graduate

Favor 67%
Oppose 26
No opinion 7

College Incomplete

Favor 73%
Oppose 20
No opinion 7

High-School Graduate

Favor 75%
Oppose 19
No opinion 6

Less Than High-School Graduate

Favor 63%
Oppose 23
No opinion 14

By Region
East

Favor 64%
Oppose 26
No opinion 10

Midwest

Favor 73%
Oppose 17
No opinion 10

South

Favor 69%
Oppose 23
No opinion 8

West

Favor 76%
Oppose 20
No opinion 4

By Age
18–29 Years

Favor 70%
Oppose 24
No opinion 6

30–49 Years

Favor 72%
Oppose 22
No opinion 6

50 Years and Over

Favor 69%
Oppose 20
No opinion 11

By Politics
Republicans

Favor 83%
Oppose 11
No opinion 6

Democrats

Favor 62%
Oppose 30
No opinion 8

Independents

Favor 69%
Oppose 22
No opinion 9

By Occupation
Professional and Business

Favor 72%
Oppose 21
No opinion 7

Clerical and Sales

Favor 78%
Oppose 16
No opinion 6

Manual Workers

Favor 69%
Oppose 24
No opinion 7

Nonlabor Force

Favor 68%
Oppose 19
No opinion 13

Selected National Trend

	Favor	Oppose	No opinion
1985			
November	75%	17%	8%
January	72	20	8
1981	66	25	9
1978	62	27	11
1976	65	28	7
1972	57	32	11
1971	49	40	11
1969	51	40	9
1966	42	47	11
1965	45	43	12
1960	51	36	13
1953	68	25	7
1937	65	35	*
1936	61	39	*

*"No opinion" was omitted in these surveys.

How strongly do you (favor/oppose) the death penalty for persons convicted of murder— very strongly or not too strongly?

Favor death penalty 70%
  Very strongly 54
  Not too strongly 16
Oppose death penalty 22
  Very strongly 13
  Not too strongly 9
No opinion 8

What do you think should be the penalty for murder—the death penalty or life imprisonment, with absolutely no possibility of parole?

Death penalty 55%
Life imprisonment 35
Other; no opinion 10

Those Who Strongly Favor Death Penalty

Death penalty 87%
Life imprisonment 11
Other; no opinion 2

Those Who Moderately Favor Death Penalty

Death penalty 46%
Life imprisonment 41
Other; no opinion 13

Those Who Strongly Oppose Death Penalty

Death penalty 2%
Life imprisonment 85
Other; no opinion 13

Those Who Moderately Oppose Death Penalty

Death penalty 3%
Life imprisonment 85
Other; no opinion 12

Note: Public support for the death penalty is near the highest point recorded in a half century of scientific polling, with seven in ten adult Americans favoring the execution of persons convicted of murder. At the same time, however, the latest Gallup Poll shows that public support for the death penalty would decline dramatically—from 70% to 55%—if life imprisonment, with no possibility of parole, were a certainty for convicted murderers.

The trend of public opinion on capital punishment is among the most volatile in Gallup annals. The highest level of support was recorded last November when 75% said they favored the death penalty for murder. The lowest level was found in 1966 when those opposing capital punishment narrowly outnumbered those in favor, 47% to 42%. Since then, public backing for the death penalty has gradually increased to the present high level.

From the end in 1977 of a de facto ten-year moratorium on capital punishment through 1983, only eleven Americans were put to death. Since

1983 the rate of executions has greatly increased; currently there are more than 1,400 inmates on death row. Thirty-nine states now have death penalty statutes on their books, but debate continues among penologists over whether the death penalty deters potential killers and whether it can be imposed fairly.

Heavy support for the death penalty is found in all major population groups, with the important exception of blacks, among whom statistically equal proportions favor and oppose it. Men are slightly more inclined than women to favor the death penalty, but no clear-cut differences of opinion are apparent on the basis of age, education, income, or geographic region. There is evidence, however, of a strong political coloration in the survey findings. Self-described Democrats favor capital punishment by a 2-to-1 margin, while among Republicans support reaches 7 to 1.

Another survey question found little equivocation in public opinion on this controversial issue. By a better than 3-to-1 ratio those who favor the death penalty say they do so "very strongly" (54%) rather than "not too strongly" (16%). Feelings are almost as intense among those in opposition, with 13% very strongly and 9% not too strongly opposed.

According to the recent audit, opinion is strongly polarized, with those strongly favoring the death penalty continuing to approve of this form of punishment. Moderate backers of capital punishment are evenly divided between those preferring execution and life imprisonment. Both strong and moderate opponents of the death penalty express an overwhelming preference (85%) for life imprisonment without parole.

MARCH 3
DEATH PENALTY

Interviewing Date: 1/10–13/86
Survey #261-G

Do you feel that the death penalty acts as a deterrent to the commitment of murder, that it lowers the murder rate, or not?

Yes 61%
No 32
No opinion 7

Those Who Favor Death Penalty

Yes 77%
No 20
No opinion 3

Those Who Strongly Favor Death Penalty

Yes 82%
No 15
No opinion 3

Those Who Moderately Favor Death Penalty

Yes 61%
No 33
No opinion 6

Those Who Oppose Death Penalty

Yes 21%
No 70
No opinion 9

Those Who Moderately Oppose
Death Penalty

Yes 26%
No 60
No opinion 14

Those Who Strongly Oppose Death Penalty

Yes 18%
No 76
No opinion 6

Asked of those who favor the death penalty for murder (70% of the sample): Suppose new evidence showed that the death penalty does not act as a deterrent to murder, that it does not lower the murder rate. Would you favor or oppose the death penalty?

Favor 73%
Oppose 19
No opinion 8

Asked of those who oppose the death penalty for murder (22% of the sample): Suppose new evidence showed that the death penalty acts as a deterrent to murder, that it lowers the murder rate. Would you favor or oppose the death penalty?

Oppose 71%
Favor 18
No opinion 11

Note: A 2-to-1 majority of Americans believes that threat of the death penalty dissuades some people from committing murder. In the latest Gallup Poll, 61% think the death penalty serves as a murder deterrent, while 32% say it does not and 7% express no opinion.

As reported in the previous audit; 70% favor the death penalty for persons convicted of murder, while 22% are opposed. The survey also found that support for the death penalty would decline to 55% if life imprisonment without parole were an alternative to execution. A similar decline in support for capital punishment, from 70% to 56%, would occur if new evidence proved that the death penalty does not act as a deterrent to murder.

When the analysis is broadened to include all three factors, hard-core support for capital punishment drops to 43%. These are people who favor the death penalty, select it over life imprisonment, and still favor execution even if it were proved not to be a murder deterrent.

The extent to which the threat of execution serves as a murder deterrent has been vigorously debated for many years, with no resolution of the issue in sight. Opponents of capital punishment point out that only about one-fifth of homicides occur during the commission of felonies, such as robberies and burglaries, while twice that proportion are committed in so-called crimes of passion, such as family arguments, or while the killers are under the influence of alcohol or drugs. The threat of execution is probably seldom considered under the latter circumstances.

The survey findings suggest that, although the weight of public opinion is that the death penalty deters prospective murderers, the principle of deterrence plays a relatively minor role in shaping basic attitudes toward capital punishment. Roughly

three-fourths of those who favor the execution of murderers say they would continue to do so even if it were proved that the death penalty was not an effective deterrent. About the same proportion of those who oppose capital punishment would still do so in the face of convincing evidence that the death penalty was an effective deterrent to murder.

Belief in the concept of deterrence declines steadily as overall attitudes toward the death penalty go from strong support to strong opposition. Eighty-two percent of persons who strongly favor the death penalty feel it acts as a deterrent. That figure, however, drops to 61% among those who only moderately favor the death penalty, to 26% among those who are moderately opposed, and 18% among strong opponents.

MARCH 9
QUALITY OF SERVICES

Interviewing Date: July 1985*; 1/10–13/86
Special Telephone Survey; Survey #261-G

We would like to learn a little more about people's impressions concerning the quality of services they receive. Using the 10-point scale on this card, on which 1 means the quality of service is poor and 10 means the quality of service is very high, how would you rate each of the following services:

Supermarkets?

10 . . . . .14%
9 17
8 27
7 16
6 9
5 8
4 3
3 3

*These findings are based on two surveys. The first comprised telephone interviews conducted by the Gallup Organization for the American Society for Quality Control.

2	1
1	1
No opinion	1

Banks?

10	18%
9	9
8	25
7	17
6	7
5	12
4	4
3	3
2	2
1	2
No opinion	1

Airlines?

10	11%
9	10
8	26
7	15
6	7
5	9
4	1
3	1
2	1
1	1
No opinion	18

Restaurants?

10	7%
9	13
8	26
7	21
6	14
5	10
4	4
3	2
2	1
1	*
No opinion	2

Hospitals?

10	15%
9	9
8	20
7	16
6	10
5	13
4	5
3	4
2	2
1	2
No opinion	4

Hotels?

10	8%
9	7
8	26
7	20
6	10
5	14
4	1
3	1
2	1
1	*
No opinion	12

Department stores?

10	8%
9	9
8	21
7	17
6	13
5	16
4	7
3	3
2	1
1	3
No opinion	2

Insurance companies?

10	11%
9	6
8	17
7	15
6	10

5	18
4	8
3	5
2	3
1	4
No opinion	3

Auto repair?

10	8%
9	5
8	13
7	13
6	12
5	20
4	8
3	6
2	4
1	6
No opinion	5

Local government?

10	6%
9	4
8	12
7	14
6	11
5	19
4	8
3	7
2	5
1	8
No opinion	6

Real estate firms?

10	4%
9	5
8	10
7	9
6	10
5	12
4	7
3	4
2	2
1	3
No opinion	34

Public transportation?

10	4%
9	4
8	9
7	10
6	8
5	11
4	7
3	6
2	4
1	9
No opinion	28

*Less than 1%

Note: Supermarkets (58%) and banks (52%) are rated highest by the U.S. public on the quality of their services, while auto repair (26%), local government (22%), real estate firms (19%), and public transportation (17%) are rated lowest. It should be noted, however, that many people were unable to rate real estate firms, public transportation, and airlines, thereby reducing the ratings, good or bad, of these services.

Overall, the most common complaint among those who within the past year or two had used a service is poor performance or failure to get work done properly (39%), followed by slow service (30%). In addition, many object to the cost of service (20%) and the indifference of service personnel (20%). It should be further noted that there are other types of problems associated with personnel (for example, inadequate qualifications and bad manners) which, if combined, would increase the proportion having personnel-related complaints.

Looking at the individual services with which consumers have had negative experiences, the problems differ by the services performed. The most frequent objection to the quality of auto repair service is the failure to get vehicles to work right (63%). Those who complain about banks or insurance companies most often cite the lack of speed with which these institutions work (29% and 31%, respectively). Slowness is also the major cause for complaint about local government, cited by 40%. Among those who believe that hospital care could be improved, 33% blame the indifference of hospital personnel. Finally, 42% of those objecting to airline service think the scheduling is handled poorly.

MARCH 13
CATHOLIC RELIGIOUS ACTIVITIES

Interviewing Date: 1/10–13/86
Survey #261-G

Asked of Catholics: By any chance, have you, yourself, done any of the following within the last thirty days?

	1986	1977	Point change
Meditated	39%	32%	+7
Said (prayed) the Rosary	38	36	+2
Attended Catholic social functions	33	21	+12
Read the Bible	32	23	+9
Went to confession	23	18	+5
Attended meetings of Catholic organizations	17	10	+7
Attended prayer meetings	12	8	+4
Participated in Catholic action or outreach programs	7	4	+3
Made retreats	4	2	+2
Attended spiritual conferences	3	2	+1
Attended marriage encounter sessions ...	2	3	-1

Note: A growing number of American Catholics are attending Catholic social functions and meetings and participating in Bible study, meditation, and other religious activities. In a 1977 survey conducted for the Catholic Press Association by the Gallup Organization, 21% said they attended Catholic social functions during a thirty-day test period. In a recent Gallup survey the figure is 33%, an increase of 12 percentage points. Bible study is up 9 points, from 23% in 1977 to 32% in 1986. Meditation increased from 32% to 39%,

while those who attended meetings of Catholic organizations rose from 10% to 17%.

Statistically similar proportions in the two surveys made confessions, attended prayer meetings, participated in Catholic action or outreach programs, made retreats, said the Rosary, attended spiritual conferences, and participated in marriage encounter sessions.

Catholics in the 1986 survey also were asked about their involvement in five additional activities. The findings show that 5% attended religious education classes during the prior thirty days, 5% participated in Bible study groups, while 4% took part in charismatic renewal, 4% in the RENEW program, and 3% were active in evangelical work.

Despite the sharp upturn since 1977 in participation in church activities and religious practices, Mass attendance has remained fairly level over the last decade. The 1985 audit shows 53% attended in a typical week.

MARCH 16
CONGRESSIONAL ELECTIONS

Interviewing Date: 1/10–13/86
Survey #261-G

Asked of registered voters: If the elections for Congress were being held today, which party would you like to see win in this congressional district—the Democratic party or the Republican party? [Those who were undecided or named another party were then asked: As of today, do you lean more to the Democratic party, or to the Republican party?]

Democratic	50%
Republican	43
Other; undecided	7

By Sex
Male

Democratic	44%
Republican	49
Other; undecided	7

Female

Democratic	55%
Republican	39
Other; undecided	6

By Ethnic Background
White

Democratic	46%
Republican	47
Other; undecided	7

Black

Democratic	82%
Republican	11
Other; undecided	7

By Education
College Graduate

Democratic	43%
Republican	51
Other; undecided	6

College Incomplete

Democratic	42%
Republican	52
Other; undecided	6

High-School Graduate

Democratic	50%
Republican	42
Other; undecided	8

Less Than High-School Graduate

Democratic	62%
Republican	31
Other; undecided	7

By Region
East

Democratic	48%
Republican	45
Other; undecided	7

Midwest

Democratic	50%
Republican	42
Other; undecided	8

South

Democratic	52%
Republican	40
Other; undecided	8

West

Democratic	49%
Republican	48
Other; undecided	3

By Age
18–29 Years

Democratic	52%
Republican	42
Other; undecided	6

30–49 Years

Democratic	50%
Republican	44
Other; undecided	6

50 Years and Over

Democratic	49%
Republican	43
Other; undecided	8

By Family Income
$25,000 and Over

Democratic	41%
Republican	51
Other; undecided	8

Under $25,000

Democratic	57%
Republican	37
Other; undecided	6

Republicans

Democratic	8%
Republican	89
Other; undecided	3

Democrats

Democratic	91%
Republican	6
Other; undecided	3

Independents

Democratic	39%
Republican	43
Other; undecided	18

Note: Whether or not the Republican party retains control of the U.S. Senate in this fall's congressional elections, President Ronald Reagan almost certainly will have to work with a heavily Democratic House of Representatives during his final two years in office. The party in control of the White House has lost an average of 48 House seats in second midterm congressional elections, beginning in 1958. Recent Gallup surveys, however, suggest that the Republicans may lose substantially fewer House seats this year than the historical precedent would indicate.

1) In the latest Gallup test election for Congress, Democratic candidates hold a narrow 50%-to-43% lead over Republicans, with 7% of registered voters choosing candidates from other parties or undecided. Similar measurements conducted early in 1982, when the last midterm congressional elections were held, gave Democratic candidates a much stronger 53%-to-39% lead over Republicans. The GOP went on to lose 26 seats in the fall elections.

2) At least part of the Republicans' poor showing in 1982 can be attributed to the economy, which was in deep recession throughout most of the year. Many economists expect the current recovery to last through the end of 1986 and perhaps beyond.

3) Although party labels are no longer as reliable an indicator of electoral strength as they once were, self-described Republicans are now considerably more numerous than in 1982, while Democrats are less so. In the latest surveys, 36% of registered voters identify themselves as Republicans, 44% Democrats, and 20% independents. In the early 1982 polls, the comparable figures were 29% Republicans, 47% Democrats, and 24% independents.

4) President Reagan's enduring popularity—63% of the public currently approve of the way he is handling the duties of his office—should not be a liability to Republican candidates for Congress. His performance ratings in early 1982 hovered below the 50% approval mark.

Democratic strategists are eyeing the traditionally Republican farm states as fertile ground for their party's congressional candidates, and many Republican incumbents there are trying to dissociate themselves from the administration's unpopular farm policy. Nevertheless, Reagan's overall job performance rating is currently as high in the Midwest as it is elsewhere in the nation.

5) A 33% plurality of Americans now believes the Republican party is better able than the Democratic party (28%) to cope with what they perceive to be the nation's most urgent problems; 27% say neither party has an advantage. In January 1982 the Democratic party held a 34% to 30% edge on this issue.

The importance to President Reagan of avoiding the fate of his second-term predecessors—counting the 1963–67 Johnson presidency as a continuation of Kennedy's and the 1974–75 Ford administration as an extension of Nixon's—is that the addition of 48 Democratic seats to their existing 255 would result in a House alignment of 303 Democrats to 132 Republicans, giving the Democrats, at least in theory, a "veto-proof" 70% majority in the House.

A shift toward Republican congressional candidates since the 1982 surveys is found in most major population groups, with the exception of Democrats and Republicans, whose monolithic choice of their own party members obviates meaningful changes, and, notably, among women who choose Democratic over Republican candidates by a wide 55%-to-39% margin. The votes of men, however, are statistically tied between Democrats

(44%) and Republicans (49%). Thus, virtually all of the Republican gain since 1982 traces to a major shift in the choices of men, while women's views are statistically unchanged.

Vote for Congress

(Based on Registered Voters)

	National	Men	Women
1986			
Democratic	50%	44%	55%
Republican	43	49	39
Other; undecided	7	7	6
1982			
Democratic	53%	50%	55%
Republican	39	40	37
Other; undecided	8	10	8

MARCH 19
NICARAGUAN REBELS

Interviewing Date: 3/4–10/86
Special Telephone Survey

President Reagan recently asked Congress to authorize $100 million in U.S. aid to the rebels seeking to overthrow the Communist government in Nicaragua, including $70 million for military purposes and $30 million for nonmilitary purposes, such as food and medical supplies. Do you think Congress should or should not authorize this new aid package?

Should 35%
Should not 52
Nonmilitary aid only (volunteered) 2
No opinion 11

By Sex
Male

Should 41%
Should not 50
Nonmilitary aid only (volunteered) 3
No opinion 6

Female

Should 30%
Should not 54
Nonmilitary aid only (volunteered) 2
No opinion 14

By Education
College

Should 38%
Should not 49
Nonmilitary aid only (volunteered) 3
No opinion 10

High School or Less

Should 34%
Should not 54
Nonmilitary aid only (volunteered) 2
No opinion 10

By Region
East

Should 34%
Should not 56
Nonmilitary aid only (volunteered) 2
No opinion 8

Midwest

Should 34%
Should not 55
Nonmilitary aid only (volunteered) 1
No opinion 10

South

Should 37%
Should not 45
Nonmilitary aid only (volunteered) 3
No opinion 15

West

Should 35%
Should not 54
Nonmilitary aid only (volunteered) 3
No opinion 8

By Age

18–29 Years

Should 46%
Should not 49
Nonmilitary aid only (volunteered) 1
No opinion 4

30–49 Years

Should 35%
Should not 53
Nonmilitary aid only (volunteered) 2
No opinion 10

50 Years and Over

Should 28%
Should not 53
Nonmilitary aid only (volunteered) 4
No opinion 15

By Income

$35,000 and Over

Should 44%
Should not 46
Nonmilitary aid only (volunteered) 2
No opinion 8

$15,000–$34,999

Should 34%
Should not ..:........................54
Nonmilitary aid only (volunteered) 3
No opinion 9

Under $15,000

Should 30%
Should not 55
Nonmilitary aid only (volunteered) 2
No opinion 13

By Politics

Republicans

Should 44%
Should not 44
Nonmilitary aid only (volunteered) 3
No opinion 9

Democrats

Should 29%
Should not 60
Nonmilitary aid only (volunteered) 2
No opinion 9

Independents

Should 34%
Should not 51
Nonmilitary aid only (volunteered) 3
No opinion 12

Note: By a vote of 52% to 35%, the public believes that Congress should refuse to authorize $100 million in aid for the American-backed rebels seeking to overthrow the leftist government of Nicaragua. The House of Representatives is expected to vote on the Reagan administration's aid proposal, which includes $70 million for military supplies and $30 million for nonmilitary purposes. Last year Congress approved $27 million in humanitarian aid for the Nicaraguan *contras*. (It is interesting to note that a small proportion —2% nationally— volunteers the opinion that Congress should authorize only the nonmilitary portion of the aid package.)

The survey, completed March 10, found Republicans evenly divided on the issue, with 44% favoring authorization of the aid program and an equal proportion opposed. Democrats oppose the plan by a 2-to-1 margin. The views of independents, as is frequently the case, mirror the national consensus, with 34% in favor and 51% opposed.

President Ronald Reagan has lobbied intensively to obtain congressional approval for his aid program, at one point saying that the United States had a "moral obligation" to provide this assistance. The president believes that it is vital to U.S. national security to prevent consolidation of a Communist base on the mainland of the Americas. Opponents contend that the *contras*, some of whom served the former Somoza dictatorship and have been accused of committing atrocities, would not present a serious military challenge to the government forces, even with additional U.S. aid.

Opposition to the administration's aid package outweighs support among most major population segments, with the exception of Republicans and groups with a strong Republican orientation—18 to 29 year olds and persons from upper-income households—who are evenly divided between those who favor congressional approval and those who oppose it.

Americans' opposition to the administration's current aid proposal parallels the findings of earlier Gallup surveys. One year ago half of those aware that the United States was backing the rebel forces in Nicaragua (38% of the total) said we should "stay completely out of the situation," while 42% thought we should "continue to help the rebel forces."

Responses to a broader question asked in April 1984 found the public narrowly favoring noninvolvement (49%) rather than the United States giving military assistance to "governments in Central America that are friendly to us" (39%).

In March 1983 those familiar with the situation in El Salvador (87% of the total) voted 3 to 1 against a Reagan request for an additional $60 million in military aid and 2 to 1 against increasing the number of U.S. advisers to the Salvadoran government.

MARCH 23
SPACE SHUTTLE PROGRAM

Interviewing Date: 3/4–10/86
Special Telephone Survey

In light of the space shuttle disaster in January in which the seven astronauts were killed, do you feel the United States should or should not continue the manned space shuttle program?

Should 80%
Should not 17
No opinion 3

By Sex
Male

Should 87%
Should not 11
No opinion 2

Female

Should 73%
Should not 23
No opinion 4

By Education
College Graduate

Should 89%
Should not 9
No opinion 2

College Incomplete

Should 88%
Should not 10
No opinion 2

High-School Graduate

Should 80%
Should not 19
No opinion 1

Less Than High-School Graduate

Should 60%
Should not 31
No opinion 9

By Age
18–29 Years

Should 88%
Should not 10
No opinion 2

30–49 Years

Should 82%
Should not 16
No opinion 2

50–64 Years

Should 70%
Should not 25
No opinion 5

65 Years and Over

Should 72%
Should not 21
No opinion 7

How much confidence do you have that NASA will be able to prevent accidents like this from happening in the future—a great deal of confidence, a fair amount, not very much, or none at all?

Great deal 38%
Fair amount 41
Not very much 13
None at all 6
No opinion 2

By Sex
Male

Great deal 46%
Fair amount 37
Not very much 10
None at all 6
No opinion 1

Female

Great deal 32%
Fair amount 44
Not very much 15
None at all 6
No opinion 3

By Education
College Graduate

Great deal 46%
Fair amount 43
Not very much 7
None at all 3
No opinion 1

College Incomplete

Great deal 45%
Fair amount 42
Not very much 9
None at all 3
No opinion 1

High-School Graduate

Great deal 37%
Fair amount 41
Not very much 15
None at all 6
No opinion 1

Less Than High-School Graduate

Great deal 25%
Fair amount 36
Not very much 19
None at all 15
No opinion 5

By Age
18–29 Years

Great deal 42%
Fair amount 40
Not very much 14
None at all 4
No opinion ....*

30–49 Years

Great deal 40%
Fair amount 43
Not very much 10
None at all 6
No opinion 1

50–64 Years

Great deal 35%
Fair amount 37
Not very much 14
None at all 10
No opinion 4

65 Years and Over

Great deal 34%
Fair amount 39
Not very much 17
None at all 6
No opinion 4

*Less than 1%

Do you feel that civilian astronauts such as journalists, politicians, and schoolteachers should or should not participate in any future space shuttle flights?

Should	69%
Should not	26
No opinion	5

By Sex
Male

Should	71%
Should not	25
No opinion	4

Female

Should	67%
Should not	27
No opinion	6

By College
College Graduate

Should	79%
Should not	20
No opinion	1

College Incomplete

Should	76%
Should not	20
No opinion	4

High-School Graduate

Should	68%
Should not	27
No opinion	5

Less Than High-School Graduate

Should	50%
Should not	38
No opinion	12

By Age
18–29 Years

Should	76%
Should not	21
No opinion	3

30–49 Years

Should	79%
Should not	17
No opinion	4

50–64 Years

Should	56%
Should not	38
No opinion	6

65 Years and Over

Should	48%
Should not	41
No opinion	11

Would you, yourself, like to be a passenger on a space shuttle flight sometime in the future?

	Would	Would not*
National	38%	62%

By Sex

Male	50%	50%
Female	26	74

By Education

College graduate	49%	51%
College incomplete	41	59
High-school graduate	34	66
Less than high-school graduate	27	73

By Age

18–29 years	47%	53%
30–49 years	45	55
50–64 years	28	72
65 years and over	17	83

*Includes small proportions, 1% nationally, who are undecided.

Note: The American people by the overwhelming margin of 80% to 17% think that the United States should continue the manned space shuttle program, despite the disaster that killed all seven *Challenger* crew members on January 28. This high level of public support is found even though many Americans have less than full confidence that the National Aeronautics and Space Administration (NASA) will be able to prevent accidents such as the recent tragedy from happening in the future. Four in ten (38%) say they have a "great deal" of confidence in NASA in this respect, but 41% say only a "fair amount," and another 19% say "not very much" or "none at all."

At the same time, however, seven in ten survey respondents (69%) think civilian astronauts, such as journalists, politicians, and schoolteachers, should participate in future space shuttle flights. Four in ten (38%), in fact, say they, themselves, would like to be a passenger, with this figure rising to 47% among adults under 30.

With public opinion an important element in determining the fate of the nation's space program, it is interesting to note that much of the support and enthusiasm for the program is centered among younger Americans, those who grew up during the space age. Persons under 50, for example, are more likely than older people to favor the continuation of the manned space shuttle program, show more confidence in NASA, are more likely to believe that civilian astronauts should participate in future flights, and show far more interest in being a passenger. However, it should be noted that an intrepid 17% of persons 65 and over would like to venture into outer space.

Women are less likely than men to want the manned space shuttle program to continue, show less confidence in NASA, and are far less likely to want to take a ride in a space vehicle. Fifty percent of men would like to go on a flight, but only 26% of women like the idea.

MARCH 27
PRESIDENT REAGAN

Interviewing Date: 3/4–10/86
Special Telephone Survey

> *How do you think Ronald Reagan will go down in history—as an outstanding president, above average, below average, or poor?*

	1986	1985
Outstanding	16%	15%
Above average	46	40
Average (volunteered)	23	27
Below average	8	9
Poor	5	5
No opinion	2	4

By Politics
Republicans

Outstanding	25%
Above average	53
Average (volunteered)	15
Below average	2
Poor	2
No opinion	3

Democrats

Outstanding	9%
Above average	35
Average (volunteered)	30
Below average	16
Poor	9
No opinion	1

Independents

Outstanding	13%
Above average	48
Average (volunteered)	26
Below average	7
Poor	5
No opinion	1

Do you approve or disapprove of the way Ronald Reagan is handling his job as president?

Approve 63%
Disapprove 26
No opinion 11

Note: In the latest survey, a growing majority of Americans (62%) thinks that President Ronald Reagan will be viewed from a historical perspective as an "outstanding" or "above average" chief executive; one year ago the figure was 55%. The latest findings are recorded at a time when Reagan enjoys a 63% job approval rating from the American public, statistically matching his performance scores since last July.

President Reagan fares much better in public expectations today, and did one year ago, than President Jimmy Carter at the end of his presidency. In December 1980, when only 34% of the public approved of Carter's performance in office and after he had been defeated by Reagan in the November election, 14% believed that Carter would go down in history as an above average or outstanding president, 37% said average, and 46% thought below average or poor.

Also, toward the close of Gerald Ford's tenure in December 1976, when his job performance rating stood at 53% approval, 25% of the public believed that he would be regarded as an above average or outstanding president, 50% as average, and 21% as below average or poor. That survey was conducted shortly after Carter defeated incumbent Ford.

	Carter Dec. 1980	Ford Dec. 1976
Outstanding	3%	5%
Above average	11	20
Average (volunteered) ...	37	50
Below average	31	15
Poor	15	6
No opinion	3	4

Views of the Reagan presidency are highly favorable in all regions of the country and among all major population groups, with the exception of blacks, who have been consistently critical of the Reagan administration. While only 11% of whites say Reagan will go down in history as a below average or poor president, 22% of blacks hold this view. At the same time, however, as many as 41% of blacks believe he will be regarded by history as above average (31%) or outstanding (10%).

Not surprisingly, sharp differences are found by political affiliation, with 78% of Republicans expecting Reagan to be viewed as an above average or outstanding president. But, even among Democrats, positive expectations (44%) outweigh negative ones (26%) by a considerable margin.

MARCH 30
THE PHILIPPINES

Interviewing Date: 3/4–10/86
Special Telephone Survey

How closely have you followed recent events in the Philippines—very closely, fairly closely, or not closely?

	Very, fairly closely
National	76%

Asked of the aware group: From what you have heard or read about it, do you think the change in government in the Philippines is in the best interests of the United States, or not?

Yes, is 76%
No, is not 12
No opinion 12

Also asked of the aware group: Do you feel the Aquino government has a better chance or not as good a chance of preventing a Communist takeover of her country than the Marcos government had?

Better chance 68%
Not as good a chance 16
About the same (volunteered) 7
No opinion 9

Increase aid 19%
Decrease aid 16
Provide same amount of aid 60
No opinion 5

Also asked of the aware group: As you may know, the United States maintains several large military bases in the Philippines that our government considers vital to U.S. interests in Southeast Asia. President Aquino has agreed to allow the United States to keep these bases at least until the present treaty expires in 1991. It has been proposed that American aid to the Aquino government be tied to an agreement that the United States can maintain its military bases in the Philippines beyond 1991. Do you approve or disapprove of this U.S. proposal?

Approve 80%
Disapprove 15
No opinion 5

Note: The latest Gallup Poll found a high level of public interest in current Philippine affairs, with 76% of Americans saying they have followed recent events there very or fairly closely. President Corazon Aquino's new Philippine government has the enthusiastic backing of the American people, who believe it to be in the best interests of the United States and to stand a better chance than the Marcos government of averting a Communist takeover of the nation. At the same time, however, the majority of American opinion is that the United States should provide only as much economic assistance to the Aquino government as it did to the deposed Marcos regime.

President Aquino's problems are many and complex. In addition to consolidating her political base, eliminating corruption, rebuilding military forces, and containing a strong Communist insurgency, she must try to revive the recession-wracked Philippine economy. The Reagan administration and the U.S. Congress have promised assistance; the amount and nature are now being debated.

Their strong sympathy for the Aquino government notwithstanding, only one-fifth of informed Americans (19%) think that the United States should increase its economic aid to the Philippines, 16% believe that U.S. aid should be reduced, and 60% say we should provide the same amount we did to the Marcos government.

President Aquino has indicated that she is leaning in favor of extending a treaty permitting the United States to maintain two huge military installations—Subic Naval Base and Clark Air Base—beyond the present 1991 expiration date. Regardless of their general stance on economic aid to the Philippines, Americans strongly approve of a proposal to link future U.S. aid to extension of the military treaty, with 80% in favor and 15% opposed.

APRIL 3
PERSONAL FINANCES

Interviewing Date: 3/4–10/86
Special Telephone Survey

We are interested in how people's financial situation may have changed. Would you say that you are financially better off now than you were a year ago, or are you financially worse off now?

Better 46%
Worse 30
Same (volunteered) 24
No opinion .... *

*Less than 1%

Selected National Trend

	Better	Worse	Same	No opinion
1986				
January	40%	30%	29%	1%
1985				
October	38	27	34	1
June	43	29	26	2
March	48	25	26	1

1984

Nov.–Dec.	43	24	32	1
July	40	25	34	1
March	36	26	37	1

1983

June	28	39	32	1
March	25	46	28	1

Now looking ahead, do you expect that at this time next year you will be financially better off than now, or worse off than now?

Better 61%
Worse 18
Same (volunteered) 16
No opinion 5

Selected National Trend

	Better	Worse	Same	No opinion
1986				
January	53%	15%	25%	7%
1985				
October	49	12	32	7
June	52	19	19	10
March	57	12	26	5
1984				
Nov.–Dec.	50	17	28	5
July	52	12	28	8
March	54	11	28	7
1983				
June	43	19	28	10
March	45	22	24	9

	Super optimists
National 37%

By Sex

Male 41%
Female 34

By Ethnic Background

White 38%
Black 27

By Education

College graduate 50%
College incomplete 44
High-school graduate 32
Less than high-school graduate 23

By Age

18–29 years 48%
30–49 years 44
50–64 years 28
65 years and over 13

By Income

$35,000 and over 51%
$15,000–$34,999 41
Under $15,000 26

By Politics

Republicans 45%
Democrats 28
Independents 40

The following is the recent trend in "super optimists," those who claim to be better off now than they were one year ago and expect to be still better off next year.

Selected National Trend

	Super optimists
1986	
March 37%
January 31
1985	
October 28
June 33
March 37
1984	
Nov.–Dec. 32

Note: The latest Gallup audit reveals a considerable improvement in consumers' perceptions of their present financial status vis-à-vis one year ago. Currently, 46% of American adults say they now are better off, 30% worse off, and 24% the same. Two months ago 40% had a positive attitude about their present financial situation, 30% were negative, and 29% neutral.

In a companion survey question regarding the public's economic expectations, 61% say they expect to be financially better off one year from now, 18% predict a downturn, and 16% believe that their situation will not change appreciably. This represents an 8-percentage point increase in consumer optimism since January when 53% thought that their finances would improve, 15% grow worse, and 25% remain the same.

In most respects the public's current financial point of view—looking both ahead and back—resembles that found in March 1985 when Americans were more optimistic than at any other time since 1976, the year in which these measurements were begun. The latest audit, however, shows significantly higher levels of pessimism than were found in the previous year's study. These increases are found in all major population groups but are especially pronounced among blacks and less well-educated and less affluent persons of all races.

Currently, almost four in ten adult Americans (37%) may be classified as "super optimists," matching the high point for this index recorded last March. Studies have shown that these people are more likely to be buyers of big-ticket discretionary items, such as houses, cars, and major appliances, and to be heavy users of credit. In the January survey, 31% qualified as super optimists.

APRIL 6
SOUTH AFRICA

Interviewing Date: 3/4–10/86
Special Telephone Survey

> How closely would you say you've followed the recent events in South Africa—very closely, fairly closely, or not very closely?

	Very, fairly closely
National	56%

> Asked of the aware group: In the South African situation, are your sympathies more with

the black population or more with the South African government?

Black population	73%
South African government	12
Both; neither (volunteered)	10
No opinion	5

By Sex
Male

Black population	71%
South African government	13
Both; neither (volunteered)	14
No opinion	2

Female

Black population	75%
South African government	10
Both; neither (volunteered)	7
No opinion	8

By Ethnic Background
White

Black population	73%
South African government	11
Both; neither (volunteered)	10
No opinion	6

Nonwhite

Black population	75%
South African government	13
Both; neither (volunteered)	8
No opinion	4

Black

Black population	76%
South African government	15
Both; neither (volunteered)	6
No opinion	3

By Education
College Graduate

Black population	77%
South African government	11
Both; neither (volunteered)	9
No opinion	3

College Incomplete

Black population	72%
South African government	13
Both; neither (volunteered)	10
No opinion	5

High-School Graduate

Black population	75%
South African government	13
Both; neither (volunteered)	7
No opinion	5

Less Than High-School Graduate

Black population	63%
South African government	8
Both; neither (volunteered)	19
No opinion	10

By Region

East

Black population	74%
South African government	8
Both; neither (volunteered)	12
No opinion	6

Midwest

Black population	75%
South African government	16
Both; neither (volunteered)	6
No opinion	3

South

Black population	67%
South African government	13
Both; neither (volunteered)	12
No opinion	8

West

Black population	79%
South African government	8
Both; neither (volunteered)	10
No opinion	3

By Age

18–29 Years

Black population	79%
South African government	14
Both; neither (volunteered)	4
No opinion	3

30–49 Years

Black population	77%
South African government	11
Both; neither (volunteered)	8
No opinion	4

50–64 Years

Black population	66%
South African government	10
Both; neither (volunteered)	13
No opinion	11

65 Years and Over

Black population	64%
South African government	10
Both; neither (volunteered)	20
No opinion	6

By Politics

Republicans

Black population	64%
South African government	13
Both; neither (volunteered)	13
No opinion	10

Democrats

Black population	83%
South African government	8
Both; neither (volunteered)	7
No opinion	2

Independents

Black population	76%
South African government	13
Both; neither (volunteered)	9
No opinion	2

Selected National Trend

	Black population	South African government	Both; neither	No opinion
1985				
October	63%	13%	18%	6%
August	67	11	8	14

Also asked of the aware group: In the last few months, do you think that protest activities in South Africa have increased, remained about the same, or decreased?

Increased	45%
Remained the same	35
Decreased	14
No opinion	6

Also asked of the aware group: As you may know, the South African government recently banned photographic coverage of protest activities because they thought that it encouraged people to commit acts of violence in order to publicize their grievances on television. Do you think the absence of television coverage has caused the number of racial protests to increase, decrease, or has not had much effect one way or the other?

Increase racial protests	28%
Not had much effect	54
Decrease racial protests	12
No opinion	6

Note: The latest Gallup Poll found an increase—from 63% last October to 73% at present—in Americans' sympathy for the black majority in South Africa. In contrast, the proportion now saying they sympathize with the South African government (12%) is virtually identical to the 13% recorded earlier.

In addition, according to the most recent Gallup audit, the vast majority of informed Americans holds the impression that racial protest activity in South Africa has either increased (45%) or remained the same (35%) during the past months, despite a government ban on television coverage

aimed at curbing such protests. Only 14% think that racial demonstrations have declined during this period. Perhaps surprisingly, in view of this blackout on television coverage, as many Americans today as before the ban (56% in each survey) say they have followed recent events in South Africa "very" or "fairly closely."

Another question in the current series found little public credence in the South African government's contention that photographic coverage encouraged protestors to commit acts of violence in order to publicize their grievances before an international television audience. Instead, the overwhelming weight of American opinion is that the absence of televised coverage has not had much effect (54%) or that it has increased (28%) the number of racial protests; only 12% attribute the ban to a decline in demonstrations.

The South African government's press restrictions unquestionably have reduced Americans' exposure to televised scenes of riots and other forms of racial protest. The media have attempted to surmount this obstacle by broadening their coverage and giving more background to their stories. Although the Pretoria government recently lifted a state-of-emergency decree imposed last July, releasing all political prisoners, it gave no sign it would soon rescind the press restrictions.

According to a recent report in the *New York Times*, during the six-month period prior to imposition of the state-of-emergency decree, an average of 1.6 South Africans died in racial incidents each day. The average rose to 3.2 deaths per day during the state of emergency, which was lifted on March 7. During the first two months of 1986, there were 3.6 killings every day. Most of the victims were black.

APRIL 10
SATISFACTION INDEX

Interviewing Date: 3/7–10/86
Special Telephone Survey

In general, are you satisfied or dissatisfied with the way things are going in the United States at this time?

Satisfied 66%
Dissatisfied 30
No opinion 4

Selected National Trend

	Satisfied	Dis-satisfied	No opinion
1985			
November	51%	46%	3%
1984			
December	52	40	8
September	48	45	7
February	50	46	4
1983			
August	35	59	6
1982			
November	24	72	4
April	25	71	4
1981			
December	27	67	6
June	33	61	6
January	17	78	5
1979			
November	19	77	4
August	12	84	4
February	26	69	5

In general, are you satisfied or dissatisfied with the way things are going in your own personal life?

Satisfied 84%
Dissatisfied 15
No opinion 1

Selected National Trend

	Satisfied	Dis-satisfied	No opinion
1985			
November	82%	17%	1%
1984			
December	79	17	4
February	79	19	2
1983			
August	77	20	3
1982			
November	75	23	2
April	76	22	2

1981			
December	81	17	2
June	81	16	3
January	81	17	2
1979			
November	79	19	2
July	73	23	4
February	77	21	2

Note: The early months of 1986 are being called the "era of good feeling," with a record number of Americans expressing satisfaction with the way things are going in the nation and in their personal lives. The latest survey shows two-thirds (66%) of all persons interviewed saying they are satisfied with what is happening in the United States, the highest percentage recorded in the seven years this measurement has been taken, up a full 15 points since last November. The low point in this trend occurred in August 1979 when only 12% were satisfied with the way things were going in the nation and 84% were dissatisfied.

At the same time, a record proportion (84%) currently are satisfied with the trend in their personal lives. This figure also is the highest in seven years, statistically matching 82% last November.

The increasingly upbeat mood found in all regions of the nation and among all major population groups doubtless reflects the public's bullish financial outlook. As reported recently, 61% expect to be financially better off one year from now, an 8-point jump in optimism since January. A companion question also showed a considerable improvement in consumers' perceptions of their present financial status compared to one year ago, with 46% saying they now are better off; in January the figure was 40%.

Finally, about four in ten (37%) may be classified as "super optimists," matching the high point for this index recorded one year ago. These are people who say they now are better off than in the past and expect to be still more prosperous in the future.

Although optimism in both national and personal dimensions has grown sharply since November among both whites and blacks, a wide disparity remains. In the latest survey 68% of whites, but only 44% of blacks, say they are satisfied with the way things are going in the nation; 86% of whites, compared to 64% of blacks, express satisfaction with their personal lives.

APRIL 13
NATIONAL DEFENSE/GOVERNMENT SPENDING

Interviewing Date: 3/4–10/86
Special Telephone Survey

At the present time, which nation do you feel is stronger in terms of nuclear weapons, the United States or the Soviet Union—or do you think they are about equal in nuclear strength?

United States 17%
Soviet Union 23
About equal 54
No opinion 6

Selected National Trend

	United States	Soviet Union	About equal	No opinion
1985				
October	21%	27%	40%	12%
February	24	23	44	9
1983				
March	15	42	35	8
1982				
April–May	17	40	32	11

There is much discussion as to the amount of money the government in Washington should spend for national defense and military purposes. How do you feel about this? Do you think we are spending too little, too much, or about the right amount?

Too little 13%
Too much 47
About right 36
No opinion 4

Selected National Trend

	Too little	Too much	About right	No opinion
1985	11%	46%	36%	7%
1983	21	37	36	6
1982	16	41	31	12
1981	51	15	22	12
1976	22	36	32	10

Of every tax dollar spent by the federal government for defense and military purposes, how many cents would you say are wasted?

	Median average
National	37¢

By Politics

Republicans ....35¢
Democrats ....36¢
Independents ....39¢

Note: A majority of Americans currently perceives the United States and the Soviet Union to be about equal in nuclear strength, the largest proportion to do so in Gallup surveys spanning the last four years. At the same time, a strong 47% plurality believes that the United States is spending too much rather than too little (13%) for defense, while 36% think that the military budget is "about the right amount." These views may be influenced, at least in part, by the perception that about one-third of each tax dollar spent for defense (37¢) is wasted.

A 54% majority currently believes that the United States and the USSR are about equal in nuclear strength, while 23% think the Soviets are stronger, and 17% say the United States holds an edge. These figures represent a dramatic shift in public opinion since Gallup's first assessment of nuclear might, in the spring of 1982. At that time, only 32% thought there was nuclear parity between the superpowers, 40% believed that the Soviet Union held an advantage, and 17% said the United States was ahead. Since 1982 the weight of public opinion has swung gradually toward the parity consensus found today. As recently as last October, only 40% believed that neither nation enjoyed a nuclear advantage.

No significant change has occurred in the past year in Americans' attitudes on defense spending. Then, as now, the heavy weight of public opinion was that it was adequate or excessive. Current views, however, are radically different from those recorded in 1981 when a majority thought that we should spend more for national defense.

To a considerable extent, attitudes toward spending are conditioned by perceptions of the relative strength of the superpowers. However, as many as one-third (33%) of those who say the Soviet Union has a nuclear advantage over the United States think that we are spending too much on defense, while 44% believe that the military budget is about right, and 21% insufficient. Details are shown in the following table:

| | Nuclear Superiority | | |
	United States (17%)	Soviet Union (23%)	About equal (54%)
Defense spending			
Too little	12%	21%	9%
Too much	49	33	54
About right	35	44	34
No opinion	4	2	3

Surveys consistently have shown that Americans believe government spending in general to be wasteful. Defense spending is no exception, with those in the current survey citing a median figure of 37¢ of every defense dollar being wasted. Perceptions of wasteful spending are linked to judgments about the adequacy of the defense budget. Those who think that too much money is now earmarked for defense, for example, cite a median figure of 48¢. Although substantially lower, the average amount of waste given by those who believe the defense appropriation is too little or about right (29¢) reveals a considerable amount of cynicism about defense spending in general, as does the lack of differentiation by political party affiliation.

APRIL 17
AIDS

Interviewing Date: 3/7–10/86
Special Telephone Survey

Have you heard or read about the disease called AIDS—Acquired Immune Deficiency Syndrome?

	Yes
National	98%

Asked of those who responded in the affirmative: Do you believe a person can get AIDS by being in a crowded place with someone who has it?

Can	6%
Cannot	81
Not sure	13

By Sex
Male

Can	7%
Cannot	79
Not sure	14

Female

Can	4%
Cannot	83
Not sure	13

By Ethnic Background
White

Can	5%
Cannot	82
Not sure	13

Nonwhite

Can	10%
Cannot	79
Not sure	11

Black

Can 11%
Cannot 76
Not sure 13

By Education
College Graduate

Can 2%
Cannot 91
Not sure 7

College Incomplete

Can 5%
Cannot 87
Not sure 8

High-School Graduate

Can 5%
Cannot 82
Not sure 13

Less Than High-School Graduate

Can 11%
Cannot 62
Not sure 27

By Region
East

Can 3%
Cannot 86
Not sure 11

Midwest

Can 6%
Cannot 81
Not sure 13

South

Can 6%
Cannot 77
Not sure 17

West

Can 6%
Cannot 83
Not sure 11

By Age
18–29 Years

Can 8%
Cannot 86
Not sure 6

30–49 Years

Can 5%
Cannot 86
Not sure 9

50–64 Years

Can 5%
Cannot 78
Not sure 17

65 Years and Over

Can 6%
Cannot 65
Not sure 29

Those Who Would Send Children to School with AIDS Victim (67%)

Can 2%
Cannot 92
Not sure 6

Those Who Would Not Send Children to School with AIDS Victim (24%)

Can 17%
Cannot 59
Not sure 24

Also asked of the aware group: A 14-year-old Indiana boy who contracted AIDS through a contaminated blood transfusion was banned from attending school classes. After a county medical officer ruled that he posed no health threat to his classmates, he went back to school, but the parents of almost half the students at his school kept their children home. If you had children of this age, would you permit them to attend classes with a child who had AIDS, or not?

Would 67%
Would not 24
No opinion 9

By Sex
Male

Would 66%
Would not 27
No opinion 7

Female

Would 67%
Would not 22
No opinion 11

By Ethnic Background
White

Would 67%
Would not 24
No opinion 9

Nonwhite

Would 64%
Would not 27
No opinion 9

Black

Would 60%
Would not 31
No opinion 9

By Education
College Graduate

Would 72%
Would not 19
No opinion 9

College Incomplete

Would 68%
Would not 23
No opinion 9

High-School Graduate

Would 68%
Would not 23
No opinion 9

Less Than High-School Graduate

Would 57%
Would not 35
No opinion 8

By Region
East

Would 64%
Would not 27
No opinion 9

Midwest

Would 69%
Would not 20
No opinion 11

South

Would 63%
Would not 27
No opinion 10

West

Would 72%
Would not 22
No opinion 6

By Age
18–29 Years

Would 64%
Would not 29
No opinion 7

30–49 Years

Would 69%
Would not 23
No opinion 8

50–64 Years

Would 71%
Would not 20
No opinion 9

65 Years and Over

Would 57%
Would not 27
No opinion 16

Note: A two-thirds majority of adults would permit their children to attend school with a student
who has AIDS, consistent with the scientific consensus that the disease cannot be transmitted by
casual social contact. One-fourth, however, would
be unwilling for a child of theirs to have a class-
mate with AIDS.

Perhaps surprisingly, the latest Gallup survey
not only found an extraordinarily high level of
public awareness of the disease (98%) but also a
very small proportion, 6%, mistakenly believing
that a person can get AIDS merely by being in a
public place with someone who has it.

The "at risk" population almost exclusively
comprises homosexual and bisexual men, intra-
venous drug users, people who receive blood
transfusions from infected donors, and the sex
partners and children of AIDS victims. Public
health officials note that, although the spread of
AIDS is rampant among the at risk groups, its
incidence outside these groups remains stable at
only 1% of reported cases. Nevertheless, there is
considerable public concern that the disease may
spread to the broader population.

As further evidence of the public's apprehension about AIDS, only one-sixth (17%) of those
who would not allow their children to attend classes
with an AIDS victim think that the disease can be
transmitted by casual social contact, 59% of this
group voice the opposite opinion, and 24% are
undecided.

Although substantial majorities in all key population groups believe that AIDS cannot be caught
by casual contact, this opinion is somewhat less
prevalent—and uncertainty more so—among older,
less well-educated, and less affluent people. Similarly, persons from these groups, which are highly
interrelated, are less likely than their counterparts
to say they would permit their children to attend
classes with a child who has AIDS.

APRIL 20
ECONOMIC SITUATION

Interviewing Date: 3/7–10/86
Special Telephone Survey

*The economy is now in the fourth year of
recovery from the recession of 1981–82. Of
course, no one knows for sure, but what is
your best guess about how long this recovery
will last before the economy turns down
again? Will the recovery end this year, early
next year, late next year, or later than that?*

This year 7%
Early next year 25
Later 58
No opinion 10

By Sex
Male

This year 8%
Early next year 23
Later 61
No opinion 8

Female

This year 5%
Early next year 26
Later 56
No opinion 13

By Age
18–29 Years

This year 7%
Early next year 27
Later 62
No opinion 4

30–49 Years

This year 6%
Early next year 26
Later 62
No opinion 6

50 Years and Over

This year 7%
Early next year 21
Later 52
No opinion 20

By Income
$35,000 and Over

This year 5%
Early next year 27
Later 61
No opinion 7

$15,000–$34,999

This year 8%
Early next year 25
Later 60
No opinion 7

Under $15,000

This year 7%
Early next year 23
Later 57
No opinion 13

By Politics
Republicans

This year 5%
Early next year 24
Later 62
No opinion 9

Democrats

This year 7%
Early next year 28
Later 54
No opinion 11

Independents

This year 7%
Early next year 23
Later 62
No opinion 8

Note: Although economists express increasing concern about the lackluster growth of the nation's economy, the public is now as bullish as ever that the recovery will continue. In the latest Gallup Poll, 83% say they expect the recovery to last at least until the end of this year, with 58% predicting that economic good times will prevail into 1988 or beyond.

Doubtless conditioned by the record duration of the recovery, as well as low inflation, declining oil prices, and lower interest rates, the public is now as optimistic as at any time since 1983 when the recovery began.

In the first Gallup assessment, in September 1983, for example, only 43% thought that the recovery would last beyond the end of 1984. In May 1984 the proportion thinking that the recovery would extend into 1986 dropped to 37%, but optimism rose to 54% last August. Now, as noted above, 58% are comparably bullish.

Conversely, in the 1983 survey, 38% thought that the recovery would start to diminish by the end of 1984; in 1984, 47% believed that it would last only until the end of 1985; and in 1985, 32% thought it would turn down by the end of 1986. Again, in the current survey, 32% say it will run out of steam by the end of next year.

Surprisingly little difference is found in the views of persons from different population groups. Less than 10% in each major segment, for example, believe that the recovery will end this year, and only about one-third think that it will end this year or next. Conversely, the heavy weight of opinion in all groups is that the recovery will last until 1988 or even beyond.

Among persons 50 and older and those whose formal education ended before graduation from high school, there is a slight tendency to hold less buoyant expectations, and relatively large proportions in these groups are undecided. And, in last year's survey, Republicans were slightly more bullish than Democrats about the recovery's duration, with 58% of the former and 50% of the latter saying it would last at least into 1987. Similarly, 12% of Republicans and 22% of Democrats thought that a downturn would occur by early this year. Today, political differences have largely disappeared, with no statistically significant variations found.

APRIL 22
TERRORISM

Interviewing Date: 4/17–18/86
Special Telephone Survey*

If Libya conducts or sponsors terrorist acts against the United States in the future, should the United States take military action again, or not?

Should 80%
Should not 10
No opinion 10

By Sex
Male

Should 85%
Should not 10
No opinion 5

Female

Should 76%
Should not 10
No opinion 14

*This study was conducted for *Newsweek* by the Gallup Poll Inc.

By Education
College Graduate

Should 72%
Should not 19
No opinion 9

College Incomplete

Should 81%
Should not 9
No opinion 10

High-School Graduate

Should 83%
Should not 7
No opinion 10

Less Than High-School Graduate

Should 83%
Should not 8
No opinion 9

By Politics
Republicans

Should 88%
Should not 6
No opinion 6

Democrats

Should 73%
Should not 13
No opinion 14

Independents

Should 80%
Should not 11
No opinion 9

Those Who Approve of the April 14 U.S. Raid on Libya (71%)

Should 93%
Should not 2
No opinion 5

Those Who Disapprove of the April 14 U.S. Raid on Libya (21%)

Should 42%
Should not 37
No opinion 21

Do you think the United States should or should not have conducted the bombing raid against Libya even if it turns out that this action does not reduce future terrorism?

Should 68%
Should not 23
No opinion 9

By Sex
Male

Should 73%
Should not 20
No opinion 7

Female

Should 65%
Should not 25
No opinion 10

By Education
College Graduate

Should 61%
Should not 36
No opinion 3

College Incomplete

Should 69%
Should not 27
No opinion 4

High-School Graduate

Should 74%
Should not 16
No opinion 10

Less Than High-School Graduate

Should 66%
Should not 21
No opinion 13

By Politics
Republicans

Should 82%
Should not 12
No opinion 6

Democrats

Should 60%
Should not 30
No opinion 10

Independents

Should 66%
Should not 25
No opinion 9

Those Who Approve of the April 14 U.S. Raid on Libya (71%)

Should 89%
Should not 5
No opinion 6

Those Who Disapprove of the April 14 U.S. Raid on Libya (21%)

Should 13%
Should not 80
No opinion 7

If Syria or Iran commits terrorist acts against the United States, do you think the United States should conduct bombing raids against them, or not?

Should 64%
Should not 22
No opinion 14

In the long run, what effect do you think the U.S. action will have on international terrorism—is terrorist activity likely to increase, decrease, or stay about the same?

Increase 40%
Decrease 31
Same 23
No opinion 6

In your opinion, what role does Libyan leader Muammar Kaddafi play in international terrorism—is he the chief sponsor of international terrorism, one of a number of Mideast leaders who sponsor terrorism, or not a sponsor of terrorism?

Chief sponsor 30%
One of a number 61
Not a sponsor 1
No opinion 8

Which one of the following future U.S. actions would you support as the principal means of dealing with Libya?

Stirring up a military coup to remove
　Kaddafi from power 42%
Supporting economic sanctions
　against Libya 34
Bombing Libyan oil fields 9
Do nothing 3
No opinion 12

Following the U.S. military action against Libya this week, are you personally a lot more concerned about the threat of terrorism in the United States, a little more concerned, or no more concerned?

A lot more concerned 39%
A little more concerned 41
No more concerned 18
No opinion 2

If you had the opportunity to travel overseas this summer, would you take the trip or refuse it because of the threat of terrorism?

Take trip 19%
Refuse 79
Don't know 2

By Age

18–29 Years

Take trip 27%
Refuse 72
Don't know 1

30–49 Years

Take trip 17%
Refuse 81
Don't know 2

50 Years and Over

Take trip 15%
Refuse 83
Don't know 2

Do you think President Reagan makes wise use of military forces to solve foreign policy problems, or do you think he is too quick to employ U.S. forces?

Wise use 62%
Too quick 26
No opinion 12

In deciding about future military retaliation against terrorism, should Congress play more of a role, less of a role, or about the same role it played in the decision this past week?

More 41%
Less 6
Same 44
Don't know 9

Do you think the military action against Libya will make it easier or more difficult to bring about peace between Israel and its Arab neighbors?

Easier 17%
More difficult 56
Have no effect (volunteered) 10
Don't know 17

Holding aside the Libyan action, do you think the Reagan administration is doing as much as it can to bring about peace in the Mideast, or not?

Is 63%
Is not 28
Don't know 9

Note: Although many Americans are doubtful that the U.S. bombing of Libya will deter terrorism, there is solid public support not only for the April 14 raid but also for further military action if Libya continues to conduct or sponsor terrorist attacks against the United States. Americans' new militancy against terrorism was revealed in a just completed Gallup survey that also found 3-to-1 public backing for last week's raid, even if it turns out not to reduce future terrorism. By an equally one-sided margin, Americans believe that the United States should bomb Syria or Iran if either nation commits terrorist acts against this country.

A *Newsweek* Poll conducted by the Gallup Organization found 71% of Americans approving of the April 14 U.S. raid on Libya, with 21% disapproving. The survey also showed that 39% think international terrorism is likely to increase as a consequence of the U.S. action, 31% say it will decrease, and 23% believe that it will stay the same.

A concurrent Gallup Poll found 8-to-1 support for future U.S. raids. While solid backing exists in all key population groups, women are slightly more reluctant than men, 76% and 85%, respectively, to sanction the further use of military force. Democrats (73%) too are slightly less likely than Republicans (88%) to approve of another Libyan strike. Aside from nonwhites, approximately one-fourth of whom oppose U.S. military action under these circumstances, opposition does not exceed 20% in any major demographic segment. Also, the relatively small group (21%) who disapprove of the April 14 raid have mixed feelings about another U.S. attack, with statistically equivalent proportions saying that the United States should (42%) and should not (37%) strike Libya again if terrorism continues.

Another question in the Gallup survey found 68% believing that the United States should have bombed Libya even if it turns out the raid was not an effective deterrent to terrorism, while 23%

express the opposite opinion. Again, majorities in all population groups subscribe to the consensus view. Finally, the last question in the series showed a 64% majority in favor of U.S. bombing raids against Syria or Iran in retaliation for terrorist acts by either nation, with 22% opposed.

In addition to minor variations in responses to these questions by sex, race, and political party affiliation, college graduates are slightly more averse than nongraduates to future raids against Libya, Syria, or Iran and somewhat more inclined to the view that the United States should not have bombed Libya if this action does not deter terrorism.

While the April 14 raid's long-term effectiveness in curbing terrorism remains to be seen, at least two terrorist incidents have occurred since then. The killing of a U.S. communications technician in the Sudan on April 18 was attributed to Libya, and the recent murders of three British and American hostages in Beirut also were directly linked to the raid.

Abroad, the French people are almost as supportive as the Americans of the U.S. air strike, although the French government refused to permit U.S. planes to fly over France on their Libyan mission. Comparatively little public approval of the raid, however, is found in either West Germany or Great Britain where the American planes are based.

U.S. Raid on Libya

	Approve	Dis- approve	No opinion
France	61%	32%	7%
Great Britain	30	66	4
West Germany	25	75	–

APRIL 27
ARMS SALES BAN

Interviewing Date: 3/7–10/86
Special Telephone Survey

Would you approve or disapprove of having the United Nations pass a resolution that would request all nations not to give or sell arms to other nations?

Approve 61%
Disapprove 28
No opinion 11

By Sex
Male

Approve 58%
Disapprove 32
No opinion 10

Female

Approve 62%
Disapprove 25
No opinion 13

By Education
College Graduate

Approve 62%
Disapprove 29
No opinion 9

College Incomplete

Approve 60%
Disapprove 28
No opinion 12

High-School Graduate

Approve 62%
Disapprove 27
No opinion 11

Less Than High-School Graduate

Approve 55%
Disapprove 32
No opinion 13

By Age
18–29 Years

Approve 62%
Disapprove 30
No opinion 8

30–49 Years

Approve 63%
Disapprove 26
No opinion 11

50 Years and Over

Approve 57%
Disapprove 29
No opinion 14

By Politics
Republicans

Approve 55%
Disapprove 33
No opinion 12

Democrats

Approve 67%
Disapprove 25
No opinion 8

Independents

Approve 63%
Disapprove 27
No opinion 10

If the United Nations were to pass such a resolution, do you think the international arms trade would be reduced a great deal, a fair amount, not very much, or not at all?

Great deal 19%
Fair amount 31
Not very much 29
Not at all 13
No opinion 8

Those Who Favor Such a UN Resolution (61%)

Great deal 23%
Fair amount 35
Not very much 28
Not at all 9
No opinion 5

Those Who Oppose Such a UN Resolution (28%)

Great deal 14%
Fair amount 24
Not very much 34
Not at all 22
No opinion 6

Note: The tremendous expansion in the sale of deadly weapons among nations has prompted a growing number of Americans to call for a UN resolution banning this traffic. A solid 61% majority of Americans, up 9 percentage points since 1981, currently approves of having the United Nations pass a resolution requesting all nations not to give or sell arms to other nations. Majority support is found among Republicans and Democrats, men and women, and at all educational and age levels.

Not surprisingly, the survey reveals considerable public skepticism about the effectiveness of a UN arms resolution. Nevertheless, one-half of all respondents believe that the arms trade would be reduced "a great deal" (19%) or "a fair amount" (31%) if such a resolution were passed. As expected, those who are in favor are far more sanguine about its effectiveness than are those who oppose the resolution; 58% of the former, compared to 38% of the latter, believe that international arms traffic would be reduced at least a fair amount.

The latest findings suggest that, while Americans tend to favor a militant U.S. posture in dealing with immediate, "brush fire" situations, such as the recent bombing raid on Libya and the 1983 Grenada incursion, they are less bellicose in long-range global affairs.

The international traffic in arms is growing rapidly. In addition to the major arms merchants in the industrialized nations, at least twenty Third World countries now manufacture highly sophisticated weapons and market them around the globe. These weapons include guided missiles, fighter planes, small attack boats, and tanks. Chief among Third World arms suppliers, with sales totaling in the billions, are China, North and South Korea, Israel, and Brazil.

MAY 1
REPUBLICAN PRESIDENTIAL CANDIDATES

Interviewing Date: 4/11–14/86
Survey #262-G

Asked of Republicans and independents: Will you please look over this list and tell me which of these persons, if any, you have heard of?

	Republicans	Independents
George Bush	95%	93%
Alexander Haig	76	67
Robert Dole	71	60
Howard Baker	64	55
Jeane Kirkpatrick	61	58
Elizabeth Dole	58	48
Jesse Helms	58	54
James Baker	56	46
Jack Kemp	47	38
Pat Robertson	42	36
William Brock	33	29
Donald Rumsfeld	31	26
Paul Laxalt	28	22
Richard Lugar	24	20
Pierre du Pont	21	16
Pete Domenici	20	18
Richard Thornburgh	20	13
Thomas Kean	19	14
Robert Packwood	18	14
James Thompson	18	14
Lewis Lehrman	11	9
Newt Gingrich	4	7
Trent Lott	3	6

Also asked of Republicans and independents: Which one would you like to see nominated as the Republican party's candidate for president in 1988? And who would be your second choice?*

	Republicans	Independents
Bush	51%	35%
Dole, R.	21	11
Baker, H.	17	14
Kemp	10	9
Haig	8	7
Kirkpatrick	7	8

Robertson	6	3
Baker, J.	4	2
Helms	3	4
Lugar	3	2
Thompson	3	3
Dole, E.	2	3
Domenici	2	2
Laxalt	2	1
Thornburgh	2	1
Brock	1	2
Du Pont	1	**
Kean	1	2
Packwood	1	1
Rumsfeld	1	**
Gingrich	**	**
Lehrman	**	**
Lott	**	**

*First and second choices are combined.
**Less than 1%

Note: Vice President George Bush remains the Republicans' early choice to be their party's standard-bearer in the 1988 presidential election. With the GOP convention more than two years away, Bush receives 51% of Republicans' nomination votes to 21% for Senate Majority Leader Robert Dole and 17% for his predecessor, former Senator Howard Baker of Tennessee.

Farther down the list of possible nominees are New York Representative Jack Kemp (the choice of 10%), former Secretary of State Alexander Haig (8%), former UN Ambassador Jeane Kirkpatrick (7%), and television evangelist Pat Robertson (6%).

None of the sixteen other persons on the list of twenty-three possible successors to President Ronald Reagan receives more than 4% of Republicans' votes for the GOP nomination. These include Treasury Secretary James Baker with 4%; Senator Jesse Helms of North Carolina, Senator Richard Lugar of Indiana, and Illinois Governor James Thompson, each with 3%. Receiving 2% are Transportation Secretary Elizabeth Dole, New Mexico Senator Pete Domenici, Nevada Senator Paul Laxalt, and Pennsylvania Governor Richard Thornburgh. Those drawing 1% or less are Labor Secretary William Brock, former Delaware Governor Pierre du Pont, New Jersey Governor Thomas

Kean, Senator Robert Packwood of Oregon, former Defense Secretary Donald Rumsfeld, Representatives Newt Gingrich of Georgia and Trent Lott of Mississippi, and New York businessman Lewis Lehrman.

Although the latest findings reveal no significant changes from those recorded in June 1985, two persons not included in last year's survey, Haig and Robertson, now rank among the top ten. These newcomers receive 8% and 6% of Republicans' votes, respectively.

The nomination contest is somewhat closer among independents, who may vote in some states' GOP primaries, but Bush nonetheless emerges as their clear early preference. The vice president is the choice of 35% of independents to 14% for Howard Baker and 11% for Robert Dole; none of the others earns more than 9%.

The following table compares the standings of the current leaders with those in last year's survey. The apparent differences, such as Robert Dole's 3-point increase and Howard Baker's 5-point decline, have no statistical significance*:

	April 1986	June 1985
Bush	51%	53%
Dole, R.	21	18
Baker, H.	17	22
Kemp	10	10
Haig	8	**
Kirkpatrick	7	9
Robertson	6	**
Baker, J.	4	5

*Based on Republicans
**Not included in 1985 test

MAY 4
DEMOCRATIC PRESIDENTIAL CANDIDATES

Interviewing Date: 4/11–14/86
Survey #262-G

Asked of Democrats and independents: Will you please look over this list and tell me which of these persons, if any, you have heard of?

	Democrats	Independents
Jesse Jackson	89%	89%
Gary Hart	81	80
Lee Iacocca	66	74
Mario Cuomo	52	51
Tom Bradley	51	50
Jay Rockefeller	47	47
Dianne Feinstein	41	38
Bill Bradley	33	33
Charles Robb	32	29
Sam Nunn	23	20
Mark White	20	24
Richard Gephardt	17	13
Dale Bumpers	16	16
Patricia Schroeder	16	22
Bruce Babbitt	13	11
Joseph Biden	8	8
Tony Coelho	6	7

Also asked of Democrats and independents: Which one would you like to see nominated as the Democratic party's candidate for president in 1988? And who would be your second choice?*

	Democrats	Independents
Hart	39%	30%
Cuomo	27	15
Jackson	18	7
Iacocca	14	24
Bradley (Tom)	7	5
Bradley (Bill)	6	5
Rockefeller	6	4
Robb	5	3
Feinstein	4	2
Bumpers	2	2
Nunn	2	1
Schroeder	2	3
White	2	5
Babbitt	1	**
Biden	1	1
Gephardt	1	1
Coelho	**	**

*First and second choices are combined.
**Less than 1%

Note: Although Senator Gary Hart of Colorado remains the Democrats' top choice to be their party's 1988 presidential nominee, the wide gap that separated Hart and runner-up New York Governor Mario Cuomo in January has narrowed considerably, and Cuomo is now in a stronger position to challenge Hart as the early nomination favorite. Hart currently receives 39% of Democrats' first and second place nomination votes to 27% for Cuomo. In a mid-January survey, Hart led Cuomo by a commanding 25-point margin, 47% to 22%.

Next on the current list of possible Democratic nominees are the Rev. Jesse Jackson and Chrysler Corporation Chairman Lee Iacocca, the choices of 18% and 14% of Democrats, respectively. Farther down the list are Los Angeles Mayor Tom Bradley with 7% of the vote, New Jersey Senator Bill Bradley (6%), West Virginia Senator Jay Rockefeller (6%), former Virginia Governor Charles Robb (5%), and San Francisco Mayor Dianne Feinstein (4%). None of the eight other persons on a list of seventeen possible contenders receives more than 2% of Democrats' votes. These include Governors Bruce Babbitt of Arizona and Mark White of Texas; Senators Joseph Biden of Delaware, Dale Bumpers of Arizona, and Sam Nunn of Georgia; and Representatives Tony Coelho of California, Richard Gephardt of Missouri, and Patricia Schroeder of Colorado.

The 1988 nomination choices of self-described independents, who may vote for Democratic candidates in states with open primaries, are markedly different from those of Democrats. The contest among independents currently is a statistical toss-up between Hart and Iacocca, with 30% and 24% of the vote, respectively. Cuomo now is a fairly distant challenger, with 15%, followed next by Jackson, with 7%. By contrast, in the January poll, Hart garnered almost as many independent votes (35%) as did runners-up Cuomo (19%) and Iacocca (18%) combined.

With almost two years remaining before the early state primaries, name recognition plays a vital role in the potential candidates' standing with the Democratic rank and file. At present, only five of the seventeen names on the list are familiar to 50% or more Democrats and independents. Conversely, eight names are recognized by one-fourth or less. The importance of name recognition is illustrated by the fact that front-runners Hart and

Cuomo are tied for the nomination lead among Democrats familiar with each man.

The following table compares the standings of the current leaders with those in the January survey*:

	April 1986	January 1986
Hart	39%	47%
Cuomo	27	22
Jackson	18	16
Iacocca	14	18

*Based on Democrats

MAY 8
PRESIDENTIAL TRIAL HEATS

Interviewing Date: 4/11–14/86
Survey #262-G

Asked of registered voters: Suppose the 1988 presidential election were being held today. If Vice President George Bush were the Republican candidate and Senator Gary Hart were the Democratic candidate, which would you like to see win? [Those who named other candidates or were undecided were then asked: As of today, do you lean more to Bush, the Republican, or to Hart, the Democrat?]

Bush	44%
Hart	46
Other; undecided	10

Selected National Trend

	Bush	Hart	Other; undecided
January 1986	45%	47%	8%
July 1985	50	39	11

Asked of registered voters: Suppose the 1988 presidential election were being held today. If Vice President George Bush were the Republican candidate and New York Governor Mario Cuomo were the Democratic candidate, which would you like to see win? [Those who named other candidates or were undecided were then asked: As of today, do

you lean more to Bush, the Republican, or to Cuomo, the Democrat?

Bush	51%
Cuomo	36
Other; undecided	13

Selected National Trend

	Bush	Cuomo	Other; undecided
January 1986	54%	34%	12%
July 1985	55	31	14

Note: If the 1988 presidential election were held now, Republican candidate George Bush and Democratic candidate Gary Hart would win about the same share of the popular vote, according to a new Gallup test election. Colorado Senator Hart currently is the choice of 46% of registered voters nationwide to 44% for Vice President Bush, with 10% naming other candidates or undecided. The latest figures are statistically unchanged from the results of a January poll in which Hart received 47% of the vote to Bush's 45%.

In a similar test, Bush now leads possible Democratic contender Mario Cuomo by a wide 51% to 36% margin. Although this appears to represent a slight weakening since January in Bush's competitive position, when he led the New York governor by 54% to 34%, the change is too small to be statistically conclusive.

The current findings represent significant improvements for both possible Democratic nominees since July 1985 when Bush led Hart by 50% to 39% and Cuomo by 55% to 31%. Since then, Hart has picked up ground against Bush among voters from widely varying demographic backgrounds and of all political stripes. Cuomo's gains also have occurred across a broad demographic spectrum.

Still, both Hart and Cuomo continue to exhibit weakness among their own party members. In the latest survey, 22% of registered Democrats say they would vote for Bush, rather than Hart (71%), if the election were held now, and 32% of self-described Democrats currently choose Bush over

Cuomo (58%). By comparison, Republicans demonstrate greater party loyalty, with 80% supporting Bush over Cuomo (11%), and 76% backing Bush over Hart (16%).

At present, no strong challenger to Vice President Bush has yet appeared. He is the current choice of 51% of Republicans for the GOP nomination. Runners-up include Senate Majority Leader Robert Dole (21%), former Tennessee Senator Howard Baker (17%), and Representative Jack Kemp of New York (10%). It should be stressed that, at this early stage in the campaign, many potential nominees are seriously hampered by a lack of familiarity to the party's rank and file. Kemp, for instance, is known to only 47% of Republicans; similarly, Hart's greater familiarity (81%) than Cuomo's (52%) among Democrats may have influenced the outcome of their test elections against Bush.

MAY 11
HANDGUN LAWS

Interviewing Date: 4/11–14/86
Survey #262-G

> In general, do you feel that the laws covering the sale of handguns should be made more strict, less strict, or kept as they are now?

More strict 60%
Less strict 8
Kept same 30
No opinion 2

By Sex
Male

More strict 53%
Less strict 14
Kept same 32
No opinion 1

Female

More strict 66%
Less strict 4
Kept same 27
No opinion 3

By Ethnic Background
White

More strict 58%
Less strict 9
Kept same 31
No opinion 2

Nonwhite

More strict 75%
Less strict 8
Kept same 17
No opinion .... *

Black

More strict 76%
Less strict 9
Kept same 15
No opinion .... *

By Education
College Graduate

More strict 65%
Less strict 8
Kept same 25
No opinion 2

College Incomplete

More strict 64%
Less strict 8
Kept same 28
No opinion .... *

High-School Graduate

More strict 57%
Less strict 8
Kept same 33
No opinion 2

Less Than High-School Graduate

More strict 55%
Less strict 10
Kept same 31
No opinion 4

By Region

East

More strict 70%
Less strict 7
Kept same 22
No opinion 1

Midwest

More strict 58%
Less strict 9
Kept same 31
No opinion 2

South

More strict 54%
Less strict 11
Kept same 32
No opinion 3

West

More strict 58%
Less strict 5
Kept same 35
No opinion 2

By Age

18–29 Years

More strict 59%
Less strict 8
Kept same 32
No opinion 1

30–49 Years

More strict 62%
Less strict 10
Kept same 27
No opinion 1

50 Years and Over

More strict 58%
Less strict 7
Kept same 31
No opinion 4

All Gun Owners

More strict 44%
Less strict 13
Kept same 41
No opinion 2

Handgun Owners Only

More strict 41%
Less strict 15
Kept same 43
No opinion 1

Nonowners

More strict 70%
Less strict 6
Kept same 22
No opinion 2

*Less than 1%

Selected National Trend

	More strict	Less strict	Kept same	No opinion
1983	59%	4%	31%	6%
1981	65	3	30	2
1980	59	6	29	6
1975	69	3	24	4

Some communities have passed laws banning the sale and possession of handguns. Would you favor or oppose having such a law in this city/community?

Favor 47%
Oppose 47
No opinion 6

By Sex

Male

Favor 39%
Oppose 57
No opinion 4

Female

Favor 55%
Oppose 38
No opinion 7

By Ethnic Background
White

Favor 45%
Oppose 49
No opinion 6

Nonwhite

Favor 59%
Oppose 35
No opinion 6

Black

Favor 59%
Oppose 34
No opinion 7

By Education
College Graduate

Favor 54%
Oppose 43
No opinion 3

College Incomplete

Favor 47%
Oppose 48
No opinion 5

High-School Graduate

Favor 45%
Oppose 48
No opinion 7

Less Than High-School Graduate

Favor 44%
Oppose 49
No opinion 7

By Region
East

Favor 62%
Oppose 34
No opinion 4

Midwest

Favor 45%
Oppose 49
No opinion 6

South

Favor 40%
Oppose 51
No opinion 9

West

Favor 43%
Oppose 55
No opinion 2

By Age
18–29 Years

Favor 47%
Oppose 47
No opinion 6

30–49 Years

Favor 50%
Oppose 47
No opinion 3

50 Years and Over

Favor 44%
Oppose 48
No opinion 8

All Gun Owners

Favor 31%
Oppose 64
No opinion 5

Handgun Owners Only

Favor 26%
Oppose 71
No opinion 3

Nonowners

Favor 58%
Oppose 36
No opinion 6

Selected National Trend

	Favor	Oppose	No opinion
1985	40%	56%	4%
1983	44	48	8

Have you heard or read about the debate in Congress over the interstate sale of handguns?

	Yes
National	59%

All persons in the sample, including the 59% who answered affirmatively, were asked: At present there is a federal law banning the sale of handguns in one state to a person or dealer from another state. Do you think this ban on interstate handgun sales should be continued, or not?

Should 67%
Should not 23
No opinion 10

By Sex
Male

Should 63%
Should not 30
No opinion 7

Female

Should 70%
Should not 18
No opinion 12

By Ethnic Background
White

Should 67%
Should not 24
No opinion 9

Nonwhite

Should 68%
Should not 17
No opinion 15

Black

Should 66%
Should not 17
No opinion 17

By Education
College Graduate

Should 77%
Should not 19
No opinion 4

College Incomplete

Should 72%
Should not 20
No opinion 8

High-School Graduate

Should 64%
Should not 26
No opinion 10

Less Than High-School Graduate

Should 59%
Should not 27
No opinion 14

By Region
East

Should 74%
Should not 18
No opinion 8

Midwest

Should	68%
Should not	24
No opinion	8

South

Should	58%
Should not	28
No opinion	14

West

Should	71%
Should not	22
No opinion	7

By Age
18–29 Years

Should	64%
Should not	26
No opinion	10

30–49 Years

Should	69%
Should not	23
No opinion	8

50 Years and Over

Should	68%
Should not	21
No opinion	11

All Gun Owners

Should	62%
Should not	29
No opinion	9

Handgun Owners Only

Should	60%
Should not	32
No opinion	8

Nonowners

Should	71%
Should not	19
No opinion	10

Those Aware of Debate

Should	70%
Should not	24
No opinion	6

Those Not Aware of Debate

Should	62%
Should not	23
No opinion	15

Note: Despite recent congressional action easing present federal handgun restrictions, the American people continue to favor stringent curbs on the sale and possession of these weapons. In the latest Gallup Poll, 60% say the laws covering the sale of handguns should be made more strict, while 30% think the present regulations are adequate and only 8% say the laws should be relaxed. Although handgun owners—comprising about one-fifth of the adult population—understandably are more reluctant to endorse stricter curbs on the sale of these weapons, 41% nonetheless do so. Only 15% call for more lenient laws, while 43% say the present laws should be kept as they are now.

Public pressure for stricter laws on handgun sales currently is as high as it has been in at least ten years, with two extraordinary exceptions: Gallup's initial measurement in October 1975, which found 69% favoring stricter laws, conducted two weeks after the second assassination attempt on President Gerald Ford; and an April 1981 assessment, in which 65% backed stricter laws, following by days the attempt on President Ronald Reagan's life.

The Gallup Poll consistently has found Americans throughout the nation and from all walks of life supportive of more stringent handgun controls but unwilling to endorse an outright ban on the sale or private possession of these weapons. A 1985 Gallup survey, for example, found 40% favoring and 56% opposed to a community ban on the sale or ownership of handguns. In the current survey, equal proportions favor and oppose (47% each) having their city or community enact such legislation. The latest findings not only represent a significant increase in public support for a ban on private sale or possession but also the first time opposition has not outweighed support. Nonowners of firearms come down heavily (58% to 36%) in favor of a community handgun ban. Surprisingly, 26% of handgun owners support such a ban as well.

In March the House of Representatives eliminated some key provisions of the 1968 Gun Control Act, under heavy pressure from the National Rifle Association; the Senate had approved these measures last year. However, gun control advocates persuaded House members to preserve the current prohibition of handgun sales across state lines, which the Senate had voted to end. Accordingly, by almost a 3-to-1 margin, the public believes the present ban on the interstate sale of handguns should be continued (67%) rather than lifted (23%), with 10% undecided. Solid public support for retention of the current federal law banning interstate sales is found in all demographic groups and in every region of the nation. Handgun owners back continuation of the ban by a 2-to-1 ratio, 60% to 32%.

MAY 15
SEAT BELTS

Interviewing Date: 4/11–14/86
Survey #262-G

Thinking about the last time you got into a car, did you use a seat belt, or not?

	Yes, used belt
National	52%

By Sex

Male	49%
Female	54

By Education

College graduate	72%
College incomplete	61
High-school graduate	46
Less than high-school graduate	34

By Region

East	59%
Midwest	47
South	38
West	69

By Age

18–24 years	45%
25–29 years	52
30–49 years	57
50–64 years	51
65 years and over	47

By Occupation

Professional and business	64%
Clerical and sales	60
Blue collar workers	46

Selected National Trend

	Yes, used belt
1985	40%
1984	25
1982	17
1977	22
1973	28

Note: The use of auto seat belts has doubled in the last two years. Currently, a 52% majority of adults reports having worn a seat belt the last time they rode in a car, twice the 25% incidence reported in Gallup's 1984 audit and sharply higher than last year's figure of 40%. As recently as 1982, only 17% used their seat belts. Although dramatic increases in seat belt use since 1984 are recorded in all major population groups, marked differences remain. Persons who attended college and those from households in which the chief wage earner is employed in a white-collar occupation are considerably more likely than their counterparts to be seat belt users. Similarly, southerners (38%) continue to lag behind those from other regions in seat belt use.

Not coincidentally, twenty-four states and the District of Columbia now have mandatory seat belt laws on the books. At this time last year only New York and New Jersey had compulsory seat belt laws, while five additional states had enacted legislation that has gone into effect since then. The recent spate of seat belt legislation doubtless reflects Transportation Secretary Elizabeth Dole's 1984 order requiring all new automobiles to be equipped with passive restraints, such as air bags or automatic seat belts, by 1989. The requirements would be waived if states with two-thirds of the U.S. population pass mandatory seat belt use laws by then.

Although states with mandatory seat belt legislation report fewer traffic fatalities since their laws took effect, auto accidents remain the third leading cause of death in the United States, trailing only cancer and heart disease. More than 44,000 people die each year in auto accidents.

MAY 18

VOLUNTARISM

Interviewing Date: 3/7–10/86
Special Telephone Survey

Do you, yourself, happen to be involved in any charity or social service activities, such as helping the poor, the sick, or the elderly?

	1986 Yes	1977 Yes
National	36%	27%

By Sex

Male	34%	24%
Female	38	29

By Education

College education	43%	38%
High school or less	31	22

By Region

East	33%	25%
Midwest	34	23
South	40	29
West	36	31

By Age

18–29 years	27%	16%
30–49 years	37	28
50 years and over	41	34

By Religion

Protestants	36%	27%
Catholics	31	26
Church members	39%	30%
Nonmembers	28	19

Selected National Trend

	Yes
1984	31%
1982	29
1977	27

Note: Although some social observers perceive Americans as becoming increasingly preoccupied with their material well-being, voluntarism—extending one's hand to those who need help—is at least as prevalent today as at any other time during the last decade. Presently one adult in three (36%) reports being involved in such charitable or social service activities as helping the poor, sick, or elderly.

The current level of voluntarism represents the highest point to date in a steadily rising trend since 1977, when the first Gallup Poll audit on this topic was conducted. In the 1977 survey, 27% were involved in charitable activities. Comparison with the 1977 findings reveals increased participation in all population segments. As in the past, church members, the college educated, and persons age 50 and older are somewhat more likely than their counterparts to engage in charitable activities. The observed differences by gender, religious preference, and geographic region are too small to be statistically conclusive.

MAY 22

PARTY BETTER FOR PEACE AND PROSPERITY

Interviewing Date: 3/7–10/86
Special Telephone Survey

Looking ahead for the next few years, which political party do you think would be more likely to keep the United States out of World War III—the Republican party or the Democratic party?

Republican 39%
Democratic 36
No difference; no opinion 25

Selected National Trend

	Republican party	Democratic party	No difference; no opinion
1985			
June	35%	37%	28%
March	39	33	28
1984			
September	38	38	24
August	36	40	24
April	30	42	28
1983	26	39	35
1982	29	38	33
1981	29	34	37
1980	25	42	33
1976	29	32	39
1972	32	28	40
1968	37	24	39
1964	22	45	33
1960	40	25	35
1956	46	16	38
1952	36	15	49
1951	28	21	51

Which political party—the Republican party or the Democratic party—do you think will do a better job of keeping the country prosperous?

Republican 51%
Democratic 33
No difference; no opinion 16

Selected National Trend

	Republican party	Democratic party	No difference; no opinion
1985			
June	44%	35%	21%
March	48	32	20
1984			
September	49	33	18
August	48	36	16
April	44	36	20
1983	33	40	27
1982	34	43	23
1981	40	31	29
1980	35	36	29
1976	23	47	30
1972	38	35	27
1968	34	37	29
1964	21	53	26
1960	31	46	23
1956	39	39	22
1952	31	35	34
1951	29	37	34

Note: More Americans now regard the Republican party as better able than the Democratic party to keep the nation prosperous than at any previous time during the past thirty-five years. Doubtless spurred by optimism about the economy as well as their own financial prospects, 51% of the public currently cite the GOP, the party in power, as the party of prosperity, while 33% name the Democrats and 16% see little difference or are undecided.

The current findings mark the first time a majority of Americans has singled out the Republican party over the Democratic party as superior in this regard in a Gallup trend that began in 1951. Republicans have held a significant advantage over Democrats on the prosperity issue only since 1984 and during President Ronald Reagan's first year in office. Prior to 1981 the Democrats enjoyed a near monopoly on this issue, at times by ratios of 3 to 1 or better. The depth of the public's perception of the GOP's superiority is illustrated by the fact that only blacks and Democrats in general currently credit the Democratic party as better able to keep the nation prosperous. Even among Democrats, as many as one in five (22%) concedes the advantage to the GOP.

At present neither political party enjoys a clear-cut lead as better able to keep the nation at peace, with the GOP named by 39% and the Democrats by 36%. One year ago the Republicans held a narrow 39% to 33% advantage, but the two parties again were nearly tied in a survey last June. With only a few exceptions, the Democrats have led on this issue for the last decade, with the lead changing hands periodically before then. The last time the GOP held an outright advantage as better able to keep the nation out of war was during the closing months of President Richard Nixon's 1972 reelection campaign.

In the latest survey, the GOP holds a slight edge as the party of peace among whites, those with family incomes of $35,000 or more, and, of course, Republicans. Again, blacks and Democrats assert that the Democratic party is superior on this issue.

MAY 25
IDEAL FAMILY SIZE

Interviewing Date: 3/7–10/86
Special Telephone Survey

What do you think is the ideal number of children for a family to have?

One	5%
Two	59
Three	17
Four or more	11
None	2
No opinion	6

By Sex
Male

One or two	61%
Three	20
Four or more	10
None; no opinion	9

Female

One or two	67%
Three	14
Four or more	12
None; no opinion	7

By Ethnic Background
White

One or two	66%
Three	17
Four or more	10
None; no opinion	7

Black

One or two	48%
Three	14
Four or more	25
None; no opinion	13

By Education
College Graduate

One or two	65%
Three	19
Four or more	5
None; no opinion	11

College Incomplete

One or two	67%
Three	21
Four or more	8
None; no opinion	4

High-School Graduate

One or two	65%
Three	15
Four or more	12
None; no opinion	8

Less Than High-School Graduate

One or two 57%
Three 14
Four or more 19
None; no opinion 10

By Age
18–29 Years

One or two 66%
Three 19
Four or more 12
None; no opinion 3

30–49 Years

One or two 71%
Three 14
Four or more 7
None; no opinion 8

50–64 Years

One or two 60%
Three 15
Four or more 13
None; no opinion 12

65 Years and Over

One or two 49%
Three 22
Four or more 20
None; no opinion 9

By Income
$35,000 and Over

One or two 69%
Three 15
Four or more 7
None; no opinion 9

$15,000–$34,999

One or two 65%
Three 20
Four or more 8
None; no opinion 7

Under $15,000

One or two 61%
Three 13
Four or more 20
None; no opinion 6

By Religion
Protestants

One or two 65%
Three 17
Four or more 11
None; no opinion 7

Catholics

One or two 61%
Three 19
Four or more 11
None; no opinion 9

By Number of Own Children
One Child

One or two 74%
Three 11
Four or more 7
None; no opinion 8

Two Children

One or two 77%
Three 13
Four or more 3
None; no opinion 7

Three Children

One or two 42%
Three 35
Four or more 12
None; no opinion 11

Four Children or More

One or two 51%
Three 16
Four or more 24
None; no opinion 9

Selected National Trend

	One; two	Three	Four or more	None; no opinion
1983	57%	21%	14%	8%
1978	50	23	17	10
1973	47	23	20	10

Note: The appeal of small families continues to grow, with almost two-thirds (64%) of Americans in the latest Gallup survey saying one or two children is the ideal number for a family to have. This is the largest proportion to express this view since Gallup began recording the public's preferences in 1936. As recently as 1973, only 47% thought one or two children was the optimal family size. Currently, only 11% cite four or more children as the ideal, the smallest proportion to do so in the fifty-year Gallup trend.

The latest Gallup findings complement recent Census Bureau estimates showing that the number of U.S. households increased by almost 9% during the five-year period ending July 1, 1985, while the population grew by less than 6%. This indicates a significant reduction in the average number of individuals per household. The continuing trend to smaller families has confounded many population experts, who had predicted a growth in family size as the baby boom generation came of childbearing age. Countervailing factors—including deferral of marriages and childbearing, divorce, the increase in single-person households, and the aging of the population, among others—have contributed to smaller household size.

In the current survey, a 59% majority believes the ideal number of children is two, while 17% prefer three, 5% one, and 2% none. Two-child families have been preferred since the early 1970s. By contrast, in the Gallup Poll's first (1936) measurement on ideal family size, 34% said that four or more children represented this ideal. By 1945, 49% chose four or more children as the best number, presaging the postwar baby boom. The percentage trended slowly downward between 1947 and 1968 but subsequently dropped sharply.

Now the ideal in all major population groups is one or two children. However, blacks are far more inclined than whites to favor large families,

as are older, less educated, and less affluent Americans. Also, Roman Catholics historically have favored larger families than have Protestants; in the 1968 survey, for instance, 50% of Catholics, compared to 37% of Protestants, cited four or more children as the ideal. In 1986, however, statistically identical proportions of Catholics and Protestants share this view.

As might be expected, there is a greater tendency for people who themselves have had large families to express a similar preference. That only one-fourth (24%) of parents of four or more children say this represents the ideal—while 51% cite one or two children as the model—may underscore the modern trend to smaller families.

MAY 29
COST OF LIVING

Interviewing Date: January–March 1986
Various Surveys

On the average, about how much does your family spend on food each week?

	Median average
National	$75

By Region

East	$80
Midwest	$69
South	$75
West	$76

By Age

18–29 years	$74
30–49 years	$81
50–64 years	$74
65 years and over	$52

By Income

$25,000 and over	$91
Under $25,000	$61

Selected National Trend

Year	Amount
1985	$75
1983	$69
1981	$62
1979	$53
1977	$48
1975	$47
1973	$37
1971	$35
1970	$34
1969	$33
1959	$29
1949	$25
1937	$11

Note: The average American family now spends about $75 each week on food, the same amount reported last year. This figure, although not significantly higher than the amounts recorded in each of the three previous years, represents the largest food budget reported since the Gallup Poll began auditing family food expenditures a half century ago. Since 1937 the weekly amount spent on food has increased almost sevenfold, from $11 in the first audit to the current $75.

During the twenty-year period between 1949 and 1969, the figure grew from $25 to $33 per week, an increase of only 32%. However, from 1970 to the present—a span of only seventeen years—food expenditures have more than doubled, from $34 to $75 per week.

Persons in the survey with annual family incomes of $25,000 or more report spending one and one-half times as much on food as do those with lower incomes. Furthermore, food bills represent a larger portion of total expenditures of families in the lower-income category than is true of upper-income households.

Food expenses take a slightly smaller bite out of the weekly budgets of Midwestern families compared to those in the East, the highest of the four regions. Also, higher average food expenses are reported by persons 30 to 49 years old, the peak childrearing years, while those 65 and older spend about two-thirds as much as the national median. This older age group, of course, includes a larger number of one- and two-person families.

JUNE 1

FAVORITE PASTIME

Interviewing Date: 4/11–14/86
Survey #262-G

What is your favorite way of spending an evening?

	1986	1974	1966	1960	1938
Watching television	33%	46%	46%	28%	*
Reading	14	14	15	10	21
Resting, relaxing	14	8	*	*	*
Home with family	13	10	5	17	7
Dining out	10	12	*	*	*
Visiting with friends	8	8	5	10	4
Movies, theater	6	9	5	6	17
Cards, games	4	8	5	6	9
Dancing	3	4	2	3	12
Listening to music, radio	3	5	2	**	9
House, yard work	3	3	*	*	*
Sewing, needlework	3	3	*	*	*

*Not available
**Less than 1%

Note: Watching television remains our most popular evening pastime, but other forms of recreation now command a greater share of Americans' free time than in earlier years. In the latest Gallup Poll, 33% say watching television is their favorite way to spend an evening, down sharply from the 46% who made this observation in each of the last two Gallup audits in 1974 and 1966.

Tied for second place this year are reading and relaxing, each named by 14%. Reading has been the most popular evening pastime of about one adult in seven for at least the last twenty years. In the first (1938) Gallup survey on the subject, however, it was the public's leading diversion, cited by 21%. Resting and relaxing has emerged as the third favorite, up from 8% in 1974.

Next in popularity this year is staying home with family and children (13%), followed by dining out (10%); both these pursuits occupy about the same levels of participants that they did in 1974. Visiting with friends is another perennial favorite, cited by 8% this year and by similar proportions since 1938. Going to the movies or theater, currently named by 6%, has roughly as many adherents as in the other postwar polls, but far fewer than in 1938, when 17% said it was their favorite way to spend an evening. Another popular current diversion is playing cards and other non-athletic games, cited by 4% this year. In earlier years games playing attracted slightly more par-ticipants. Currently named by 3% each are danc-ing, listening to music, doing chores around the house or yard, and sewing.

Not surprisingly, the relative popularity of many of the pastimes varies considerably by gender, age, education, and family income. Women, for instance, are more avid readers than men, as are better educated and more affluent persons of both sexes. In fact, reading edges out watching tele-vision as the most popular diversion among col-lege graduates. Television viewing becomes progressively more popular as age increases, with 26% of young adults (18 to 24 years) compared to 47% of persons 65 and older naming it as their favorite. Older people also are more likely to be involved in church-related activities.

Dining out and movie- and theater-going are more popular among the young, the better edu-cated, and the more affluent. Several of the top national pastimes appear to be about equally pop-ular, however, with persons from widely diverse socioeconomic backgrounds. These include play-ing cards and other nonathletic games, resting and relaxing, visiting with friends, and listening to music.

JUNE 5
HONESTY AND STANDARDS OF BEHAVIOR

Interviewing Date: 4/11–14/86
Survey #262-G

On the whole, would you say you are satisfied or dissatisfied with the honesty and standards of behavior of people in this country today?

Satisfied 33%
Dissatisfied 63
No opinion 4

By Sex
Male

Satisfied 35%
Dissatisfied 61
No opinion 4

Female

Satisfied 30%
Dissatisfied 65
No opinion 5

By Ethnic Background
White

Satisfied 34%
Dissatisfied 62
No opinion 4

Black

Satisfied 21%
Dissatisfied 73
No opinion 6

By Education
College Graduate

Satisfied 43%
Dissatisfied 55
No opinion 2

College Incomplete

Satisfied 32%
Dissatisfied 64
No opinion 4

High-School Graduate

Satisfied 31%
Dissatisfied 64
No opinion 5

Less Than High-School Graduate

Satisfied 27%
Dissatisfied 68
No opinion 5

By Age
18–29 Years

Satisfied 35%
Dissatisfied 60
No opinion 5

30–49 Years

Satisfied 36%
Dissatisfied 60
No opinion 4

50 Years and Over

Satisfied 26%
Dissatisfied 70
No opinion 4

By Income
$25,000 and Over

Satisfied 39%
Dissatisfied 59
No opinion 2

Less Than $25,000

Satisfied 29%
Dissatisfied 66
No opinion 5

By Religion
Protestants

Satisfied 31%
Dissatisfied 66
No opinion 3

Catholics

Satisfied 33%
Dissatisfied 62
No opinion 5

By Moral Values
Traditional

Satisfied 26%
Dissatisfied 69
No opinion 6

Moderate

Satisfied 37%
Dissatisfied 60
No opinion 3

Liberal

Satisfied 33%
Dissatisfied 64
No opinion 3

Selected National Trend

	Satisfied	Dissatisfied	No opinion
1973	22%	72%	6%
1963	34	58	8

Note: Amid widespread recent reports of unethical and illegal activities in many areas of public life, almost two-thirds of Americans express dissatisfaction with the honesty and standards of behavior of their compatriots. In the latest Gallup assessment, 63% say that, on the whole, they are dissatisfied with the honesty of people in this country, while only about one-half that proportion, 33%, are satisfied.

The current findings are similar to those recorded in the first (1963) Gallup measurement but represent a modest improvement over the results of a Gallup Poll taken at the height of the Watergate affair in 1973. In that survey, dissatisfaction outweighed satisfaction by better than a 3-to-1 ratio, 72% to 22%.

Although majorities in all major population groups express dissatisfaction with the current ethical climate in the United States, somewhat greater concern is voiced by blacks, persons age 50 and older, the less affluent and less well educated, and people holding traditional moral values. The apparent differences by gender and religion are too small to be statistically meaningful.

The generally low ethical ratings they attribute to their fellow Americans are reflected in the poor marks the public gave most occupations tested in a 1985 survey. Asked to rate people in twenty-four different fields in terms of their honesty and ethical standards, a majority assigned very high or high ratings to only six: the clergy, pharmacists, medical doctors, dentists, college teachers, and engineers.

JUNE 8
NATIONAL DEFENSE

Interviewing Date: 4/11–14/86
Survey #262-G

In your opinion, which of the following increases the chances of nuclear war more— a continuation of the nuclear arms buildup here and in the Soviet Union, or the United States falling behind the Soviet Union in nuclear weaponry?

Continued arms buildup 39%
United States falling behind 47
No opinion 14

By Sex
Male

Continued arms buildup 38%
United States falling behind 51
No opinion 11

Female

Continued arms buildup 39%
United States falling behind 45
No opinion 16

By Ethnic Background
White

Continued arms buildup 39%
United States falling behind 49
No opinion 12

Nonwhite

Continued arms buildup 40%
United States falling behind 37
No opinion 23

Black

Continued arms buildup 38%
United States falling behind 39
No opinion 23

By Education
College Graduate

Continued arms buildup 48%
United States falling behind 47
No opinion 5

College Incomplete

Continued arms buildup 39%
United States falling behind 50
No opinion 11

High-School Graduate

Continued arms buildup 42%
United States falling behind 48
No opinion 10

Less Than High-School Graduate

Continued arms buildup 28%
United States falling behind 44
No opinion 28

By Region
East

Continued arms buildup 39%
United States falling behind 48
No opinion 13

Midwest

Continued arms buildup 44%
United States falling behind 41
No opinion 15

South

Continued arms buildup 32%
United States falling behind 53
No opinion 15

West

Continued arms buildup 41%
United States falling behind 46
No opinion 13

By Age
18–29 Years

Continued arms buildup 43%
United States falling behind 47
No opinion 10

30–49 Years

Continued arms buildup 42%
United States falling behind 47
No opinion 11

50 Years and Over

Continued arms buildup 33%
United States falling behind 48
No opinion 19

By Politics
Republicans

Continued arms buildup 36%
United States falling behind 56
No opinion 8

Democrats

Continued arms buildup 40%
United States falling behind 45
No opinion 15

Independents

Continued arms buildup 40%
United States falling behind 43
No opinion 17

Selected National Trend

	Continued arms buildup	United States falling behind	No opinion
October 1985	33%	45%	22%
February 1985	41	43	16
March 1983	38	47	15

*The Soviet Union has had a ban on under-
ground tests of nuclear weapons since last
August. The United States has rejected such
a ban and has conducted eight underground
tests since then. The Reagan administration
argues that these tests are necessary to
develop new weapons and to assure the reli-
ability of existing weapons. Do you think the
United States should or should not agree to
a ban on nuclear testing if the Soviet Union
continues their ban?*

Should agree 56%
Should not 35
No opinion 9

By Sex
Male

Should agree 57%
Should not 37
No opinion 6

Female

Should agree 55%
Should not 33
No opinion 12

By Ethnic Background
White

Should agree 56%
Should not 35
No opinion 9

Nonwhite

Should agree 56%
Should not 34
No opinion 10

Black

Should agree 55%
Should not 33
No opinion 12

By Education
College Graduate

Should agree 65%
Should not 31
No opinion 4

College Incomplete

Should agree 54%
Should not 38
No opinion 8

High-School Graduate

Should agree 58%
Should not 34
No opinion 8

Less Than High-School Graduate

Should agree 50%
Should not 36
No opinion 14

By Region
East

Should agree 63%
Should not 28
No opinion 9

Midwest

Should agree 61%
Should not 33
No opinion 6

South

Should agree 44%
Should not 42
No opinion 14

West

Should agree 61%
Should not 35
No opinion 4

By Age
18–29 Years

Should agree 59%
Should not 33
No opinion 8

30–49 Years

Should agree 58%
Should not 35
No opinion 7

50 Years and Over

Should agree 52%
Should not 36
No opinion 12

By Politics
Republicans

Should agree 51%
Should not 43
No opinion 6

Democrats

Should agree 58%
Should not 33
No opinion 9

Independents

Should agree 59%
Should not 31
No opinion 10

Greater War Risk
Continued Arms Buildup

Should agree 74%
Should not 22
No opinion 4

United States Falling Behind

Should agree 44%
Should not 48
No opinion 8

Note: Despite President Ronald Reagan's contention that U.S. underground nuclear testing is vital to the nation's security, a majority of Americans favors a ban on further U.S. tests if the Soviet Union continues its test moratorium, which began last August. In the latest Gallup Poll, 56% believe that the United States should go along with the Soviet moratorium on nuclear testing, while 35% disagree and 9% are undecided. Americans of all political persuasions support a bilateral agreement, although Republicans' views are more evenly divided than are those of Democrats and independents.

Other factors also influence public opinion on the issue. College graduates, for example, support the proposed halt to more U.S. weapons tests by a 2-to-1 ratio, 65% to 31%. Southerners are closely divided, with 44% in favor and 42% opposed, while persons living outside the South strongly favor the proposal, 61% to 32%.

The survey, however, found no evidence that Americans are ready to abandon the strong military posture fostered by the Reagan administration since its inception. As in previous surveys, a plurality currently believes our falling behind the Soviet Union in nuclear weaponry would increase the chances of nuclear war more than would continuation of the arms race between the superpowers. Somewhat greater political polarization is found on this question than on the proposal for a bilateral test ban, with substantially more Republicans than either Democrats or independents citing U.S. nuclear inferiority as a potentially greater threat to world peace. As expected, the 47% who think the possible loss of U.S. nuclear strength constitutes a greater war risk are more reluctant to endorse the test moratorium than are the 39% who fear the arms buildup more. Among the former, statistically equivalent proportions favor (44%) and oppose (48%) our ending the test program. Among the latter, 74% favor the proposal and 22% oppose it.

Americans from all walks of life and all political leanings consistently have favored an agreement between the United States and the Soviet Union for an immediate, verifiable freeze on the testing, production, and deployment of nuclear weapons, at times by margins of better than 5 to 1. In the most recent (1984) Gallup assessment, 78% favored and 18% opposed a bilateral freeze. At least 70% support was found in five earlier polls.

JUNE 12
VALUES ON SOCIAL ISSUES

Interviewing Date: 4/11–14/86
Survey #262-G

Some people have very traditional values about such matters as sex, morality, family life, and religion. If 1 represents someone who has very traditional, old-fashioned values and 7 represents someone who has very liberal, modern values about these matters, where on this scale would you place yourself?

Traditional (1, 2) 36%
Moderate (3, 4, 5) 52
Liberal (6, 7) 11
No opinion 1

By Sex
Male

Traditional (1, 2) 31%
Moderate (3, 4, 5) 54
Liberal (6, 7) 14
No opinion 1

Female

Traditional (1, 2) 41%
Moderate (3, 4, 5) 49
Liberal (6, 7) 9
No opinion 1

By Ethnic Background

White

Traditional (1, 2) 37%
Moderate (3, 4, 5) 52
Liberal (6, 7) 10
No opinion 1

Black

Traditional (1, 2) 35%
Moderate (3, 4, 5) 50
Liberal (6, 7) 15
No opinion .... *

By Education

College Graduate

Traditional (1, 2) 27%
Moderate (3, 4, 5) 62
Liberal (6, 7) 11
No opinion .... *

College Incomplete

Traditional (1, 2) 30%
Moderate (3, 4, 5) 58
Liberal (6, 7) 12
No opinion .... *

High-School Graduate

Traditional (1, 2) 34%
Moderate (3, 4, 5) 53
Liberal (6, 7) 12
No opinion 1

Less Than High-School Graduate

Traditional (1, 2) 54%
Moderate (3, 4, 5) 35
Liberal (6, 7) 10
No opinion 1

By Region

East

Traditional (1, 2) 31%
Moderate (3, 4, 5) 58
Liberal (6, 7) 10
No opinion 1

Midwest

Traditional (1, 2) 33%
Moderate (3, 4, 5) 55
Liberal (6, 7) 11
No opinion 1

South

Traditional (1, 2) 45%
Moderate (3, 4, 5) 43
Liberal (6, 7) 11
No opinion 1

West

Traditional (1, 2) 34%
Moderate (3, 4, 5) 53
Liberal (6, 7) 13
No opinion .... *

By Age

18–29 Years

Traditional (1, 2) 20%
Moderate (3, 4, 5) 58
Liberal (6, 7) 21
No opinion 1

30–49 Years

Traditional (1, 2) 33%
Moderate (3, 4, 5) 55
Liberal (6, 7) 11
No opinion 1

50 Years and Over

Traditional (1, 2) 52%
Moderate (3, 4, 5) 43
Liberal (6, 7) 4
No opinion 1

By Politics

Republicans

Traditional (1, 2) 38%
Moderate (3, 4, 5) 53
Liberal (6, 7) 9
No opinion .... *

Democrats

Traditional (1, 2) 40%
Moderate (3, 4, 5) 51
Liberal (6, 7) 8
No opinion 1

Independents

Traditional (1, 2) 28%
Moderate (3, 4, 5) 53
Liberal (6, 7) 18
No opinion 1

By Religion
Protestants

Traditional (1, 2) 41%
Moderate (3, 4, 5) 51
Liberal (6, 7) 7
No opinion 1

Catholics

Traditional (1, 2) 29%
Moderate (3, 4, 5) 56
Liberal (6, 7) 14
No opinion 1

By Political Philosophy
Left of Center

Traditional (1, 2) 32%
Moderate (3, 4, 5) 53
Liberal (6, 7) 15
No opinion . . . . *

Middle of the Road

Traditional (1, 2) 31%
Moderate (3, 4, 5) 58
Liberal (6, 7) 10
No opinion 1

Right of Center

Traditional (1, 2) 45%
Moderate (3, 4, 5) 46
Liberal (6, 7) 9
No opinion . . . . *

*Less than 1%

Note: On values relating to sex, morality, family life, and religion, the views of most Americans are somewhere between extremely conservative and extremely liberal, although the weight of opinion is decidedly on the conservative side. About one-half of survey respondents (52%) place themselves in moderate positions on a 7-point scale designed to measure social values, while 36% take positions on the right and 11% on the left.

The survey suggests that the Democratic and Republican parties, in seeking to win votes on social issues with a strong moral content, start with an even advantage: 38% of Republicans place themselves on the traditional side, 53% in moderate positions, and 9% on the liberal side. These figures almost exactly match those for Democrats: 40%, 51%, and 8%, respectively.

Protestants (41%) are considerably more likely to lean to the right on the values scale than are Catholics (29%). Little difference in this regard is found between whites and blacks, with 37% of whites and 35% of blacks placing themselves on the traditional side of the scale.

The college educated tend to eschew either strongly liberal or strongly conservative positions, with three college graduates in five (62%) opting for moderate points on the scale. However, traditional values also outweigh liberal ones among this group by a 27% to 11% margin. Persons whose formal education ended before high-school graduation come down strongly (54% to 10%) in favor of traditional values. The survey also shows women, older persons, and Southerners to be more traditionally oriented than their opposite numbers.

Those surveyed who indicate that their political philosophy is right of center are somewhat more inclined than others to place themselves on the traditional side of the values scale. Nevertheless, the overall differences on the two scales are not as pronounced as might be expected.

JUNE 15
PRESIDENT REAGAN

Interviewing Date: 5/16–19/86
Special Telephone Survey

Do you approve or disapprove of the way Ronald Reagan is handling his job as president?

Approve 68%
Disapprove 23
No opinion 9

Selected National Trend

	Approve	Dis-approve	No opinion
1986			
April 11–14	62%	29%	9%
March 7–10	63	26	11
January 10–13	64	27	9

The following table compares Reagan's current standing with those of his predecessors in May of the second year of their second or elective term:

Presidential Performance Ratings

Incumbent	Dates	Approve	Disap-prove	No opinion
Reagan	May 1986	68%	23%	9%
Nixon	May 1974	25	61	14
Johnson	May* 1966	48	33	19
Eisenhower	May 1958	53	32	15
Truman	May 1950	37	44	19

*Two-survey average

The table below shows Reagan's job approval ratings in May of each of the last six years, by major population groups. The trend reveals virtually unanimous Republican support—through good years and bad—as well as majority backing from Democrats in the current and 1981 surveys. The now familiar "gender gap," the greater tendency of men than women to approve of Reagan's job performance, is evident throughout the trend, as are politically oriented factors such as race, income, and education.

The president's apparently greater recent popularity with younger Americans (age 18 to 29 years) than with those over age 30 may be ascribed to statistical variability. His average job ratings for 1986 to date, as well as for earlier years, have been the same among both the 18- to 29- and 30- to 49-year age groups and only marginally lower among those age 60 and older.

Reagan Approval Ratings

(Percent Approving in May of Each Year)

	'86	'85	'84	'83	'82	'81
National	68%	55%	54%	43%	45%	68%

By Sex

	'86	'85	'84	'83	'82	'81
Male	74%	57%	58%	50%	47%	70%
Female	62	53	50	36	43	65

By Ethnic Background

	'86	'85	'84	'83	'82	'81
White	72%	60%	58%	47%	51%	73%
Black	31	18	11	13	13	27

By Education

	'86	'85	'84	'83	'82	'81
College	71%	63%	62%	54%	52%	72%
High school	69	51	51	40	45	68
Grade school	44	37	37	33	31	55

By Region

	'86	'85	'84	'83	'82	'81
East	69%	50%	52%	39%	44%	64%
Midwest	67	54	51	41	51	70
South	68	57	54	46	37	69
West	67	59	59	50	49	68

By Age

	'86	'85	'84	'83	'82	'81
18–29 years	74%	60%	53%	41%	41%	65%
30–49 years	71	56	55	44	47	72
50 years and over	62	50	53	44	46	65

By Income*

Upper	77%	63%	62%	51%	55%	79%
Lower	60	49	45	36	38	60

By Politics

Republicans	88%	87%	85%	79%	80%	92%
Democrats	51	24	32	22	22	51
Independents	69	55	55	47	51	70

*Upper-income households in the 1986 and 1985 surveys are defined as those with $25,000 or more in total family earnings; for 1981 to 1984, $20,000 or more.

Note: Borne by a strong wave of consumer optimism, President Ronald Reagan is riding a crest of public support unprecedented in Gallup Poll annals. In a just completed survey, 68% of adult Americans approve of the way Reagan is handling his presidential duties, while 23% disapprove and 9% are undecided.

The president's current job performance rating not only is the highest recorded during his entire tenure, matching the job score he received exactly five years ago during the "honeymoon" period of his first year in office, but it also breaks a historical precedent. Each of Reagan's postwar predecessors who won reelection (Nixon and Eisenhower), or who was elected to his own term after nonelective presidential service (Johnson and Truman), saw his popularity erode sharply as his tenure progressed.

President Reagan's strong current standing doubtless reflects the record duration of the economic recovery as well as low oil prices, low inflation, and low interest rates. As reported recently, 83% in a March Gallup Poll said they expected the recovery to last at least until the end of this year, with 58% predicting that economic good times would prevail into 1988 or beyond. In the same survey, Americans expressed a bullish outlook toward their personal financial situation, with 46% saying they now are better off than they

were a year ago and 61% expecting to be more prosperous next year than they are now.

JUNE 19
POLITICAL IDEOLOGY

Interviewing Date: 4/11–14/86
Survey #262-G

People who are conservative in their political views are referred to as being right of center and people who are liberal in their political views are referred to as being left of center. Which one of these categories best describes your own political position? [Respondents were handed a card listing eight categories.]

Far left	3%
Substantially left of center	4
Moderately left of center 13	
Liberal subtotal	20%
Slightly left of center 13	
Middle of the road* 10	
Slightly right of center 22	
Moderate subtotal	45
Moderately right of center 19	
Substantially right of center	6
Far right	3
Conservative subtotal	28
No opinion	7

*Volunteered

By Sex
Male

Liberal	19%
Moderate	46
Conservative	29
No opinion	6

Female

Liberal	21%
Moderate	45
Conservative	27
No opinion	7

By Ethnic Background

White

Liberal 19%
Moderate 45
Conservative 29
No opinion 7

Black

Liberal 27%
Moderate 49
Conservative 14
No opinion 10

By Education

College Graduate

Liberal 23%
Moderate 42
Conservative 34
No opinion 1

College Incomplete

Liberal 19%
Moderate 51
Conservative 24
No opinion 6

High-School Graduate

Liberal 21%
Moderate 47
Conservative 26
No opinion 6

Less Than High-School Graduate

Liberal 17%
Moderate 41
Conservative 29
No opinion 13

By Region

East

Liberal 19%
Moderate 49
Conservative 23
No opinion 9

Midwest

Liberal 20%
Moderate 44
Conservative 32
No opinion 4

South

Liberal 17%
Moderate 48
Conservative 26
No opinion 9

West

Liberal 26%
Moderate 39
Conservative 31
No opinion 4

By Age

18–29 Years

Liberal 26%
Moderate 44
Conservative 23
No opinion 7

30–49 Years

Liberal 20%
Moderate 47
Conservative 26
No opinion 7

50 Years and Over

Liberal 14%
Moderate 45
Conservative 34
No opinion 7

By Income

$25,000 and Over

Liberal 22%
Moderate 46
Conservative 30
No opinion 2

Under $25,000

Liberal 19%
Moderate 45
Conservative 26
No opinion 10

By Politics

Republicans

Liberal 11%
Moderate 42
Conservative 43
No opinion 4

Democrats

Liberal 26%
Moderate 48
Conservative 19
No opinion 7

Independents

Liberal 21%
Moderate 49
Conservative 23
No opinion 7

Selected National Trend

	Liberal	Moderate	Conser- vative	No opinion
1984	17%	41%	31%	11%
1982	17	40	33	10
1981	18	43	30	9
1980	19	40	30	11
1979	21	42	26	11
1978	21	35	27	17
1977	20	39	29	12
1976	21	41	26	12

Note: Despite a dramatic shift since 1980 in political affiliation, in which the Democratic party's historic advantage over the Republican party virtually disappeared, Americans' basic political orientation—the proportions describing their political views in conservative, moderate, and liberal terms—is almost exactly the same today as

it has been for the last decade. In a recent (mid-April) Gallup Poll, 28% describe their basic political ideology as right of center, 45% in centrist or moderate terms, and 20% as left of center. In a March 1976 survey, when Gallup adopted its current question wording, the findings were statistically identical: 30% gave their orientation as conservative, 42% as moderate, and 18% as liberal.

The stability of Americans' descriptions of their political ideology is illustrated by the following table, which shows no significant difference in the public's orientation during the tenure of Presidents Ronald Reagan and Jimmy Carter. (To facilitate comparisons, those who did not express opinions are excluded.)

	Liberal	Moderate	Conservative
1981–86	20%	46%	34%
1977–80	23	45	32

This stability helps explain the public's intransigence on school prayer, gun control, abortion, federal aid to parochial schools, and other longstanding issues.

Comparison of the 1986 and 1976 findings shows relatively minor shifts in political ideology on the part of most population groups. In both surveys, for example, substantially more young adults (18 to 29 years) expressed liberal views than did their elders, while far fewer described themselves in conservative terms.

While the gain in Republican affiliation since 1976 has occurred among all population groups—including those with a heavily Democratic orientation—as well as from all points on the ideological spectrum, by far the greatest shift toward the GOP has come from the right. In 1976 only 30% of those who described themselves in conservative terms were self-identified Republicans, while 38% said they were Democrats and 32% independents. Today, fully one-half of conservatives (50%) claim allegiance to the GOP, 28% to the Democratic party, and 22% say they are independents.

The same interim has seen modest Republican gains among liberals (from 12% to 19%) and moderates (from 24% to 29%). Details are shown below:

	Political Party Affiliation		
	Repub-licans	Demo-crats	Inde-pendents
*Totals**			
1986	32%	38%	30%
1976	23	46	31
Political Ideology			
Liberal			
1986	19%	53%	28%
1976	12	51	37
Moderate			
1986	29%	42%	29%
1976	24	46	30
Conservative			
1986	50%	28%	22%
1976	30	38	32

*Excludes persons who said they belonged to other parties or had no party allegiance.

JUNE 22
COST OF LIVING

Interviewing Date: 1/10–13; 3/7–10/86
Survey #261-G; Special Telephone Survey

> *Asked of nonfarm families: What is the smallest amount of money a family of four (husband, wife, and two children) needs each week to get along in this community?*

	Median average
National	$349

Selected National Trend

	Median average
1985	$302
1983	296
1981	277
1979	223
1977	199
1975	161
1973	149
1971	127
1969	120

1967	101
1961	84
1954	60
1950	50
1947	43
1937	30

> *Asked of nonfarm families: What is the smallest amount of money your family needs each week to get along in this community?*

	Median average
National	$300

By Region

East	$302
Midwest	299
South	298
West	302

By Income

$25,000 and over	$400
Under $25,000	249

Note: Americans believe it now takes at least $349 per week for a husband, wife, and two children to make ends meet. This is the highest figure recorded in Gallup surveys on this topic, which began in 1937, and represents a 15% increase over last year's estimate of $302.

Unlike the public's perceptions of living costs for a hypothetical family of four, respondents' median average of the minimum weekly amount needed for their own families, $300, is virtually unchanged from last year's figure of $298. No significant differences are found by geographic region.

The Gallup Poll's annual audits of the public's perceptions of living costs generally have paralleled the Consumer Price Index (CPI) compiled by the U.S. Bureau of Labor Statistics. According to this index, living costs rose only 2.3% during the twelve-month period ending in March.

Although the latest Gallup surveys provide no internal evidence to explain the difference between the Gallup and CPI cost of living indexes, several possible explanations have been advanced. Paul K. Perry, president and chief statistician emeritus of the Gallup Organization, notes that the annual increments in the public's perceptions of living costs from 1982 through 1985 were very small, averaging less than 1% per year, while the CPI increased by more than 4% per year, on average, during this period. Thus, this year's median figure of $349 may represent the public's perceptions as "catching up" with the "real" cost of living, as measured by the CPI.

That this catching-up process occurred this year also may be attributed to Americans' extraordinarily bullish current expectations for the nation's economy (as determined by recent Gallup surveys), which have created a climate of economic euphoria. This era of good feeling has influenced consumers to raise their sights as to what constitutes an adequate standard of living for a four-person family and hence to raise their estimates of minimum living costs.

JUNE 26
CIGARETTE SMOKING

Interviewing Date: 6/9–16/86
Special Telephone Survey

Have you, yourself, smoked any cigarettes in the past week?

	Yes
National	31%

By Sex

Male	35%
Female	28

By Ethnic Background

White	31%
Black	34

By Education

College graduate	23%
College incomplete	25
High-school graduate	33
Less than high-school graduate	45

By Region

East	31%
Midwest	29
South	35
West	29

By Age

18–29 years	27%
30–49 years	37
50–64 years	35
65 years and over	23

By Income

$35,000 and over	28%
$15,000–$34,999	30
Under $15,000	39

Selected National Trend

	Yes
1985	35%
1983	38
1981	35
1977	38
1972	43
1969	40
1957	42
1949	44
1944	41

Note: Cigarette smoking has declined to its lowest incidence in the Gallup Poll's forty-two-year trend, but at least three adult Americans in ten still cling to the habit. In the latest Gallup audit, 31% report having smoked cigarettes during the week prior to being interviewed. This is the lowest level of adult smoking recorded since Gallup began conducting these audits in 1944.

Dr. C. Everett Koop, U.S. surgeon general, has set his sights on a "smokeless society" by the year 2000. Yet, the proportion of smokers in the adult population has declined only gradually since the historic 1964 report linking smoking and serious illnesses such as cancer and heart disease.

As in Gallup audits since 1977, more men (35%) than women (28%) are smokers. In earlier surveys, there were far more men than women smokers: in 1954, for example, 57% of men but only 32% of women said they smoked cigarettes.

Education is closely related to whether or not people smoke. In the current audit, only 23% of college graduates are cigarette smokers, with the proportion rising to 33% among high-school graduates and to 45% among those whose formal education did not include a high-school diploma.

Although the current survey found modest declines in smoking among most groups, a significant 11-percentage point drop occurred among young adults (18 to 29 years), from 38% in 1985 to 27% today. Smokers under age 30 also tend to be lighter smokers, with 58% in this age group, compared to 39% of those over 30, claiming to smoke less than one pack of cigarettes per day.

Although the proportion of America's teenagers who experiment with cigarette smoking has not changed over the past four years, there has been a steady decrease in the number of cigarettes they smoke daily, according to the latest Gallup Youth Survey. Thirteen percent of the teens surveyed say they smoked cigarettes during the week preceding the interview. This proportion has been constant since 1983. However, in 1983, teen smokers puffed an average of 11 cigarettes per day. The average dropped to 7 in 1984 and is now down to only 5 cigarettes per day.

JUNE 29
SALT II

Interviewing Date: 6/9–16/86
Special Telephone Survey

Have you heard or read about SALT II, the 1979 strategic arms limitation treaty between the United States and the Soviet Union?

	Yes
National	67%

Asked of those who replied in the affirmative: Do you happen to know whether or not the United States has ratified this treaty?

	Has not ratified
National	32%*

*Based on the total sample

Asked of the informed group, those who had heard or read about SALT II and who knew that the United States has not ratified this treaty: Do you think the Soviet Union has or has not lived up to the terms of the treaty?

Has	6%
Has not	81
No opinion	13

Also asked of the informed group: Do you think the United States has or has not lived up to the terms of the treaty?

Has	36%
Has not	53
No opinion	11

Also asked of the informed group: The Reagan administration announced that it no longer feels bound by SALT II and that it may abandon the treaty's nuclear weapons limits. Do you approve or disapprove of this decision?

Approve	45%
Disapprove	47
No opinion	8

Also asked of the informed group: Do you think this decision is likely to increase or decrease the chances of a nuclear war?

Increase chances	44%
Decrease chances	22
No difference (volunteered)	28
No opinion	6

Also asked of the informed group: Do you think this decision will help or hurt the United States in reaching future agreements with the Soviet Union on strategic arms?

Will help 35%
Will hurt 45
No difference (volunteered) 14
No opinion 6

Also asked of the informed group: Do you think this decision is likely to increase the arms race a great deal, quite a lot, not very much, or not at all?

A great deal 7%
Quite a lot 27
Not very much 48
Not at all 15
No opinion 3

Also asked of the informed group: At the present time, which nation do you feel is stronger in terms of nuclear weapons, the United States or the Soviet Union—or do you think they are about equal in nuclear strength?

United States 19%
Soviet Union 21
About equal 52
No opinion 8

Note: Among informed Americans opinion is evenly divided between approval and disapproval of President Ronald Reagan's tentative decision to abandon SALT II, the 1979 strategic arms limitation treaty between the United States and the Soviet Union.

In a survey conducted shortly after the signing of the SALT II agreement in June 1979 by President Jimmy Carter and Soviet Premier Leonid Brezhnev, 53% of informed Americans favored Senate ratification of the treaty and 30% were opposed. This compares to 60% in favor and 20% opposed in a survey conducted earlier in March, prior to the Vienna Conference that year.

By the fall of 1979, however, informed support had declined, and a survey at that time showed the informed public to be evenly divided on the desirability of Senate ratification of the treaty, with 39% in favor and 43% opposed. Despite a marked deterioration in Soviet-American relations

brought about by the Soviet invasion of Afghanistan and demands for a stronger defense posture toward the Russians, the American public, in March 1980, remained evenly divided about the desirability of Senate ratification: 43% in favor, 43% opposed.

JULY 3
LEGAL DRINKING AGE

Interviewing Date: 6/9–16/86
Special Telephone Survey

Would you favor or oppose a national law that would raise the legal drinking age in all states to 21?

Favor 80%
Oppose 17
No opinion 3

By Sex
Male

Favor 76%
Oppose 22
No opinion 2

Female

Favor 84%
Oppose 13
No opinion 3

By Education
College Graduate

Favor 83%
Oppose 14
No opinion 3

College Incomplete

Favor 83%
Oppose 15
No opinion 2

High-School Graduate

Favor 79%
Oppose 19
No opinion 2

Less Than High-School Graduate

Favor 79%
Oppose 19
No opinion 2

By Age
18–29 Years

Favor 72%
Oppose 27
No opinion 1

30–49 Years

Favor 82%
Oppose 16
No opinion 2

50 Years and Over

Favor 86%
Oppose 11
No opinion 3

States Where Legal Age Is 21

Favor 82%
Oppose 16
No opinion 2

States Where Legal Age Is Under 21

Favor 72%
Oppose 24
No opinion 4

Selected National Trend

	Favor	Oppose	No opinion
1984	79%	18%	3%
1982	77	20	3

In 1984 a law was passed requiring all states to raise their legal drinking age to 21 or face reductions in federal highway funds. At present, nine states and the District of Columbia permit legal drinking under age 21. Would you favor or oppose having the federal government start withholding funds from these states if they fail to raise their drinking age to 21 by October first?

Favor 64%
Oppose 32
No opinion 4

By Sex
Male

Favor 60%
Oppose 38
No opinion 2

Female

Favor 67%
Oppose 27
No opinion 6

By Education
College Graduate

Favor 65%
Oppose 32
No opinion 3

College Incomplete

Favor 67%
Oppose 31
No opinion 2

High-School Graduate

Favor 66%
Oppose 31
No opinion 3

Less Than High-School Graduate

Favor 56%
Oppose 34
No opinion 10

By Age

18–29 Years

Favor 58%
Oppose 40
No opinion 2

30–49 Years

Favor 65%
Oppose 32
No opinion 3

50 Years and Over

Favor 68%
Oppose 25
No opinion 7

States Where Legal Age Is 21

Favor 66%
Oppose 30
No opinion 4

States Where Legal Age Is Under 21

Favor 54%
Oppose 41
No opinion 5

Note: Americans' willingness to join the national crusade against drunk driving is epitomized by their overwhelming support for a national law that would raise the drinking age in all states to 21. In the latest Gallup Poll, 80% express approval for such a law, while 17% are opposed. The national consensus includes large majorities from population groups that would be most directly affected if a national drinking-age law were enacted—young adults (18 to 29 years) and residents of states where persons under 21 still can drink alcoholic beverages legally.

At present, the individual states are free to set their own minimum drinking-age laws. In 1984, however, the federal government passed a law requiring that all states raise their legal drinking age to 21 or face reductions in their U.S. highway funds. States that are not in compliance by October 1 risk losing 5% of their share of the $10.6 billion in road construction·funds in 1987 and 10% in 1988. Although some state officials have complained about federal "blackmail," the statute thus far has withstood all legal challenges.

Strong public support is found for withholding highway funds from states that fail to comply with the 1984 law, with 64% in favor and 32% opposed. Somewhat greater opposition is expressed by men, young adults, and residents of noncomplying states. However, solid majorities in all major population groups favor the measure.

Public support for a uniform 21-year legal drinking age doubtless stems from evidence of widespread alcohol abuse on the part of young people, including the grim statistic that 40% of those killed each year in alcohol-related highway accidents are under age 25.

JULY 6
PRIDE IN AMERICA

Interviewing Date: 6/9–16/86
Special Telephone Survey

> *How proud are you to be an American—very proud, quite proud, not very proud, or not at all proud?*

Very proud 89%
Quite proud 10
Not very proud 1
Not at all proud .... *
No opinion .... *

*Less than 1%

> *How much confidence do you have in the future of the United States—quite a lot, some, very little, or none at all?*

Quite a lot 76%
Some 19
Very little 4
None at all .... *
No opinion 1

By Sex

Male

Quite a lot 78%
Some 16
Very little 4
None at all 1
No opinion 1

Female

Quite a lot 74%
Some 22
Very little 3
None at all .... *
No opinion 1

By Ethnic Background

White

Quite a lot 77%
Some 18
Very little 3
None at all 1
No opinion 1

Nonwhite

Quite a lot 65%
Some 27
Very little 8
None at all .... *
No opinion .... *

Black

Quite a lot 64%
Some 27
Very little 9
None at all .... *
No opinion .... *

By Education

College Graduate

Quite a lot 77%
Some 21
Very little 2
None at all .... *
No opinion .... *

College Incomplete

Quite a lot 79%
Some 18
Very little 2
None at all .... *
No opinion 1

High-School Graduate

Quite a lot 76%
Some 18
Very little 4
None at all 1
No opinion 1

Less Than High-School Graduate

Quite a lot 69%
Some 22
Very little 6
None at all 1
No opinion 2

By Region

East

Quite a lot 78%
Some 18
Very little 2
None at all 1
No opinion 1

Midwest

Quite a lot 72%
Some 21
Very little 4
None at all 1
No opinion 2

South

Quite a lot 75%
Some 18
Very little 5
None at all .... *
No opinion 2

West

Quite a lot	79%
Some	17
Very little	2
None at all	1
No opinion	1

By Age

18–29 Years

Quite a lot	70%
Some	25
Very little	4
None at all	1
No opinion	*

30–49 Years

Quite a lot	76%
Some	21
Very little	3
None at all	*
No opinion	*

50 Years and Over

Quite a lot	80%
Some	13
Very little	4
None at all	*
No opinion	3

*Less than 1%

In general, are you satisfied or dissatisfied with the way things are going in the United States at this time?

Satisfied	69%
Dissatisfied	26
No opinion	5

By Sex

Male

Satisfied	74%
Dissatisfied	23
No opinion	3

Female

Satisfied	66%
Dissatisfied	28
No opinion	6

By Ethnic Background

White

Satisfied	72%
Dissatisfied	24
No opinion	4

Nonwhite

Satisfied	51%
Dissatisfied	42
No opinion	7

Black

Satisfied	42%
Dissatisfied	50
No opinion	8

By Education

College Graduate

Satisfied	72%
Dissatisfied	25
No opinion	3

College Incomplete

Satisfied	74%
Dissatisfied	22
No opinion	4

High-School Graduate

Satisfied	70%
Dissatisfied	24
No opinion	6

Less Than High-School Graduate

Satisfied	60%
Dissatisfied	35
No opinion	5

By Region

East

Satisfied 72%
Dissatisfied 25
No opinion 3

Midwest

Satisfied 68%
Dissatisfied 29
No opinion 3

South

Satisfied 67%
Dissatisfied 26
No opinion 7

West

Satisfied 72%
Dissatisfied 23
No opinion 5

By Age

18–29 Years

Satisfied 78%
Dissatisfied 20
No opinion 2

30–49 Years

Satisfied 72%
Dissatisfied 22
No opinion 6

50 Years and Over

Satisfied 61%
Dissatisfied 34
No opinion 5

Selected National Trend

	Satisfied	Dis-satisfied	No opinion
1986			
March	66%	30%	4%
1985			
November	51	46	3
1984			
December	52	40	8
February	50	46	4
1983			
August	35	59	6
1982			
November	24	72	3
1981			
December	27	67	6
January	17	78	5
1979			
November	19	77	4
August	12	84	4

Do you display an American flag outside your home on national holidays or other days during the year?

Yes 43%
No 47
Don't have flag (volunteered) 7
No place to hang flag (volunteered) 3

By Sex

Male

Yes 45%
No 48
Don't have flag (volunteered) 5
No place to hang flag (volunteered) 2

Female

Yes 41%
No 47
Don't have flag (volunteered) 9
No place to hang flag (volunteered) 3

By Ethnic Background

White

Yes 43%
No 47
Don't have flag (volunteered) 7
No place to hang flag (volunteered) 3

Nonwhite

Yes 37%
No 52
Don't have flag (volunteered) 9
No place to hang flag (volunteered) 2

Black

Yes 33%
No 55
Don't have flag (volunteered) 9
No place to hang flag (volunteered) 3

By Education

College Graduate

Yes 37%
No 56
Don't have flag (volunteered) 5
No place to hang flag (volunteered) 2

College Incomplete

Yes 43%
No 50
Don't have flag (volunteered) 4
No place to hang flag (volunteered) 3

High-School Graduate

Yes 48%
No 43
Don't have flag (volunteered) 6
No place to hang flag (volunteered) 3

Less Than High-School Graduate

Yes 38%
No 45
Don't have flag (volunteered) 15
No place to hang flag (volunteered) 2

By Region

East

Yes 45%
No 45
Don't have flag (volunteered) 6
No place to hang flag (volunteered) 4

Midwest

Yes 47%
No 46
Don't have flag (volunteered) 5
No place to hang flag (volunteered) 2

South

Yes 35%
No 50
Don't have flag (volunteered) 11
No place to hang flag (volunteered) 4

West

Yes 47%
No 47
Don't have flag (volunteered) 5
No place to hang flag (volunteered) 1

By Age

18–29 Years

Yes 35%
No 59
Don't have flag (volunteered) 3
No place to hang flag (volunteered) 3

30–49 Years

Yes 40%
No 52
Don't have flag (volunteered) 7
No place to hang flag (volunteered) 1

50 Years and Over

Yes 51%
No 34
Don't have flag (volunteered) 11
No place to hang flag (volunteered) 4

Note: The celebration of the centennial of the Statue of Liberty comes at a time when American patriotism and confidence in the future are running high. In the latest nationwide Gallup Poll:

1) Nine in ten (89%) say they are "very proud" to be Americans, up 9 points from a 1981 survey.

2) Three in four Americans (76%) express they have "quite a lot" of confidence in the future of

the United States, while far fewer, 19%, say "some" and only 4% "very little." By comparison, a 1974 survey found 68% saying quite a lot.

3) Seven in ten (69%) express satisfaction with the way things are going in the nation, the highest level recorded since this measurement was started in 1979.

4) As further indication of growing patriotism, four in ten Americans (43%) say they display a flag on national holidays or other days during the year, up from 30% in 1984.

Patriotism is running high among all population groups, with little difference found on the basis of sex, race, age, education, family income, or region. Even among those who are dissatisfied with the way things are going in the nation, eight in ten say they are very proud to be Americans. Socioeconomic differences on confidence in the future are slightly more pronounced, but large majorities in each group nevertheless express a high degree of confidence.

The upsurge in patriotism and confidence in the nation reflects in considerable measure the public's bullish financial outlook, which is more optimistic today than at any other time in the previous decade. However, Americans are keenly alert to the many problems confronting our nation. In fact, when asked to name the most important issues facing the nation today, only 4% are unable to name a problem. Leading the list of concerns are international tensions and the fear of war, unemployment, the budget deficit, high living costs, poverty and hunger, farm problems, a perceived moral and religious decline, crime, and problems of the elderly.

JULY 10
DAYLIGHT SAVING TIME

Interviewing Date: 6/9–16/86
Special Telephone Survey

At present, daylight saving time in most states extends from the last Sunday in April to the last Sunday in October. Would you approve or disapprove of extending daylight saving time another three or four weeks each year

by having it start on the first Sunday of April instead of the last Sunday?

Approve 62%
Disapprove 25
No opinion 13

By Sex
Male

Approve 64%
Disapprove 24
No opinion 12

Female

Approve 60%
Disapprove 26
No opinion 14

By Education
College Graduate

Approve 63%
Disapprove 26
No opinion 11

College Incomplete

Approve 66%
Disapprove 23
No opinion 11

High-School Graduate

Approve 64%
Disapprove 25
No opinion 11

Less Than High-School Graduate

Approve 53%
Disapprove 29
No opinion 18

By Region
East

Approve 75%
Disapprove 14
No opinion 11

Midwest

Approve 56%
Disapprove 32
No opinion 12

South

Approve 58%
Disapprove 28
No opinion 14

West

Approve 59%
Disapprove 26
No opinion 15

By Age
18–29 Years

Approve 69%
Disapprove 22
No opinion 9

30–49 Years

Approve 64%
Disapprove 25
No opinion 11

50–64 Years

Approve 58%
Disapprove 29
No opinion 13

65 Years and Over

Approve 51%
Disapprove 27
No opinion 22

By Income
$35,000 and Over

Approve 70%
Disapprove 22
No opinion 8

$15,000–$34,999

Approve 64%
Disapprove 24
No opinion 12

Under $15,000

Approve 51%
Disapprove 32
No opinion 17

By Community Size
500,000 and Over

Approve 65%
Disapprove 24
No opinion 11

50,000–499,999

Approve 63%
Disapprove 20
No opinion 17

2,500–49,999

Approve 58%
Disapprove 30
No opinion 12

Under 2,500; Rural

Approve 58%
Disapprove 29
No opinion 13

Note: Extension of daylight saving time, a system that has aroused public passions since colonial days, finally has achieved broad public acceptance. In the latest Gallup Poll, 62% approve and 25% disapprove of extending daylight time for an additional three or four weeks each year by having it begin on the first Sunday in April instead of the last Sunday, as at present. It would still end on the last Sunday of October. President Ronald Reagan is expected to sign a bill with these provisions, recently passed by both houses of Congress.

Sponsors of the bill cite increased opportunities for daylight recreation, as well as energy conservation, crime reduction, and highway safety. Opponents point to the fact that an additional hour of afternoon daylight in the early spring entails a compensating hour of early morning darkness, creating a hardship for some people, including farmers and children going to school.

The federal government instituted daylight saving time, often called "war time," early in World War II as an energy conservation measure and to extend daylight working hours. A 1942 Gallup Poll found almost 2-to-1 public support for year-round daylight time for "as long as the war lasts." However, from the first Gallup inquiry until the current survey, southerners and residents of rural areas throughout the nation consistently have opposed it.

After the war, Gallup surveys periodically probed public reaction to daylight time. In a 1956 poll, approval outweighed disapproval by a 57% to 43% ratio, with the undecided vote allocated. Approval ranged from a high of 78% in cities with populations of 500,000 or more, to 51% in towns with fewer than 2,500 inhabitants, to 24% among residents of rural areas. A similar 1957 Gallup Poll found 59% to 41% national support for daylight time. Regionally, support was highest in the East (82%), followed by 57% in the West, 51% in the Midwest, and 39% in the South.

To conserve energy, Congress put most of the nation on year-round daylight saving time for two years, effective January 1974. Another bill, signed in October 1974, however, restored standard time to a nine-month period. This system was ended in 1975, and the nation returned to the present end-of-April-to-end-of-October regimen.

In the current survey, support for extending daylight saving time is slightly higher among younger, better educated, and more affluent respondents, even when allowance is made for the higher levels of nonresponse on the part of their opposite numbers. However, aside from greater backing in the East, little difference is found by region or community size.

JULY 13
ARMS CONTROL

Interviewing Date: 2/1–3/6/86 (U.S. only 2/10–24/86)
Special Survey*

How important do you think it is that the United States and the Soviet Union sign an arms control treaty within a few years from now?

	Very important	Important	Unimportant	Very unimportant	No reply
Argentina	42%	30%	7%	5%	16%
Belgium	46	26	11	7	11
Brazil	59	17	4	8	12
Canada	64	23	6	2	5
Denmark	58	24	6	3	9
Finland	60	32	5	1	1
France	52	33	7	4	3
Great Britain	65	19	6	3	7
India	42	38	9	3	8
Ireland	64	18	6	1	11
Japan	42	42	6	3	8
Netherlands	66	24	4	2	4
Nigeria	29	20	10	3	38
Norway	58	31	3	2	6
Portugal	43	29	5	2	21
South Africa	56	26	10	7	1
South Korea	37	51	6	2	4
Spain	44	15	7	9	25

*All results are based on national samples except Argentina (Greater Buenos Aires), Brazil (São Paulo and Rio areas), India (literates in four main cities), South Africa (whites only, metropolitan areas), Uruguay (six metropolitan areas), and Nigeria (only urban). There is a total of 22,950 interviews, and the survey covers major regions of the world. Some columns do not add to 100% due to rounding.

Turkey	33	35	4	6	22
United States	62	25	6	2	5
Uruguay	31	35	14	7	13

Have you heard or read about the resumption of arms control talks between the leaders of the Soviet Union and the United States?

	Yes	No	No reply
Argentina	54%	31%	15%
Belgium	66	25	9
Brazil	37	63	–
Canada	71	24	5
Denmark	84	11	5
Finland	83	15	2
France	70	28	2
Great Britain	70	28	2
India	78	17	5
Ireland	70	22	8
Japan	62	33	5
Netherlands	87	11	2
Nigeria	31	40	29
Norway	77	17	5
Portugal	62	17	21
South Africa	74	26	–
South Korea	54	46	–
Spain	60	28	12
Turkey	37	39	25
United States	77	21	3
Uruguay	39	55	6

Asked of the aware group: Do you think such arms control talks between the United States and the Soviet Union have increased or decreased the chance of a nuclear war? Or doesn't it make any difference?

	In- creased	De- creased	No dif- ference	No reply
Argentina	9%	29%	33%	29%
Belgium	7	42	37	14
Brazil	31	33	20	16
Canada	8	45	35	12
Denmark	3	59	24	14
Finland	7	48	35	9
France	6	38	48	8
Great Britain	6	43	44	7
India	20	40	37	3
Ireland	8	46	35	11
Japan	13	30	50	7
Netherlands	3	59	35	3
Nigeria	10	29	14	47
Norway	4	66	21	9
Portugal	9	41	13	37
South Africa	10	39	48	3
South Korea	16	62	16	6
Spain	11	26	37	26
Turkey	6	18	49	27
United States	7	36	45	12
Uruguay	20	21	37	22

Not counting your own ideas about this, do you think that most people in our (this) country feel that the chance of nuclear war has increased, decreased, or has remained the same as a consequence of these arms control talks?

	In- creased	De- creased	No change	No reply
Argentina	14%	20%	31%	35%
Belgium	13	35	37	15
Brazil	24	27	30	19
Canada	18	27	44	11
Denmark	10	38	34	18
Finland	18	29	46	7
France	9	26	49	16
Great Britain	13	27	48	12
India	22	35	33	10
Ireland	16	33	38	13
Japan	12	24	58	6
Netherlands	5	56	35	4
Nigeria	13	27	13	47
Norway	10	48	32	10
Portugal	10	27	18	45
South Africa	18	25	53	3
South Korea	17	57	19	7
Spain	16	15	42	27
Turkey	9	14	45	32
United States	15	26	48	11
Uruguay	21	14	39	26

How often do you talk with others about the chances of a nuclear war—hardly ever, perhaps once a month, about once a week or more often, or almost every day?

	Never; hardly ever	About once a month	Once a week; more often	Daily	No reply
Argentina	65%	16%	5%	3%	11%
Belgium	63	21	10	2	4
Brazil	85	3	6	3	3
Canada	59	27	9	3	2
Denmark	61	23	8	4	4
Finland	46	36	12	5	1
France	71	22	3	3	1
Great Britain	64	22	8	4	2
India	39	27	15	13	6
Ireland	70	18	4	2	6
Japan	70	22	3	2	3
Netherlands	62	26	7	2	3
Nigeria	37	11	4	13	35
Norway	58	23	11	2	6
Portugal	51	19	6	4	20
South Africa	76	17	5	2	–
South Korea	70	26	3	1	–
Spain	66	13	8	4	9
Turkey	51	11	8	3	28
United States	56	26	13	4	1
Uruguay	77	15	3	2	2

Here is a list of various sources of information. Which of these is for you personally the most important source of information about problems of rearmament and disarmament?

	Newspapers	Magazines	Books	Radio	Television	Talks/people
Argentina	37%	4%	5%	7%	28%	3%
Belgium	25	4	2	7	54	2
Brazil	46	14	9	35	75	13
Canada	29	3	2	9	52	2
Denmark	36	1	2	20	59	5
Finland	37	2	1	9	47	1
France	22	7	4	11	46	4
Great Britain	25	1	2	6	57	5
India	68	6	1	6	15	2
Ireland	31	3	2	13	59	5
Japan	52	1	1	2	39	1
Netherlands	39	4	2	10	57	4
Nigeria	22	4	–	27	14	2
Norway	35	1	1	19	59	3
Portugal	14	2	1	7	55	3
South Africa	33	4	2	6	50	2
South Korea	32	2	1	5	52	2
Spain	26	2	2	19	41	2
Turkey	32	4	1	5	39	3
United States	27	9	2	6	50	3
Uruguay	12	10	4	22	42	5

And which of these sources is the least important for you personally?

	Newspapers	Magazines	Books	Radio	Television	Talks/people
Argentina	5%	8%	16%	6%	10%	24%
Belgium	9	12	20	4	5	34
Brazil	7	34	37	19	7	24
Canada	7	14	34	6	3	31
Denmark	5	41	25	2	5	9
Finland	4	19	42	3	3	19
France	12	8	20	4	7	35
Great Britain	15	20	29	7	4	19
India	3	3	13	13	7	31
Ireland	8	24	27	8	2	25
Japan	2	26	19	4	2	34
Netherlands	9	14	35	9	5	25
Nigeria	7	3	7	9	15	19
Norway	–	8	46	17	6	5
Portugal	6	8	22	2	2	28
South Africa	10	9	29	8	4	36
South Korea	5	27	26	8	2	20
Spain	10	22	15	5	10	18
Turkey	5	14	14	4	3	23
United States	9	19	28	7	5	26
Uruguay	16	10	24	3	7	31

Note: In a major international survey on nuclear arms control, Americans rank near the top in the importance they place on concluding an arms agreement with the Soviet Union. Yet far fewer in this country than in most of the twenty other nations studied believe that the arms control negotiations between the United States and the USSR have reduced the chance of nuclear war. The international inquiry, which included interviews with almost 23,000 adult residents of twenty-one free world nations around the globe, was conducted by Gallup International Research Institutes.

In response to the first question in the survey, statistically equivalent proportions in the Netherlands (66%), Great Britain (65%), Canada (64%), the Republic of Ireland (64%), and the United States (62%) said they thought it was "very important" for the United States and the Soviet Union to sign an arms control treaty within the next few years. An additional one-fifth to one-quarter in each of these nations said that the conclusion of an arms treaty was "important." Majorities in Finland (60%), Brazil (59%), Denmark (58%), Norway (58%), South Africa (56%), and France (52%) also assigned the highest level of importance to completing the treaty.

For the twenty-one nations as a whole, 50% described the treaty as "very important," 28% as "important," and 11% as either "unimportant" (7%) or "very unimportant" (4%). The 11% balance was undecided or failed to answer the question. In the United States, solid majorities in all key population groups said they thought the treaty was very important.

In sharp contrast to the importance they place on concluding an arms treaty, Americans are highly skeptical about how effective the nuclear arms negotiations between the superpowers have been in reducing international tensions. Although Americans share the lead with the citizens of other nations in their belief that it is very important to reach an arms agreement with the Soviet Union, they rank fourteenth on the list of twenty-one in the percentage who think the arms talks have "decreased the chance of nuclear war." Roughly one-third of Americans (36%) fall into this category, while a 45% plurality thinks the arms talks "haven't made any difference," and 7% say the talks have increased the chance of nuclear war.

By comparison, the weight of public opinion in eight of the ten other nations in which majorities believe it is very important to conclude an arms pact is that the disarmament negotiations have decreased the chance of war. Only in France and

South Africa do pluralities agree with the American consensus that the negotiations have not diminished the chance of war. For all twenty-one nations in the study, the prevailing view about the arms talks is positive (41%) rather than neutral (34%) or negative (10%).

Although most Americans share the national consensus on this issue, young adults (18 to 29 years) are more likely to view the talks as not having made any contribution to reducing the chance of war (56%) and less apt to perceive a positive effect (31%) than are their elders. Among those over 30, the comparable figures are 42% and 38%, respectively.

JULY 17
SPEED LIMIT

Interviewing Date: 6/19–16/86
Special Telephone Survey

Do you favor or oppose keeping the present 55-mile-per-hour speed limit on the highways of the nation?

Favor 66%
Oppose 32
No opinion 2

By Sex
Male

Favor 55%
Oppose 44
No opinion 1

Female

Favor 76%
Oppose 21
No opinion 3

By Education
College Graduate

Favor 61%
Oppose 36
No opinion 3

College Incomplete

Favor 62%
Oppose 37
No opinion 1

High-School Graduate

Favor 70%
Oppose 28
No opinion 2

Less Than High-School Graduate

Favor 68%
Oppose 30
No opinion 2

By Region
East

Favor 74%
Oppose 24
No opinion 2

Midwest

Favor 64%
Oppose 36
No opinion .... *

South

Favor 65%
Oppose 33
No opinion 2

West

Favor 61%
Oppose 36
No opinion 3

By Age
18–29 Years

Favor 63%
Oppose 36
No opinion 1

30–49 Years

Favor 65%
Oppose 33
No opinion 2

50 Years and Over

Favor 70%
Oppose 28
No opinion 2

By Income
$35,000 and Over

Favor 58%
Oppose 40
No opinion 2

$25,000–$34,999

Favor 68%
Oppose 30
No opinion 2

Under $15,000

Favor 70%
Oppose 28
No opinion 2

Those Who Obey the 55-Mile-per-Hour Limit All or Most of the Time

Favor 77%
Oppose 22
No opinion 1

Those Who Obey the 55-Mile-per-Hour Limit Not Very Often or Never

Favor 29%
Oppose 69
No opinion 2

*Less than 1%

Selected National Trend

	Favor	Oppose	No opinion
1984	71%	25%	4%
1982	76	21	3
1981	75	23	2
1980	81	17	2
1979	71	26	3
1977	76	22	2
1974	73	24	3

From your own observations, would you say that most drivers obey the 55-mile-per-hour speed limit all of the time, most of the time, not very often, or never?

All of the time	1%
Most of the time	30
Not very often	62
Never	6
No opinion	1

Would you say that you, yourself, obey the 55-mile-per-hour speed limit all of the time, most of the time, not very often, or never?

All of the time	17%
Most of the time	54
Not very often	20
Never	4
Don't drive	5

Do you think the 55-mile-per-hour speed limit has saved lives, or not?

Yes, has	79%
No, has not	15
Don't know	6

Note: Despite a growing perception that the 55-mile-per-hour national speed limit is widely disobeyed, a two-thirds' majority of Americans favors retaining this law. Current public support, however, is the lowest since the law was imposed in 1974. In the latest Gallup Poll, 66% favor keeping the national speed limit, while 32% would like to see it repealed. Support for the law grew intermittently, from 73% in the first Gallup assessment, conducted shortly after the 1973 Arab embargo of oil shipments to the United States, to a peak of 81% in 1980. Since then public backing gradually has tailed off.

Until recently, opposition to the law has been relatively muted because of its success in reducing gasoline consumption and auto fatalities. Now that there is an oversupply of oil and lower retail gas prices, however, critics of the national speed limit have stepped up their demands for its repeal.

Americans' continuing support for the 55-mph limit can be ascribed, in large measure, to the overwhelming national consensus (79% to 15%) that this limit saves lives, with heavy majorities in all demographic groups sharing this opinion. Even among those who oppose the national speed limit, a 55% majority concedes the law's effectiveness in this regard. A federal study estimated that 3,000 to 5,000 lives are saved each year by keeping the 55-mph law rather than going to a 65-mph standard.

A 1978 federal law requires that at least 50% of the motorists in each state comply with the law. Failure to meet this requirement could cause noncomplying states to lose some of their federal funds for highway construction and repair. Nevertheless, many states have found ways to circumvent the law. Montana, for example, imposes only a $5 fine on motorists driving up to 70 miles per hour. The issue gained currency when the U.S. Department of Transportation recently announced it would withhold up to 10% of federal highway funds from Arizona and Vermont because more than one-half of the motorists in these states exceeded the 55-mph limit last year.

JULY 20
TAX REFORM

Interviewing Date: 6/9–16/86
Special Telephone Survey

As you may know, the Senate Finance Committee recently approved a major tax reform program. From everything that you have heard or read about it, do you think the amount of taxes you now pay would go down a lot, go down a little, go up a little, go up a lot, or stay about the same if the Senate plan were put into effect?

Go down 22%
Go up 34
Stay the same 30
No opinion 14

By Sex
Male

Go down 24%
Go up 35
Stay the same 31
No opinion 10

Female

Go down 20%
Go up 33
Stay the same 30
No opinion 17

By Income
$35,000 and Over

Go down 25%
Go up 37
Stay the same 28
No opinion 10

$15,000–$34,999

Go down 23%
Go up 33
Stay the same 32
No opinion 12

Under $15,000

Go down 19%
Go up 34
Stay the same 31
No opinion 16

By Politics
Republicans

Go down 24%
Go up 30
Stay the same 32
No opinion 14

Democrats

Go down 23%
Go up 38
Stay the same 27
No opinion 12

Independents

Go down 19%
Go up 35
Stay the same 32
No opinion 14

Selected National Trend*

	Go down	Go up	Stay the same	No opinion
1985				
August	11%	46%	30%	13%
June	25	32	29	14

*The wording of the question referred to the administration's proposal.

Do you think the Senate plan would make for a fairer distribution of the tax load among all taxpayers, one that's less fair, or wouldn't it be much different from the present system?

Fairer than old 25%
Not as fair 17
Not much different 40
No opinion 18

By Sex
Male

Fairer than old 29%
Not as fair 17
Not much different 39
No opinion 15

Female

Fairer than old	22%
Not as fair	17
Not much different	40
No opinion	21

By Income

$35,000 and Over

Fairer than old	32%
Not as fair	19
Not much different	34
No opinion	15

$15,000–$34,999

Fairer than old	26%
Not as fair	16
Not much different	42
No opinion	16

Under $15,000

Fairer than old	18%
Not as fair	20
Not much different	43
No opinion	19

By Politics

Republicans

Fairer than old	30%
Not as fair	14
Not much different	36
No opinion	20

Democrats

Fairer than old	18%
Not as fair	22
Not much different	40
No opinion	20

Independents

Fairer than old	31%
Not as fair	13
Not much different	45
No opinion	11

Selected National Trend*

	Fairer than old	Not as fair	Not much different	No opinion
1985				
August	25%	20%	40%	15%
June	29	22	34	15

*The wording of the question referred to the administration's proposal.

The Senate plan would greatly reduce basic personal tax rates. Most people would pay only 15%, and the top tax rate for individuals would be 27% versus the present 50%. In return, it would eliminate many deductions that are presently allowed. Please tell me whether you approve or disapprove of each of the following changes:

Employees with pensions would no longer be able to deduct the cost of Individual Retirement Accounts (IRAs) from their tax returns, although the income from IRAs would not be taxed until withdrawn?

Approve	33%
Disapprove	58
No opinion	9

By Income

$35,000 and Over

Approve	31%
Disapprove	63
No opinion	6

$15,000–$34,999

Approve	36%
Disapprove	58
No opinion	6

Under $15,000

Approve	32%
Disapprove	53
No opinion	15

Interest on car loans or credit card bills would no longer be deductible for most people?

Approve 33%
Disapprove 60
No opinion 7

By Income

$35,000 and Over

Approve 38%
Disapprove 59
No opinion 3

$15,000–$34,999

Approve 35%
Disapprove 61
No opinion 4

Under $15,000

Approve 27%
Disapprove 63
No opinion 10

Capital gains from the sale of property such as stocks and bonds would be taxed as ordinary income and would no longer qualify for lower tax rates?

Approve 45%
Disapprove 46
No opinion 9

By Income

$35,000 and Over

Approve 47%
Disapprove 49
No opinion 4

$15,000–$34,999

Approve 47%
Disapprove 45
No opinion 8

Under $15,000

Approve 39%
Disapprove 48
No opinion 13

Tax shelters such as real estate partnerships would no longer qualify for favorable tax treatment?

Approve 53%
Disapprove 37
No opinion 10

By Income

$35,000 and Over

Approve 57%
Disapprove 38
No opinion 5

$15,000–$34,999

Approve 59%
Disapprove 34
No opinion 7

Under $15,000

Approve 44%
Disapprove 38
No opinion 18

Now that we've had a chance to discuss some of the details of the Senate's tax reform program, would you say that you approve or disapprove of it?

	Before Senate Finance Committee discussion*	After Senate Finance Committee discussion**	Point change
Approve	38%	48%	+ 10
Disapprove	36	38	+ 2
No opinion	26	14	− 12

By Income**

$35,000 and Over

Approve 53%
Disapprove 37
No opinion 10

$15,000–$34,999

Approve 51%
Disapprove 38
No opinion 11

Under $15,000

Approve 40%
Disapprove 40
No opinion 20

By Politics**
Republicans

Approve 55%
Disapprove 31
No opinion 14

Democrats

Approve 42%
Disapprove 45
No opinion 13

Independents

Approve 50%
Disapprove 37
No opinion 13

Perceived Effect on Own Taxes**
Would Go Down

Approve 68%
Disapprove 25
No opinion 7

Would Go Up

Approve 34%
Disapprove 54
No opinion 12

Stay the Same

Approve 57%
Disapprove 32
No opinion 11

Perceived Fairness of Senate Plan**
Fairer Than Old

Approve 80%
Disapprove 14
No opinion 6

Not As Fair

Approve 28%
Disapprove 64
No opinion 8

Not Much Different

Approve 44%
Disapprove 45
No opinion 11

*August 1985 survey
**Current survey

Note: Although the stage in Washington clearly is set for the most extensive overhaul of the nation's tax system since World War II, public reaction to the tax reform program is generally unenthusiastic. To some extent, this may be attributed to the public's lack of familiarity or misunderstanding of the tax proposals now being debated by congressional conferees. More importantly, Americans are highly skeptical that the new tax system will reduce their own taxes or eliminate the inequities of the present system.

These observations are based on the findings of a recent Gallup Poll that probed Americans' opinions about key provisions of the tax bill passed last month by the U.S. Senate by a 97-to-3 vote. Most of the provisions studied are expected to emerge from the current House-Senate conference in or near their original Senate form.

The survey gave respondents two opportunities to express their overall reactions to the tax reform proposal, before and after detailed discussion of specific elements of the Senate program. At the start of interviewing, 38% said they approved, 36% disapproved, and 26% were undecided about the tax reform proposal. At the conclusion of the survey, 48% were in favor, 38% opposed, and 14% were undecided. Thus, exposure to some of the plan's basic features resulted in a 10-point shift from neutral to positive assessments, with no decline in negative views.

A further indication of the public's lack of enthusiasm is that, even among those who approve of the plan, relatively few show much conviction, with 19% saying they approve "very strongly," compared to 29% who approve "not so strongly." On the other hand, public opinion is fairly evenly divided between strong (21%) and moderate (17%) disapproval.

When the responses of the six in ten surveyed who said they had followed the recent discussions about tax reform either "very closely" (17%) or "fairly closely" (44%) are analyzed, the same ratios of approval and disapproval are found on both the "before" and "after" assessment questions, although fewer were undecided. Men, those over 30, the college educated, and the affluent are more likely to have followed the subject very closely, but the proportion claiming to have done so does not exceed 26% in any major population group.

By shifting some of the present tax burden from individuals to corporations and by eliminating many preferential deductions, the new tax program is expected to remove some 6 million working poor from the federal income tax rolls altogether and to bring tax relief to the vast majority of other taxpayers.

Despite the consensus of lawmakers that the tax reform program will be fairer than the present system, the survey found:

1) Almost two-thirds of the public (64%) think the taxes they now pay either would go up (34%) or stay the same (30%) if the tax reform program were put into effect. Only 22% say their taxes would go down. These findings are strikingly similar to those recorded in a June 1985 Gallup Poll, when the program in question was the Reagan administration's tax proposal.

2) Only 25% in the current survey believe the Senate plan would provide a more equitable distribution of the tax load among all taxpayers, while 40% think it would not be much different, and 17% say the new tax code would not be as fair as the present system. Again, these findings closely resemble those recorded one year ago, with reference to the administration's proposal. At least some of the public's antipathy toward the Senate

tax reform proposal can be traced to the proposed elimination of some presently allowed deductions.

3) Of four specific deductions that may be altered or discontinued under the tax reform bill, only one, the elimination of tax shelters such as real estate partnerships, receives majority approval, 53% to 37%. The public is evenly divided on the desirability of taxing capital gains from the sale of property as ordinary income, with 45% approving and 46% disapproving.

4) Two other provisions of the Senate bill—eliminating the deduction for Individual Retirement Accounts (IRAs) for employees with pensions and ending the deduction for interest on car loans and credit card bills—were voted down by a margin of almost 2 to 1.

JULY 24
NUCLEAR POWER PLANTS

Interviewing Date: 6/9–16/86
Special Telephone Survey

In order to meet the future power needs of the nation, how important do you feel it is to have more nuclear power plants—extremely important, somewhat important, not too important, or not at all important?

Extremely important 15%
Somewhat important 35
Not too important 20
Not at all important 26
No opinion 4

By Sex
Male

Extremely important 21%
Somewhat important 32
Not too important 21
Not at all important 23
No opinion 3

Female

Extremely important	9%
Somewhat important	38
Not too important	20
Not at all important	28
No opinion	5

By Ethnic Background

White

Extremely important	15%
Somewhat important	36
Not too important	20
Not at all important	25
No opinion	4

Nonwhite

Extremely important	13%
Somewhat important	28
Not too important	22
Not at all important	33
No opinion	4

Black

Extremely important	14%
Somewhat important	22
Not too important	22
Not at all important	37
No opinion	5

By Education

College Graduate

Extremely important	15%
Somewhat important	35
Not too important	20
Not at all important	27
No opinion	3

College Incomplete

Extremely important	15%
Somewhat important	43
Not too important	20
Not at all important	20
No opinion	2

High-School Graduate

Extremely important	14%
Somewhat important	35
Not too important	19
Not at all important	28
No opinion	4

Less Than High-School Graduate

Extremely important	16%
Somewhat important	25
Not too important	25
Not at all important	26
No opinion	8

By Region

East

Extremely important	15%
Somewhat important	33
Not too important	19
Not at all important	30
No opinion	3

Midwest

Extremely important	13%
Somewhat important	35
Not too important	25
Not at all important	24
No opinion	3

South

Extremely important	16%
Somewhat important	35
Not too important	18
Not at all important	4
No opinion	7

West

Extremely important	15%
Somewhat important	28
Not too important	20
Not at all important	25
No opinion	2

By Age

18–29 Years

Extremely important 15%
Somewhat important 39
Not too important 25
Not at all important 20
No opinion 1

30–49 Years

Extremely important 11%
Somewhat important 35
Not too important 19
Not at all important 32
No opinion 3

50 Years and Over

Extremely important 18%
Somewhat important 32
Not too important 19
Not at all important 24
No opinion 7

By Politics

Republicans

Extremely important 19%
Somewhat important 39
Not too important 19
Not at all important 20
No opinion 3

Democrats

Extremely important 13%
Somewhat important 31
Not too important 21
Not at all important 30
No opinion 5

Independents

Extremely important 12%
Somewhat important 37
Not too important 21
Not at all important 27
No opinion 3

Selected National Trend

	1979	1976
Extremely important	30%	34%
Somewhat important	33	37
Not too important	13	10
Not at all important	17	8
No opinion	7	11

*Do you feel that nuclear power plants oper-
ating today are safe enough with the present
safety regulations, or do you feel that their
operations should be cut back until more strict
regulations can be put into practice?*

Safe enough 25%
Should cut back 66
No opinion 9

By Sex

Male

Safe enough 36%
Should cut back 55
No opinion 9

Female

Safe enough 15%
Should cut back 76
No opinion 9

By Ethnic Background

White

Safe enough 26%
Should cut back 65
No opinion 9

Nonwhite

Safe enough 18%
Should cut back 73
No opinion 9

Black

Safe enough 13%
Should cut back 76
No opinion 11

By Education
College Graduate

Safe enough 33%
Should cut back 57
No opinion 10

College Incomplete

Safe enough 25%
Should cut back 69
No opinion 6

High-School Graduate

Safe enough 26%
Should cut back 66
No opinion 8

Less Than High-School Graduate

Safe enough 15%
Should cut back 73
No opinion 12

By Region
East

Safe enough 23%
Should cut back 72
No opinion 5

Midwest

Safe enough 24%
Should cut back 65
No opinion 11

South

Safe enough 23%
Should cut back 65
No opinion 12

West

Safe enough 31%
Should cut back 63
No opinion 6

By Age
18–29 Years

Safe enough 27%
Should cut back 66
No opinion 7

30–49 Years

Safe enough 24%
Should cut back 69
No opinion 7

50 Years and Over

Safe enough 25%
Should cut back 64
No opinion 11

By Politics
Republicans

Safe enough 31%
Should cut back 59
No opinion 10

Democrats

Safe enough 18%
Should cut back 74
No opinion 8

Independents

Safe enough 28%
Should cut back 66
No opinion 6

Selected National Trend

	Safe enough	Should cut back	No opinion
1980	30%	55%	15%
1979	24	66	10
1976	34	40	26

As of today, how do you feel about the construction of a nuclear power plant in this area—that is, within five miles of here? Would you be against the construction of such a plant in this area, or not?

Would be against 73%
Would not be against 23
No opinion 4

By Sex
Male

Would be against 65%
Would not be against 32
No opinion 3

Female

Would be against 80%
Would not be against 15
No opinion 5

By Ethnic Background
White

Would be against 71%
Would not be against 25
No opinion 4

Nonwhite

Would be against 81%
Would not be against 15
No opinion 4

Black

Would be against 80%
Would not be against 16
No opinion 4

By Education
College Graduate

Would be against 72%
Would not be against 25
No opinion 3

College Incomplete

Would be against 70%
Would not be against 26
No opinion 4

High-School Graduate

Would be against 74%
Would not be against 23
No opinion 3

Less Than High-School Graduate

Would be against 75%
Would not be against 19
No opinion 6

By Region
East

Would be against 75%
Would not be against 21
No opinion 4

Midwest

Would be against 72%
Would not be against 27
No opinion 1

South

Would be against 71%
Would not be against 24
No opinion 5

West

Would be against 74%
Would not be against 21
No opinion 5

By Politics
Republicans

Would be against 64%
Would not be against 31
No opinion 5

Democrats

Would be against 81%
Would not be against 15
No opinion 4

Would be against 72%
Would not be against 26
No opinion 2

Selected National Trend

	Would be against	Would not be against	No opinion
1979	60%	33%	7%
1976	45	42	13

Note: Americans' misgivings about the safety of nuclear power plants, which began to recede within months after the 1979 accident at Three-Mile Island, were revived by the recent explosion at the Soviet nuclear reactor at Chernobyl. In fact, more Americans today (73%) than in the immediate aftermath of the Three-Mile Island accident (60%) say they would oppose the construction of a nuclear power plant within five miles of where they live.

The latest survey also found an increase since 1980, from 55% to 66%, in public sentiment favoring a cutback in nuclear power operations until stricter safety regulations can be effected. The current findings reveal far more apprehension than recorded in the first Gallup Poll on the subject. In that 1976 assessment, before any major nuclear mishap had occurred, 40% called for stricter safety regulations, 34% thought nuclear power plants were safe enough, and 26% were undecided.

Another question in the nuclear power series found a further decline in the public's perceptions that more nuclear generating plants should be built "in order to meet the future power needs of the nation." In the 1976 poll, 34% thought this was "extremely important," with the percentage dropping to 30% in 1979 and 15% at present. Since the demand for electric power has declined in the past ten years and there is now a plentiful supply of alternate fuel sources, it is not possible to determine to what extent the Chernobyl accident contributed to Americans' present outlook on nuclear generating capacity.

There is no doubt, however, that the public's perceptions of the danger of nuclear plants and the need for more such plants are interrelated. Only 9% of those in the current survey who say that present nuclear operations should be cut back, compared to 28% of those who believe the plants operating now are safe enough, consider the need for more nuclear plants to be "extremely important." Conversely, 33% of the former, but only 9% of the latter, characterize the need for more plants as "not at all important."

Although the Chernobyl explosion undoubtedly revived Americans' fears about the danger of nuclear plants, the future of nuclear power in the United States was already in question. According to an article in *National Journal,* no new nuclear plants have been ordered since 1978, and all orders placed between 1974 and 1977 have been canceled. Currently, 100 plants are operating in the United States, generating about 16% of the nation's electricity. When the 27 plants now under construction are completed, nuclear energy will account for about 20% of total capacity.

Aside from the political issues involved, economic factors may rule out future construction of U.S. nuclear generators. Although the uranium fuel used has remained cheap, the cost of building and operating these plants has soared, compared with the cost of coal-fired ones. Thus, additional nuclear plants may be unable to compete with other energy sources solely on the basis of economics.

The latest survey found strong differences of opinion by gender, with 76% of women and 55% of men favoring a cutback of presently operating reactors. Similarly, 80% of women and 65% of men are opposed to having a nuclear plant built near their homes.

As in past surveys, there is a political dimension to the public's current attitudes toward nuclear power. Although Republicans and Democrats share the same basic convictions on the three issues studied, Democrats are more likely than Republicans to think that the construction of additional nuclear power plants is "not too" or "not at all important," 51% to 39%. Also, more Democrats (74%) than Republicans (59%) believe that nuclear operations should be cut back until stricter regulations can be effected. Finally, more Democrats

(81%) than Republicans (64%) express opposition to the construction of a nuclear plant near home.

The Chernobyl accident also had a strong impact on public opinion in Canada. Currently, 40% of Canadians believe nuclear power generation should be stopped completely, 37% think no further plants should be built, and 13% say nuclear generation should be increased. In a 1980 survey the comparable figures were: stopped, 27%, no further plants, 27%, and increased, 30%. Also, the current Canadian Gallup Poll found 71% opposed to construction of a nuclear plant in their area, and an additional 17% anxious; a 1976 survey showed 35% opposed and 23% apprehensive.

JULY 27
POLITICAL AFFILIATION

Interviewing Date: January–June 1986
Various Surveys*

*In politics, as of today, do you consider yourself a Republican, a Democrat, or an independent?***

Republican 32%
Democrat 39
Independent 29

By Sex
Male

Republican 33%
Democrat 36
Independent 31

Female

Republican 31%
Democrat 42
Independent 37

*Findings are based on more than 5,900 interviews.
**Those saying they have no party preference, or who named other parties (3% in the latest surveys), are excluded.

By Ethnic Background
White

Republican 35%
Democrat 35
Independent 30

Black

Republican 9%
Democrat 73
Independent 18

Hispanic

Republican 24%
Democrat 49
Independent 27

By Education
College Graduate

Republican 39%
Democrat 31
Independent 30

College Incomplete

Republican 40%
Democrat 31
Independent 29

High-School Graduate

Republican 30%
Democrat 39
Independent 31

Less Than High-School Graduate

Republican 23%
Democrat 53
Independent 24

By Region
East

Republican 32%
Democrat 39
Independent 29

Midwest

Republican 31%
Democrat 35
Independent 34

South

Republican 31%
Democrat 43
Independent 26

West

Republican 37%
Democrat 38
Independent 25

By Age
18–29 Years

Republican 35%
Democrat 33
Independent 32

30–49 Years

Republican 30%
Democrat 38
Independent 32

50–64 Years

Republican 31%
Democrat 44
Independent 25

65 Years and Over

Republican 35%
Democrat 45
Independent 20

By Income
$35,000 and Over

Republican 39%
Democrat 32
Independent 29

$15,000–$34,999

Republican 32%
Democrat 37
Independent 31

Under $15,000

Republican 27%
Democrat 47
Independent 26

By Occupation
Professional and Business

Republican 39%
Democrat 31
Independent 30

Other White Collar

Republican 35%
Democrat 36
Independent 29

Blue Collar Workers

Republican 27%
Democrat 42
Independent 31

Skilled Workers Only

Republican 29%
Democrat 38
Independent 33

Unskilled Workers Only

Republican 26%
Democrat 45
Independent 29

By Labor Union Household
Labor Union Members

Republican 26%
Democrat 44
Independent 30

Nonlabor Union Members

Republican 34%
Democrat 38
Independent 28

Selected National Trend

	Republican	Democrat	Independent
1985	33%	38%	29%
1984	31	40	29
1982	26	45	29
1980	24	46	30
1976	23	47	30
1968	27	46	27
1964	25	53	22
1960	30	47	23
1954	34	46	20
1950	33	45	22
1946	40	39	21
1937	34	50	16

Note: During the first six months of 1986, the Democratic party held a slim 7-percentage point lead over the Republican party in rank-and-file membership, unchanged from the numerical superiority enjoyed by the Democrats during the final months of 1985. Thus the strong upturn in consumer optimism observed earlier this year, which might be expected to benefit the party in power, has failed to increase the Republican party's grassroots strength.

This anomaly is heightened by the results of a March Gallup Poll, in which a majority of Americans, for the first time in a thirty-five-year trend, cited the Republican party as better able than the Democratic party to keep the nation prosperous. Prior to and during the 1981–82 recession, the Democrats enjoyed a near monopoly on this issue, at times by ratios of 3 to 1 or better.

During the first half of 1986, 39% of voting-age Americans described themselves as Democrats, 32% as Republicans, and 29% as independents. The comparable figures for the October–December 1985 period are 40% Democrats, 33% Republicans, and 27% independents. As recently as early 1985, the two parties were nearly equal in strength, with 37% identifying themselves as Democrats, 35% as Republicans, and 28% as independents.

Americans' improved outlook for the economy was expressed in several ways in the March survey. First, 83% said they expected the recovery to last at least until the end of this year, with 58% predicting that economic good times would prevail into 1988 or beyond. The public was as optimistic then as at any time since 1983 when the recovery began. Second, 61% said they would be financially better off one year from now, compared to 18% who predicted a downturn; only 16% thought their situation would not change much. This represented an 8-percentage point increase in consumer optimism since January when 53% believed their finances would improve, 15% grow worse, and 25% remain the same.

The early months of 1985 saw the Democratic party's historic advantage over the Republican party virtually disappear, with almost as many adult Americans describing themselves as Republicans (35%) as Democrats (37%). As the year wore on, however, the Democratic party regained support, culminating in the 7-point advantage recorded during the last quarter of 1985 and the first half of 1986. The 2-percentage point gap in party affiliation observed during the first quarter of 1985 is the closest the two parties have come to numerical parity in forty years.

The largest Democratic advantage during President Ronald Reagan's tenure occurred during the second quarter of 1983 when the nation was still recovering from the recession. At that time, there were twice as many nominal Democrats (46%) as Republicans (23%).

The first quarter of 1985 also brought the Republicans unaccustomed but short-lived leadership in key demographic groups. In earlier periods the Republicans could claim small pluralities over the Democrats only among college graduates, upper-income groups, and those from households in which the chief wage earner was employed in business or the professions.

By early 1985 the GOP also led among whites, 18 to 29 year olds, persons who attended but did not graduate from college, and midwesterners. In addition, the two parties were at a virtual standoff, not only nationally and among voters of both sexes but also among high-school graduates, middle-income groups, skilled blue collar workers, nonunion households, and westerners. In the latest surveys, the GOP has retained an edge in party membership only among the college educated, persons from business and professional households, and those with annual family incomes of $35,000 or more.

Currently, statistically equivalent numbers of Democratic and Republican loyalists can be found among men, whites, 18 to 29 year olds, persons from homes in which the chief wage earner is employed in a clerical or sales position, and residents of the Midwest and West. And Democrats presently outnumber Republicans among women, blacks, Hispanics, persons 30 and older, the less well educated and less affluent, blue collar workers, persons from both union and nonunion households, and residents of the East and South.

JULY 31
PERSONAL FINANCES

Interviewing Date: 7/11–14/86
Survey #266-G

We are interested in how people's financial situation may have changed. Would you say that you are financially better off now than you were a year ago, or are you financially worse off now?

Better 39%
Worse 25
Same (volunteered) 35
No opinion 1

By Sex
Male

Better 39%
Worse 24
Same (volunteered) 37
No opinion .... *

Female

Better 40%
Worse 26
Same (volunteered) 33
No opinion 1

By Ethnic Background
White

Better 40%
Worse 24
Same (volunteered) 35
No opinion 1

Nonwhite

Better 37%
Worse 34
Same (volunteered) 27
No opinion 2

Black

Better 39%
Worse 36
Same (volunteered) 23
No opinion 2

By Education
College Graduate

Better 53%
Worse 16
Same (volunteered) 31
No opinion .... *

College Incomplete

Better 45%
Worse 22
Same (volunteered) 32
No opinion 1

High-School Graduate

Better 41%
Worse 27
Same (volunteered) 31
No opinion 1

Less Than High-School Graduate

Better 21%
Worse 34
Same (volunteered) 43
No opinion 2

By Region

East

Better 43%
Worse 19
Same (volunteered) 38
No opinion .... *

Midwest

Better 39%
Worse 24
Same (volunteered) 36
No opinion 1

South

Better 36%
Worse 31
Same (volunteered) 32
No opinion 1

West

Better 41%
Worse 25
Same (volunteered) 34
No opinion .... *

By Age

18–29 Years

Better 54%
Worse 26
Same (volunteered) 20
No opinion .... *

30–49 Years

Better 45%
Worse 26
Same (volunteered) 28
No opinion 1

50–64 Years

Better 29%
Worse 25
Same (volunteered) 46
No opinion .... *

65 Years and Over

Better 18%
Worse 24
Same (volunteered) 55
No opinion 3

By Income

$40,000 and Over

Better 34%
Worse 15
Same (volunteered) 31
No opinion .... *

$25,000–$39,999

Better 48%
Worse 20
Same (volunteered) 32
No opinion .... *

$15,000–$24,999

Better 38%
Worse 27
Same (volunteered) 34
No opinion 1

Under $15,000

Better 28%
Worse 34
Same (volunteered) 37
No opinion 1

By Occupation

Professional and Business

Better 50%
Worse 19
Same (volunteered) 30
No opinion 1

Other White Collar

Better 46%
Worse 25
Same (volunteered) 29
No opinion .... *

Unskilled Workers

Better 40%
Worse 31
Same (volunteered) 29
No opinion .... *

By Labor Union Household
Labor Union Members

Better 40%
Worse 26
Same (volunteered) 33
No opinion 1

Nonlabor Union Members

Better 39%
Worse 25
Same (volunteered) 35
No opinion 1

*Less than 1%

Selected National Trend

	Better	Worse	Same	No opinion
1986				
June	46%	25%	28%	1%
March	46	30	24	*
January	40	30	29	1
1985				
October	38	27	34	1
June	43	29	26	2
March	48	25	26	1
1984				
Nov.–Dec.	43	24	32	1
July	40	25	34	1
March	36	26	37	1
1983				
June	28	39	32	1
March	25	46	28	1

Now looking ahead, do you expect that at this time next year you will be financially better off than now, or worse off than now?

Better 51%
Worse 15
Same (volunteered) 28
No opinion 6

The following are the findings among "super optimists," those who claim to be better off now than they were one year ago and expect to be still better off next year.

	Super optimists
National	31%

By Sex

| Male .... | 32% |
| Female .... | 30 |

By Ethnic Background

White 32%
Black 27

By Education

College graduate 45%
College incomplete 36
High-school graduate 32
Less than high-school graduate 15

By Region

East 32%
Midwest 33
South 29
West 32

By Age

18–29 years 46%
30–49 years 38
50–64 years 21
65 years and over 9

By Income

$40,000 and over	.....................48%
$25,000–$39,999	38
$15,000–$24,999	29
Under $15,000	18

By Politics

Republicans	........................39%
Democrats	28
Independents	27

Selected National Trend

	Super optimists
1986	
June	.........................37%
March	37
January	31
1985	
October	28
June	33
March	37
1984	
Nov.–Dec.	32
July	31
March	28
1983	
June	20
March	18

Note: Consumers' financial optimism, which remained strong throughout the first half of the year, is now showing signs of cooling off. Still, optimism outweighs pessimism by a wide margin. The latest figures represent a substantial decrease since March in the proportion who are bullish in their financial outlook—from 61% to 51%—and a sharp increase—from 16% to 28%—in those who believe their economic status will not change much in the coming year. Outright pessimism, 15% in the current survey, is statistically unchanged from March.

The public's buoyant financial outlook led to heavy consumer spending for big-ticket discretionary items, which has been the mainstay of the economy so far this year, according to Jay Schmiedeskamp, chief economist of the Gallup Organization. The decline in consumer optimism found in the latest survey may be a portent of reduced discretionary spending, Schmiedeskamp believes.

In response to another survey question, 39% see an improvement in their current financial status vis-à-vis one year ago, 25% claim to be worse off, and 35% perceive no change. Again, comparison with surveys conducted in June and March reveals a decline in those saying they are better off and an increase in those who think their financial situation is about the same as it was one year ago. The proportion saying they are worse off has not changed significantly.

The current survey also marks a decline in "super optimists," from 37% in March and June to 31% at present. Studies have shown that those in this group tend to be young, well educated, affluent, and are likely to be heavy buyers of houses, cars, major appliances, and other discretionary items.

The current level of extreme optimism is the lowest found in Gallup surveys since January. It is, however, far higher than those recorded in 1982 and 1983 when the nation was recovering from recession.

AUGUST 3
PRESIDENT REAGAN

Interviewing Date: 7/11–14/86
Survey #266-G

Do you approve or disapprove of the way Ronald Reagan is handling his job as president?

Approve	...........................63%
Disapprove	28
No opinion	 9

By Sex
Male

Approve	...........................69%
Disapprove	26
No opinion	 5

Female

Approve 58%
Disapprove 30
No opinion 12

By Ethnic Background
White

Approve 66%
Disapprove 25
No opinion 9

Black

Approve 36%
Disapprove 56
No opinion 8

By Education
College Graduate

Approve 64%
Disapprove 33
No opinion 3

College Incomplete

Approve 73%
Disapprove 20
No opinion 7

High-School Graduate

Approve 65%
Disapprove 22
No opinion 13

Less Than High-School Graduate

Approve 52%
Disapprove 37
No opinion 11

By Region
East

Approve 66%
Disapprove 27
No opinion 7

Midwest

Approve 61%
Disapprove 30
No opinion 9

South

Approve 64%
Disapprove 26
No opinion 10

West

Approve 64%
Disapprove 28
No opinion 8

By Age
18–24 Years

Approve 67%
Disapprove 24
No opinion 9

25–29 Years

Approve 73%
Disapprove 19
No opinion 8

30–49 Years

Approve 65%
Disapprove 27
No opinion 8

50–64 Years

Approve 58%
Disapprove 32
No opinion 10

65 Years and Over

Approve 59%
Disapprove 32
No opinion 9

By Income

$40,000 and Over

Approve 69%
Disapprove 26
No opinion 5

$25,000–$39,999

Approve 53%
Disapprove 25
No opinion 7

$15,000–$24,999

Approve 66%
Disapprove 26
No opinion 8

Under $15,000

Approve 54%
Disapprove 33
No opinion 13

By Politics

Republicans

Approve 88%
Disapprove 6
No opinion 6

Democrats

Approve 44%
Disapprove 47
No opinion 9

Independents

Approve 55%
Disapprove 25
No opinion 10

Selected National Trend

	Approve	Disapprove	No opinion
1986			
June 9–16	64%	26%	10%
June 6–9	61	29	10
May 16–19	68	23	9
April 11–14	62	29	9
March 7–10	63	26	11
January 10–13	64	27	9
1985	61	30	9
1984	56	35	9
1983	44	46	10
1982	44	46	10
1981	58	28	14

Now let me ask you about some specific foreign and domestic problems. As I read off each problem, would you tell me whether you approve or disapprove of the way President Reagan is handling that problem:

Economic conditions in this country?

Approve 49%
Disapprove 43
No opinion 8

Unemployment?

Approve 42%
Disapprove 47
No opinion 11

Federal budget deficit?

Approve 32%
Disapprove 52
No opinion 16

Foreign policy?

Approve 51%
Disapprove 35
No opinion 14

Relations with the Soviet Union?

Approve 60%
Disapprove 27
No opinion 13

Nuclear disarmament negotiations with the Soviet Union?

Approve 51%
Disapprove 33
No opinion 16

Situation in the Middle East?

Approve 47%
Disapprove 34
No opinion 19

Situation in Nicaragua?

Approve 34%
Disapprove 46
No opinion 20

Note: A solid majority of Americans continues to approve of President Ronald Reagan's handling of the duties of his office, despite a substantial recent decline in consumers' financial optimism. In the latest Gallup Poll, 63% approve of the president's overall job performance, while 28% disapprove, and 9% are undecided. These ratings, although not significantly different from those recorded last month, are slightly below his peak of 68% approval in May. As consistently has been the case since he took office, Reagan currently receives higher marks for his overall job performance than for his handling of many specific areas of responsibility.

The most recent survey also found evidence that consumers' financial optimism, which remained strong throughout the first half of the year, is starting to cool off. Fewer today than in either March or June say they are better off now than they were one year ago, and fewer think they will be more prosperous next year than they are at present. Presidential popularity and the political fortunes of the party in control of the White House tend to ebb and flow with the economic climate. Thus, a further weakening in consumer optimism could lead to erosion of Reagan's popularity and have an important bearing on the November midterm elections as well.

Not surprisingly, there is a strong political coloration to the public's assessment of the president's overall job performance, as well as his handling of specific problems. Republicans strongly endorse Reagan's general leadership (88% approve) and his handling of Soviet relations (79%), economic conditions (73%), foreign policy (71%), the disarmament talks (69%), and the Middle East situation (67%). Somewhat fewer approve of his handling of unemployment (63%). The president's conduct of the Nicaraguan situation and his handling of the budget deficit receive the approval of 55% and 50% of Republicans, respectively.

Reagan's overall job rating from Democrats is 44% approval (only half that of Republicans). For his handling of the eight specific issues tested, Democratic approval ranges from a high of 47%, for Soviet relations, to a low of 21%, for the budget deficit.

AUGUST 7
DEMOCRATIC PRESIDENTIAL CANDIDATES

Interviewing Date: 7/11–14/86
Survey #266-G

Asked of Democrats and Democratic-leaning independents: Will you please look over this list and tell me which of these persons you have heard of? Now will you please tell me which of these persons you know something about?

	Heard of	Know something about
Jesse Jackson	89%	71%
Gary Hart	80	53
Lee Iacocca	70	57
Mario Cuomo	53	37
Tom Bradley	47	27
Jay Rockefeller	47	22
Dianne Feinstein	36	24
Bill Bradley	35	18
Charles Robb	30	17
Mark White	25	12

Sam Nunn	24	12	
Patricia Schroeder	21	9	
Dale Bumpers	20	9	
Bill Clinton	14	6	
Richard Gephardt	14	5	
Bruce Babbitt	13	5	
Joseph Biden	9	4	
Tony Coelho	7	2	
None of the above	3	8	

Bradley (Tom)	7	8
Rockefeller	6	6
Robb	3	4
Feinstein	4	4
White	3	5
Others	*	*
Don't know	**	**

*All others on the list were chosen by 2% or fewer.
**Not available

Also asked of Democrats and Democratic-leaning independents: Which one would you like to see nominated as the Democratic party's candidate for president in 1988? And who would be your second choice?

The following results are based on first and second choices combined:

Hart	34%
Iacocca	26
Cuomo	22
Jackson	17
Bradley (Bill)	7
Bradley (Tom)	7
Rockefeller	6
Robb	3
Feinstein	3
White	3
Others	*
Don't know	21

*All others on the list were chosen by 2% or fewer.

Selected National Trend

	April 1986	January 1986
Hart	40%	46%
Iacocca	16	17
Cuomo	26	23
Jackson	16	15
Bradley (Bill)	6	7

Interviewing Date: 6/9–16/86
Special Telephone Survey

Asked of Democrats and Democratic-leaning independents: Suppose the choice for president in the Democratic convention in 1988 narrows down to Senator Gary Hart and New York Governor Mario Cuomo. Which one would you prefer to have the Democratic convention select?

Hart	55%
Cuomo	30
Undecided	15

Asked of Democrats and Democratic-leaning independents: Suppose the choice for president in the Democratic convention in 1988 narrows down to Senator Gary Hart and the Reverend Jesse Jackson. Which one would you prefer to have the Democratic convention select?

Hart	75%
Jackson	14
Undecided	11

Asked of Democrats and Democratic-leaning independents: Suppose the choice for president in the Democratic convention in 1988 narrows down to Senator Gary Hart and businessman Lee Iacocca. Which one would you prefer to have the Democratic convention select?

Hart 59%
Iacocca 28
Undecided 13

Note: Although Colorado Senator Gary Hart remains the early leader for the 1988 Democratic presidential nomination, Chrysler Corporation Chairman Lee Iacocca now trails the senator by a slim 8-point margin. As recently as April, Iacocca was a distant third in the nomination contest, with Hart leading runner-up New York Governor Mario Cuomo by 15 points and Iacocca by 25. In the latest Gallup Poll, Hart receives 34% of the combined first- and second-place nomination votes of Democrats and Democratic-leaning independents, compared to 26% for Iacocca and 22% for Cuomo.

Iacocca's television coverage over the July 4 weekend and his role as the chief fund-raiser for the restoration of the Statue of Liberty doubtless enhanced his appeal as a possible Democratic candidate. Although Iacocca has denied interest in the nomination, his supporters are pressing his candidacy.

Next on the list of possible Democratic nominees is the Reverend Jesse Jackson, the choice of 17%; New Jersey Senator Bill Bradley and Los Angeles Mayor Tom Bradley, each with 7%; and West Virginia Senator Jay Rockefeller, with 6%. Former Virginia Governor Charles Robb, San Francisco Mayor Dianne Feinstein, and Texas Governor Mark White are selected by 3% each. None of the eight other persons on the list of eighteen Democrats mentioned as possible nominees receives more than 2% of the vote.

With almost two years remaining before the early state primaries, name recognition plays a vital role in the potential candidates' standing with the rank and file. At present, only four of the eighteen names on the list are familiar to 50% or more Democrats and independent leaners. Conversely, nine names are recognized by one-fourth or fewer. In addition, only Jackson (71%), Iacocca (57%), and Hart (53%) are sufficiently well known so that one-half or more in the survey says they "know something about" each man. Substantially fewer make this claim about Cuomo (37%) and the others on the list.

AUGUST 10
REPUBLICAN PRESIDENTIAL CANDIDATES

Interviewing Date: 7/11–14/86
Survey #266-G

Asked of Republicans and Republican-leaning independents: Will you please look over this list and tell me which of these persons you have heard of? Now will you please tell me which of these persons you know something about?

	Heard of	Know something about
George Bush	93%	82%
Alexander Haig	73	53
Robert Dole	67	45
Jeane Kirkpatrick	59	41
Howard Baker	58	38
Jesse Helms	55	35
Elizabeth Dole	53	36
James Baker	46	25
Pat Robertson	44	33
Jack Kemp	39	25
William Brock	28	14
Paul Laxalt	26	16
Donald Rumsfeld	26	11
Robert Packwood	22	13
Richard Lugar	21	12
Pete Domenici	17	9
Richard Thornburgh	16	9
Pierre du Pont	15	7
William Armstrong	14	6
Thomas Kean	14	7
James Thompson	12	8
None of the above	3	6

Also asked of Republicans and Republican-leaning independents: Which one would you like to see nominated as the Republican party's candidate for president in 1988? And who would be your second choice?

The following results are based on first and second choices combined:

Bush 53%
Dole, R. 16
Baker, H. 12
Haig 10
Kemp 9
Kirkpatrick 9
Robertson 8
Thornburgh 4
Dole, E. 3
Helms 3
Others . . . . *
Don't know 20

*All others on the list were chosen by 2% or fewer.

Selected National Trend

	April 1986
Bush	51%
Dole, R.	19
Baker, H.	18
Haig	8
Kemp	10
Kirkpatrick	7
Robertson	6
Thornburgh	1
Dole, E.	2
Helms	3
Others	*
Don't know	14

*All others on the list were chosen by 2% or fewer.

Interviewing Date: 6/9–16/86
Special Telephone Survey

Asked of Republicans and Republican-leaning independents: Suppose the choice for president in the Republican convention in 1988 narrows down to Vice President George Bush and Senator Bob Dole. Which one would you prefer to have the Republican convention select?

Bush 59%
Dole 21
Undecided 20

Asked of Republicans and Republican-leaning independents: Suppose the choice for president in the Republican convention in 1988 narrows down to Vice President George Bush and former Senator Howard Baker. Which one would you prefer to have the Republican convention select?

Bush 59%
Baker 23
Undecided 18

Asked of Republicans and Republican-leaning independents: Suppose the choice for president in the Republican convention in 1988 narrows down to Vice President George Bush and Representative Jack Kemp. Which one would you prefer to have the Republican convention select?

Bush 65%
Kemp 16
Undecided 19

Note: Vice President George Bush continues to hold a commanding lead for the 1988 Republican presidential nomination, with no strong challengers apparent at this early stage in the selection process. In the latest Gallup Poll, Bush receives 53% of Republicans' and Republican-leaning independents' combined first- and second-place nomination votes. Runners-up are Senate Majority Leader Robert Dole, with 16%, former Senator Howard Baker, with 12%, and former Secretary of State Alexander Haig, with 10%.

Farther down the list are Representative Jack Kemp and former U.S. Ambassador to the United Nations Jeane Kirkpatrick, with 9% each, followed by television evangelist Pat Robertson (8%), Governor Richard Thornburgh (4%), and Transportation Secretary Elizabeth Dole and Senator Jesse Helms, with 3% each. None of the eleven other persons on a list of twenty-one Republicans mentioned as possible nominees receives more than 2% of the votes.

In light of Bush's better than 3-to-1 current nationwide advantage over his nearest potential rival, it is not surprising that the vice president also is the top nomination choice of Republicans and Republican-leaning independents from widely disparate socioeconomic and geographic backgrounds. Further, it should be stressed that Bush is the clear current favorite among all Republican-oriented voter groups, despite comparatively minor variations in other prospective nominees' political profiles.

Some of the runners-up, however, exhibit pockets of comparative strength that, while insufficient to put them into strong current contention with Bush, may represent areas of opportunity as the campaign progresses. The most obvious of these is Robertson's relatively strong current standing with the three in ten Republicans and Republican-leaning independents who describe themselves as "born again" or evangelical Christians. Robertson receives 20% of evangelicals' nomination votes, placing him second to Bush, with 43%. Bush is the choice of 57% of non-evangelicals, compared to Robertson's 3%.

Senator Dole, who ranks a distant second to Bush nationwide, exhibits somewhat greater strength in his native Midwest than he does elsewhere in the nation, as does Robertson in the South. Also, nomination support for Dole and Howard Baker is slightly stronger among older Republicans and leaders (50 and older), while Haig's backing is skewed toward younger voters (18 to 29 year olds). And Kemp fares relatively better among men, 13% of whom name him as their first or second choice for the nomination; only 4% of women do likewise.

With almost two years remaining before the early state primaries, name recognition plays a vital role in potential candidates' standing with the rank and file. At present, only seven of the twenty-one names on the list are familiar to 50% or more Republicans and Republican-leaning independents. In addition, only Bush (82%) and Haig (53%) are sufficiently well known so that one-half or more of this group says they "know something about" each man. Substantially fewer make this claim about the others on the list.

Although he remains among the top challengers, Howard Baker's competitive position has slipped slightly since the earlier poll, from 17% to 12%. This finding is buttressed by a decline, from 50% in a June 1985 survey to 38% today,

in the percentage of Republicans and Republican leaners who claim to "know something about" Baker. Among the prospective candidates included in both the 1985 and current lists, the former Senate majority leader is the only one to suffer a significant decline in this key measurement.

AUGUST 14
SEXUAL VIOLENCE IN MOVIES AND MAGAZINES

Interviewing Date: 7/11–14/86
Survey #266-G

As I read you some items, please tell me if you feel each one should be totally banned for sale to adults, sold to adults as long as there is no public display, or sold to adults with no restrictions:

Sale or rental of video cassettes featuring sexual violence?

Totally banned 73%
No public display 19
No restrictions 6
No opinion 2

By Sex
Male

Totally banned 66%
No public display 23
No restrictions 9
No opinion 2

Female

Totally banned 79%
No public display 15
No restrictions 4
No opinion 2

By Ethnic Background
White

Totally banned 73%
No public display 19
No restrictions 6
No opinion 2

Black

Totally banned	66%
No public display	25
No restrictions	7
No opinion	2

By Education

College Graduate

Totally banned	66%
No public display	23
No restrictions	10
No opinion	1

College Incomplete

Totally banned	72%
No public display	19
No restrictions	7
No opinion	2

High-School Graduate

Totally banned	75%
No public display	19
No restrictions	4
No opinion	2

Less Than High-School Graduate

Totally banned	74%
No public display	16
No restrictions	6
No opinion	4

By Region

East

Totally banned	69%
No public display	23
No restrictions	6
No opinion	2

Midwest

Totally banned	79%
No public display	13
No restrictions	6
No opinion	2

South

Totally banned	72%
No public display	21
No restrictions	6
No opinion	1

West

Totally banned	70%
No public display	20
No restrictions	7
No opinion	3

By Age

18–24 Years

Totally banned	57%
No public display	30
No restrictions	11
No opinion	2

25–29 Years

Totally banned	63%
No public display	29
No restrictions	5
No opinion	3

30–49 Years

Totally banned	74%
No public display	19
No restrictions	6
No opinion	1

50–64 Years

Totally banned	78%
No public display	15
No restrictions	5
No opinion	2

65 Years and Over

Totally banned	81%
No public display	11
No restrictions	4
No opinion	4

By Income

$40,000 and Over

Totally banned 70%
No public display 20
No restrictions 8
No opinion 2

$25,000–$39,999

Totally banned 74%
No public display 19
No restrictions 6
No opinion 1

$15,000–$24,999

Totally banned 73%
No public display 20
No restrictions 6
No opinion 1

Under $15,000

Totally banned 74%
No public display 17
No restrictions 6
No opinion 3

By Politics

Republicans

Totally banned 75%
No public display 18
No restrictions 5
No opinion 2

Democrats

Totally banned 73%
No public display 19
No restrictions 6
No opinion 2

Independents

Totally banned 71%
No public display 19
No restrictions 8
No opinion 2

By Religion

Protestants

Totally banned 78%
No public display 17
No restrictions 4
No opinion 1

Catholics

Totally banned 70%
No public display 20
No restrictions 7
No opinion 3

By Occupation

Professional and Business

Totally banned 73%
No public display 18
No restrictions 8
No opinion 1

Other White Collar

Totally banned 75%
No public display 16
No restrictions 4
No opinion 5

Skilled Workers

Totally banned 68%
No public display 25
No restrictions 6
No opinion 1

Unskilled Workers

Totally banned 71%
No public display 22
No restrictions 6
No opinion 1

Theaters showing movies that depict sexual violence?

Totally banned 74%
No public display 18
No restrictions 6
No opinion 2

By Sex

Male

Totally banned 69%
No public display 22
No restrictions 8
No opinion 1

Female

Totally banned 80%
No public display 14
No restrictions 4
No opinion 2

By Ethnic Background

White

Totally banned 75%
No public display 18
No restrictions 5
No opinion 2

Black

Totally banned 71%
No public display 23
No restrictions 6
No opinion .... *

By Education

College Graduate

Totally banned 66%
No public display 27
No restrictions 7
No opinion .... *

College Incomplete

Totally banned 74%
No public display 19
No restrictions 5
No opinion 2

High-School Graduate

Totally banned 78%
No public display 15
No restrictions 5
No opinion 2

Less Than High-School Graduate

Totally banned 77%
No public display 15
No restrictions 5
No opinion 3

By Region

East

Totally banned 71%
No public display 22
No restrictions 4
No opinion 3

Midwest

Totally banned 79%
No public display 13
No restrictions 6
No opinion 2

South

Totally banned 76%
No public display 17
No restrictions 6
No opinion 1

West

Totally banned 71%
No public display 20
No restrictions 7
No opinion 2

By Age

18–24 Years

Totally banned 62%
No public display 24
No restrictions 12
No opinion 2

25–29 Years

Totally banned 63%
No public display 31
No restrictions 6
No opinion .... *

30–49 Years

Totally banned	75%
No public display	18
No restrictions	5
No opinion	2

50–64 Years

Totally banned	79%
No public display	15
No restrictions	3
No opinion	3

65 Years and Over

Totally banned	84%
No public display	9
No restrictions	4
No opinion	3

By Income

$40,000 and Over

Totally banned	74%
No public display	18
No restrictions	7
No opinion	1

$25,000–$39,999

Totally banned	74%
No public display	21
No restrictions	4
No opinion	1

$15,000–$24,999

Totally banned	73%
No public display	19
No restrictions	6
No opinion	2

Under $15,000

Totally banned	77%
No public display	15
No restrictions	6
No opinion	2

By Politics

Republicans

Totally banned	76%
No public display	18
No restrictions	4
No opinion	2

Democrats

Totally banned	76%
No public display	17
No restrictions	6
No opinion	1

Independents

Totally banned	72%
No public display	19
No restrictions	6
No opinion	3

By Religion

Protestants

Totally banned	79%
No public display	15
No restrictions	5
No opinion	1

Catholics

Totally banned	71%
No public display	21
No restrictions	5
No opinion	3

By Occupation

Professional and Business

Totally banned	72%
No public display	20
No restrictions	6
No opinion	2

Other White Collar

Totally banned	73%
No public display	19
No restrictions	5
No opinion	3

Skilled Workers

Totally banned 72%
No public display .22
No restrictions 5
No opinion 1

Unskilled Workers

Totally banned 74%
No public display .17
No restrictions 7
No opinion 2

*Less than 1%

Magazines that show sexual violence?

Totally banned 76%
No public display .18
No restrictions 4
No opinion 2

By Sex
Male

Totally banned 71%
No public display .22
No restrictions 6
No opinion 1

Female

Totally banned 81%
No public display .15
No restrictions 2
No opinion 2

By Ethnic Background
White

Totally banned 77%
No public display .17
No restrictions 4
No opinion 2

Black

Totally banned 68%
No public display .25
No restrictions 5
No opinion 2

By Education
College Graduate

Totally banned 70%
No public display .25
No restrictions 5
No opinion . . . . *

College Incomplete

Totally banned 76%
No public display .18
No restrictions 4
No opinion 2

High-School Graduate

Totally banned 79%
No public display .16
No restrictions 3
No opinion 2

Less Than High-School Graduate

Totally banned 75%
No public display .17
No restrictions 5
No opinion 3

By Region
East

Totally banned 71%
No public display .22
No restrictions 4
No opinion 3

Midwest

Totally banned 79%
No public display .15
No restrictions 4
No opinion 2

South

Totally banned 76%
No public display .19
No restrictions 4
No opinion 1

West

Totally banned 76%
No public display 18
No restrictions 4
No opinion 2

By Age
18–24 Years

Totally banned 59%
No public display 30
No restrictions 9
No opinion 2

25–29 Years

Totally banned 70%
No public display 24
No restrictions 6
No opinion .... *

30–49 Years

Totally banned 77%
No public display 18
No restrictions 4
No opinion 1

50–64 Years

Totally banned 80%
No public display 14
No restrictions 3
No opinion 3

65 Years and Over

Totally banned 84%
No public display 10
No restrictions 2
No opinion 4

By Income
$40,000 and Over

Totally banned 77%
No public display 16
No restrictions 5
No opinion 2

$25,000–$39,999

Totally banned 76%
No public display 20
No restrictions 3
No opinion 1

$15,000–$24,999

Totally banned 74%
No public display 19
No restrictions 5
No opinion 2

Under $15,000

Totally banned 76%
No public display 18
No restrictions 4
No opinion 2

By Politics
Republicans

Totally banned 78%
No public display 18
No restrictions 2
No opinion 2

Democrats

Totally banned 76%
No public display 18
No restrictions 5
No opinion 1

Independents

Totally banned 74%
No public display 19
No restrictions 5
No opinion 2

By Religion
Protestants

Totally banned 80%
No public display 16
No restrictions 3
No opinion 1

Catholics

Totally banned 74%
No public display .20
No restrictions 3
No opinion 3

By Occupation

Professional and Business

Totally banned 75%
No public display .19
No restrictions 5
No opinion 1

Other White Collar

Totally banned 79%
No public display .15
No restrictions 3
No opinion 3

Skilled Workers

Totally banned 75%
No public display .21
No restrictions 4
No opinion . . . . *

Unskilled Workers

Totally banned 71%
No public display .22
No restrictions 6
No opinion 1

*Less than 1%

Magazines that show nudity?

Totally banned 29%
No public display .51
No restrictions 18
No opinion 2

By Sex

Male

Totally banned 21%
No public display .54
No restrictions 24
No opinion 1

Female

Totally banned 37%
No public display .48
No restrictions 13
No opinion 2

By Ethnic Background

White

Totally banned 28%
No public display .51
No restrictions 19
No opinion 2

Black

Totally banned 33%
No public display .51
No restrictions 15
No opinion 1

By Education

College Graduate

Totally banned 15%
No public display .59
No restrictions 26
No opinion . . . . *

College Incomplete

Totally banned 24%
No public display .53
No restrictions 21
No opinion 2

High-School Graduate

Totally banned 27%
No public display .56
No restrictions 16
No opinion 1

Less Than High-School Graduate

Totally banned 48%
No public display .36
No restrictions 13
No opinion 3

By Region

East

Totally banned 26%
No public display 53
No restrictions 19
No opinion 2

Midwest

Totally banned 28%
No public display 54
No restrictions .,....................17
No opinion 1

South

Totally banned 37%
No public display 46
No restrictions 16
No opinion 1

West

Totally banned 24%
No public display 53
No restrictions 22
No opinion 1

By Age

18–24 Years

Totally banned 15%
No public display 57
No restrictions 27
No opinion 1

25–29 Years

Totally banned 15%
No public display 61
No restrictions 24
No opinion .... *

30–49 Years

Totally banned 23%
No public display 57
No restrictions 19
No opinion 1

50–64 Years

Totally banned 37%
No public display 48
No restrictions 14
No opinion 1

65 Years and Over

Totally banned 52%
No public display 35
No restrictions 10
No opinion 3

By Income

$40,000 and Over

Totally banned 14%
No public display 62
No restrictions 22
No opinion 2

$25,000–$39,999

Totally banned 26%
No public display 55
No restrictions 19
No opinion .... *

$15,000–$24,999

Totally banned 28%
No public display 52
No restrictions 18
No opinion 2

Under $15,000

Totally banned 42%
No public display 40
No restrictions 16
No opinion 2

By Politics

Republicans

Totally banned 34%
No public display 51
No restrictions 13
No opinion 2

Democrats

Totally banned 32%
No public display .48
No restrictions 19
No opinion 1

Independents

Totally banned 20%
No public display .57
No restrictions 21
No opinion 2

By Religion
Protestants

Totally banned 35%
No public display .51
No restrictions 13
No opinion 1

Catholics

Totally banned 22%
No public display .52
No restrictions 24
No opinion 2

By Occupation
Professional and Business

Totally banned 20%
No public display .58
No restrictions 21
No opinion 1

Other White Collar

Totally banned 25%
No public display .52
No restrictions 21
No opinion 2

Skilled Workers

Totally banned 23%
No public display .58
No restrictions 18
No opinion 1

Unskilled Workers

Totally banned 29%
No public display .49
No restrictions 21
No opinion 1

*Less than 1%

Magazines that show adults having sexual relations?

Totally banned 49%
No public display .40
No restrictions 9
No opinion 2

By Sex
Male

Totally banned 41%
No public display .46
No restrictions 12
No opinion 1

Female

Totally banned 58%
No public display .34
No restrictions 5
No opinion 3

By Ethnic Background
White

Totally banned 50%
No public display .39
No restrictions 9
No opinion 2

Black

Totally banned 44%
No public display .46
No restrictions 7
No opinion 3

By Education

College Graduate

Totally banned 41%
No public display .51
No restrictions 8
No opinion . . . . *

College Incomplete

Totally banned 44%
No public display .43
No restrictions 11
No opinion 2

High-School Graduate

Totally banned 50%
No public display .41
No restrictions 8
No opinion 1

Less Than High-School Graduate

Totally banned 60%
No public display .28
No restrictions 8
No opinion 4

By Region

East

Totally banned 47%
No public display .43
No restrictions 7
No opinion 3

Midwest

Totally banned 50%
No public display .40
No restrictions 8
No opinion 2

South

Totally banned 53%
No public display .38
No restrictions 8
No opinion 1

West

Totally banned 47%
No public display .39
No restrictions 12
No opinion 2

By Age

18–24 Years

Totally banned 32%
No public display .50
No restrictions 17
No opinion 1

25–29 Years

Totally banned 34%
No public display .51
No restrictions 15
No opinion . . . . *

30–49 Years

Totally banned 43%
No public display .49
No restrictions 7
No opinion 1

50–64 Years

Totally banned 63%
No public display .29
No restrictions 6
No opinion 2

65 Years and Over

Totally banned 71%
No public display .20
No restrictions 4
No opinion 5

By Income

$40,000 and Over

Totally banned 41%
No public display .48
No restrictions 10
No opinion 1

$25,000–$39,999

Totally banned 46%
No public display 48
No restrictions 6
No opinion .... *

$15,000–$24,999

Totally banned 51%
No public display 38
No restrictions 8
No opinion 3

Under $15,000

Totally banned 57%
No public display 30
No restrictions 10
No opinion 3

By Politics
Republicans

Totally banned 54%
No public display 38
No restrictions 6
No opinion 2

Democrats

Totally banned 51%
No public display 38
No restrictions 10
No opinion 1

Independents

Totally banned 42%
No public display 46
No restrictions 9
No opinion 3

By Religion
Protestants

Totally banned 56%
No public display 37
No restrictions 6
No opinion 1

Catholics

Totally banned 43%
No public display 44
No restrictions 10
No opinion 3

By Occupation
Professional and Business

Totally banned 43%
No public display 46
No restrictions 10
No opinion 1

Other White Collar

Totally banned 53%
No public display 34
No restrictions 11
No opinion 2

Skilled Workers

Totally banned 41%
No public display 51
No restrictions 7
No opinion 1

Unskilled Workers

Totally banned 45%
No public display 42
No restrictions 11
No opinion 2

*Less than 1%

Theaters showing X-rated movies?

Totally banned 43%
No public display 38
No restrictions 16
No opinion 3

By Sex
Male

Totally banned 34%
No public display 43
No restrictions 21
No opinion 2

Female

Totally banned 51%
No public display .34
No restrictions 11
No opinion 4

By Ethnic Background
White

Totally banned 43%
No public display .38
No restrictions 16
No opinion 3

Black

Totally banned 40%
No public display .42
No restrictions 16
No opinion 2

By Education
College Graduate

Totally banned 29%
No public display .52
No restrictions 18
No opinion 1

College Incomplete

Totally banned 39%
No public display .42
No restrictions 17
No opinion 2

High-School Graduate

Totally banned 42%
No public display .38
No restrictions 16
No opinion 4

Less Than High-School Graduate

Totally banned 56%
No public display .26
No restrictions 13
No opinion 5

By Region
East

Totally banned 42%
No public display .41
No restrictions 14
No opinion 3

Midwest

Totally banned 41%
No public display .42
No restrictions 14
No opinion 3

South

Totally banned 48%
No public display .33
No restrictions 17
No opinion 2

West

Totally banned 39%
No public display .37
No restrictions 21
No opinion 3

By Age
18–24 Years

Totally banned 25%
No public display .49
No restrictions 23
No opinion 3

25–29 Years

Totally banned 31%
No public display .47
No restrictions 19
No opinion 3

30–49 Years

Totally banned 38%
No public display .43
No restrictions 16
No opinion 3

50–64 Years

Totally banned 53%
No public display 33
No restrictions 12
No opinion 2

65 Years and Over

Totally banned 63%
No public display 22
No restrictions 11
No opinion 4

By Income

$40,000 and Over

Totally banned 32%
No public display 48
No restrictions 17
No opinion 3

$25,000–$39,999

Totally banned 39%
No public display 45
No restrictions 14
No opinion 2

$15,000–$24,999

Totally banned 43%
No public display 32
No restrictions 21
No opinion 4

Under $15,000

Totally banned 51%
No public display 33
No restrictions 13
No opinion 3

By Politics

Republicans

Totally banned 46%
No public display 40
No restrictions 12
No opinion 2

Democrats

Totally banned 45%
No public display 35
No restrictions 17
No opinion 3

Independents

Totally banned 36%
No public display 43
No restrictions 18
No opinion 3

By Religion

Protestants

Totally banned 48%
No public display 37
No restrictions 13
No opinion 2

Catholics

Totally banned 40%
No public display 40
No restrictions 16
No opinion 4

By Occupation

Professional and Business

Totally banned 33%
No public display 46
No restrictions 19
No opinion 2

Other White Collar

Totally banned 40%
No public display 39
No restrictions 16
No opinion 5

Skilled Workers

Totally banned 40%
No public display 44
No restrictions 14
No opinion 2

Unskilled Workers

Totally banned 39%
No public display 38
No restrictions 19
No opinion 4

Sale or rental of X-rated video cassettes for home viewing?

Totally banned 36%
No public display 43
No restrictions 19
No opinion 2

By Sex
Male

Totally banned 29%
No public display 46
No restrictions 24
No opinion 1

Female

Totally banned 43%
No public display 40
No restrictions 14
No opinion 3

By Ethnic Background
White

Totally banned 36%
No public display 44
No restrictions 18
No opinion 2

Black

Totally banned 35%
No public display 45
No restrictions 18
No opinion 2

By Education
College Graduate

Totally banned 23%
No public display 54
No restrictions 22
No opinion 1

College Incomplete

Totally banned 31%
No public display 46
No restrictions 21
No opinion 2

High-School Graduate

Totally banned 36%
No public display 44
No restrictions 18
No opinion 2

Less Than High-School Graduate

Totally banned 50%
No public display 32
No restrictions 14
No opinion 4

By Region
East

Totally banned 34%
No public display 47
No restrictions 16
No opinion 3

Midwest

Totally banned 37%
No public display 43
No restrictions 17
No opinion 3

South

Totally banned 41%
No public display 40
No restrictions 17
No opinion 2

West

Totally banned 30%
No public display 42
No restrictions 26
No opinion 2

By Age

18–24 Years

Totally banned 18%
No public display 52
No restrictions 28
No opinion 2

25–29 Years

Totally banned 20%
No public display 58
No restrictions 20
No opinion 2

30–49 Years

Totally banned 33%
No public display 48
No restrictions 18
No opinion 1

50–64 Years

Totally banned 44%
No public display 40
No restrictions 14
No opinion 2

65 Years and Over

Totally banned 58%
No public display 24
No restrictions 12
No opinion 6

By Income

$40,000 and Over

Totally banned 27%
No public display 49
No restrictions 22
No opinion 2

$25,000–$39,999

Totally banned 31%
No public display 52
No restrictions 17
No opinion .... *

$15,000–$24,999

Totally banned 37%
No public display 41
No restrictions 19
No opinion 3

Under $15,000

Totally banned 44%
No public display 34
No restrictions 18
No opinion 4

By Politics

Republicans

Totally banned 40%
No public display 42
No restrictions 16
No opinion 2

Democrats

Totally banned 38%
No public display 42
No restrictions 18
No opinion 2

Independents

Totally banned 29%
No public display 45
No restrictions 23
No opinion 3

By Religion

Protestants

Totally banned 42%
No public display 41
No restrictions 15
No opinion 2

Catholics

Totally banned 29%
No public display 47
No restrictions 21
No opinion 3

By Occupation

Professional and Business

Totally banned	28%
No public display	48
No restrictions	22
No opinion	2

Other White Collar

Totally banned	33%
No public display	48
No restrictions	16
No opinion	3

Skilled Workers

Totally banned	30%
No public display	52
No restrictions	18
No opinion	*

Unskilled Workers

Totally banned	37%
No public display	38
No restrictions	24
No opinion	1

*Less than 1%

*Sale or rental of video cassettes featuring sexual acts involving children?**

Totally banned	92%
No public display	5
No restrictions	2
No opinion	1

*Not asked in 1985

Do you think the standards in your community regarding the sale of sexually explicit material should be stricter than they are now, not as strict, or kept as they are now?

Stricter	45%
Not as strict	5
Kept as they are	43
No opinion	7

By Sex

Male

Stricter	40%
Not as strict	6
Kept as they are	48
No opinion	6

Female

Stricter	49%
Not as strict	3
Kept as they are	39
No opinion	9

By Ethnic Background

White

Stricter	44%
Not as strict	5
Kept as they are	44
No opinion	7

Black

Stricter	45%
Not as strict	6
Kept as they are	37
No opinion	12

By Education

College Graduate

Stricter	33%
Not as strict	6
Kept as they are	53
No opinion	8

College Incomplete

Stricter	41%
Not as strict	5
Kept as they are	49
No opinion	5

High-School Graduate

Stricter	44%
Not as strict	4
Kept as they are	45
No opinion	7

Less Than High-School Graduate

Stricter 58%
Not as strict 4
Kept as they are 29
No opinion 9

By Region

East

Stricter 46%
Not as strict 3
Kept as they are 45
No opinion 6

Midwest

Stricter 43%
Not as strict 3
Kept as they are 46
No opinion 8

South

Stricter 51%
Not as strict 5
Kept as they are 36
No opinion 8

West

Stricter 38%
Not as strict 7
Kept as they are 49
No opinion 6

By Age

18–24 Years

Stricter 31%
Not as strict 8
Kept as they are 58
No opinion 3

25–29 Years

Stricter 33%
Not as strict 9
Kept as they are 54
No opinion 4

30–49 Years

Stricter 42%
Not as strict 4
Kept as they are 47
No opinion 7

50–64 Years

Stricter 54%
Not as strict 3
Kept as they are 34
No opinion 9

65 Years and Over

Stricter 58%
Not as strict 2
Kept as they are 27
No opinion 13

By Income

$40,000 and Over

Stricter 36%
Not as strict 3
Kept as they are 55
No opinion 6

$25,000–$39,999

Stricter 41%
Not as strict 6
Kept as they are 48
No opinion 5

$15,000–$24,999

Stricter 48%
Not as strict 5
Kept as they are 40
No opinion 7

Under $15,000

Stricter 50%
Not as strict 4
Kept as they are 37
No opinion 9

By Politics

Republicans

Stricter 48%
Not as strict 5
Kept as they are 41
No opinion 6

Democrats

Stricter 47%
Not as strict 4
Kept as they are 40
No opinion 9

Independents

Stricter 37%
Not as strict 5
Kept as they are 51
No opinion 7

By Religion

Protestants

Stricter 49%
Not as strict 4
Kept as they are 40
No opinion 7

Catholics

Stricter 45%
Not as strict 4
Kept as they are 45
No opinion 6

By Occupation

Professional and Business

Stricter 37%
Not as strict 5
Kept as they are 52
No opinion 6

Other White Collar

Stricter 40%
Not as strict 7
Kept as they are 43
No opinion 10

Skilled Workers

Stricter 43%
Not as strict 5
Kept as they are 48
No opinion 4

Unskilled Workers

Stricter 47%
Not as strict 4
Kept as they are 44
No opinion 5

Selected National Trend

	1985	1977
Stricter	43%	45%
Not as strict	4	6
Kept as they are	48	35
No opinion	5	14

In determining whether a book, magazine, or movie is obscene, do you think there should be a single, nationwide standard, or do you think each community should have its own standard?

Nationwide 45%
Community 43
None 7
No opinion 5

Selected National Trend

	1985	1977
Nationwide	47%	45%
Community	43	39
None	5	9
No opinion	5	7

Note: A growing majority of Americans supports an outright ban on the portrayal of sexual violence in magazines, movies, and video cassettes. In the latest survey, 73% want a ban in their communities on the sale or rental of video cassettes displaying sexual violence (up 10 points from a March 1985 poll), 74% a ban on theaters that feature movies depicting sexual violence (up 6 points), and 76% a ban on magazines that show sexual violence (up 3 points). Of the roughly one-fourth who oppose such a ban, only a very small proportion, 4% to 6%, want no restrictions whatsoever.

The public is more liberal when it comes to the presentation of nonviolent sex, but here, too, there has been an increase in favor of community restrictions. Fewer than one-half of Americans favors a ban on magazines that show nudity or adults having sexual relations, theaters presenting X-rated movies, and the sale or rental of X-rated cassettes for home viewing. More people today than in 1985, however, favor some kind of restriction in the case of most of these activities, either a ban or no public display. Heavy majority support, 92%, is found for a ban on the sale or rental of video cassettes featuring sexual acts involving children.

The public continues to oppose a relaxation in community standards regarding the sale of sexually explicit material. Currently, 45% say local standards should be tougher, compared to 5% who think they should be less strict; 43% believe they should be kept as they are now. Little change in views has occurred on this question from two earlier surveys—1985 and 1977. The survey also reveals a close division of opinion on the question of whether there should be a single nationwide standard in determining obscenity, or whether each community should set its own standards. Only one person in fourteen (7%) says there should be no standards whatsoever.

Men and women hold sharply different views on the eight activities surveyed in the latest poll, with men an average of 12 points less likely to favor a ban. Sharp differences also are recorded on the basis of age, with young adults (18 to 29) holding far more liberal views than their elders. Catholics are consistently more liberal than are

Protestants, largely because of the conservative position held by evangelicals within the Protestant group.

AUGUST 17
PRESIDENTIAL TRIAL HEATS

Interviewing Date: 7/11–14/86
Survey #266-G

Asked of registered voters: Suppose the 1988 presidential election were being held today. If Vice President George Bush were the Republican candidate and Senator Gary Hart were the Democratic candidate, which would you like to see win? [Those who named other candidates or were undecided were then asked: As of today, do you lean more to Bush, the Republican, or to Hart, the Democrat?]

Bush	45%
Hart	45
Other; undecided	10

By Politics*
Republicans

Bush	77%
Hart	16
Other; undecided	7

Democrats

Bush	18%
Hart	72
Other; undecided	10

*Includes independents who lean toward each party

Selected National Trend

	Bush	Hart	Other; undecided
1986			
April	44%	46%	10%
January	45	47	8
1985			
July	50	39	11

Asked of registered voters: Suppose the 1988 presidential election were being held today.

If Vice President George Bush were the Republican candidate and New York Governor Mario Cuomo were the Democratic candidate, which would you like to see win? [Those who named other candidates or were undecided were then asked: As of today, do you lean more to Bush, the Republican, or to Cuomo, the Democrat?]

Bush 53%
Cuomo 37
Other; undecided 10

By Politics*

Republicans

Bush 81%
Cuomo 14
Other; undecided 5

Democrats

Bush 30%
Cuomo 59
Other; undecided 11

*Includes independents who lean toward each party

Selected National Trend

	Bush	Cuomo	Other; undecided
1986			
April	51%	36%	13%
January	54	34	12
1985			
July	55	31	14

Asked of registered voters: Suppose the 1988 presidential election were being held today. If Vice President George Bush were the Republican candidate and Chrysler Corporation Chairman Lee Iacocca were the Democratic candidate, which would you like to see win? [Those who named other candidates or were undecided were then asked: As of today, do you lean more to Bush, the Republican, or to Iacocca, the Democrat?]

Bush 42%
Iacocca 48
Other; undecided 10

By Politics*

Republicans

Bush 62%
Iacocca 30
Other; undecided 8

Democrats

Bush 27%
Iacocca 63
Other; undecided 10

*Includes independents who lean toward each party

Note: Chrysler Corporation Chairman Lee Iacocca has overtaken Vice President George Bush in the latest Gallup Poll test race and currently leads 48% to 42% among registered voters. Iacocca now also runs a better race against Bush than does either Senator Gary Hart of Colorado or New York Governor Mario Cuomo. Bush and Hart are in a dead heat, 45% to 45%, while the vice president holds a 53%-to-37% lead over Cuomo. Republican voters stand solidly behind Bush in races against Hart and Cuomo but desert the GOP side in considerable numbers in the Bush-Iacocca contest.

Both Hart and Cuomo have improved their standing from one year ago in test races against Bush, but little movement has been recorded in 1986 in either race. Iacocca's gains have been the most dramatic; this time last year he trailed Bush 35% to 52%. Iacocca's current showing undoubtedly reflects his television coverage over the July 4 weekend and his role as the chief fund-raiser for the restoration of the Statue of Liberty. Although he has denied interest in the nomination, his supporters are pressing for Iacocca's nomination.

As reported last week by the Gallup Poll, Iacocca has registered gains on Senator Hart as the choice of Democrats for the presidential nomination, although he continues to trail 26% to Hart's 34% among a field of eighteen. Next after Iacocca on the current list are Cuomo with 22% and Jackson with 17%. As recently as April, Iacocca was a distant third in the nomination contest, with Hart leading runner-up Cuomo by 14 points and Iacocca by 24.

AUGUST 21
CONGRESSIONAL ELECTIONS

Interviewing Date: 7/11–14/86
Survey #266-G

Asked of registered voters: If the elections for Congress were being held today, which party would you like to see win in this congressional district—the Democratic party or the Republican party? [Those who were undecided or named another party were then asked: As of today, do you lean more to the Democratic party, or to the Republican party?]

Republican 40%
Democratic 54
Other; undecided 6

Selected National Trend

	Repub-lican	Demo-cratic	Other; undecided
1986			
June	43%	49%	8%
April	40	50	10
January	43	50	7
1985			
October	42	48	10

Note: With the congressional elections little more than ten weeks away, growing public concern over the economy appears to be giving a solid boost to Democratic candidates nationwide. The latest Gallup survey of congressional strength shows registered voters picking Democratic candidates over Republicans by the margin of 54% to 40%, with 6% choosing other candidates or undecided. This represents a gain for Democrats over an earlier series of 1986 surveys, which showed a 50%-to-43% Democratic lead, with 7% undecided.

Democratic gains are likely due to growing economic fears. A recent Gallup report showed a sharp drop in the number of people who expect to be better off financially next year—down from 61% in March to 51% in July. Economic worries, however, do not appear to have hurt Ronald Reagan's personal popularity, which continues to hold steady at 63% in the most recent Gallup survey.

The shift to the Democratic side in the latest survey has been largely among independents—10 points compared to only 2 points among Republicans and 1 point among Democrats. While independent voters include a high percentage of "swing voters" who might return to the GOP side in the weeks ahead, the present outlook is for a heavily Democratic House of Representatives.

Survey findings cannot be projected to specific seat gains or losses, but it is instructive to note that a 56%-to-44% Democratic margin in the popular vote in the 1982 elections resulted in a 26-seat loss for the GOP that fall. (On a two-way basis, with the undecided vote allocated equally to both major parties, the current survey shows a 57%-to-43% Democratic advantage.)

The party in control of the White House has lost an average of 48 House seats in second midterm congressional elections beginning in 1958, counting the 1963–67 Johnson presidency as a continuation of Kennedy's and the 1974–75 Ford presidency as an extension of Nixon's.

AUGUST 24
MOST IMPORTANT PROBLEM

Interviewing Date: 7/11–14/86
Survey #266-G

What do you think is the most important problem facing this country today?

Unemployment 23%
International tensions; fear of war 20
Budget deficit 13
Drug abuse 8
Economy (general) 7
Poverty; hunger 6
Crime 3

Moral, religious decline in society 3
All others 24
No opinion 3
                                        110%*

*Total adds to more than 100% due to multiple responses.

All of those who named a problem were then asked: Which political party do you think can do a better job of handling the problem you have just mentioned—the Republican party or the Democratic party?

Republican party 33%
Democratic party 36
No difference (volunteered) 21
No opinion 10

Selected National Trend

	Repub- lican	Demo- cratic	No dif- ference	No opinion
1986				
January	33%	28%	27%	12%
1985				
May	37	31	23	9
January	39	29	24	8
1984				
August	39	37	16	8
June	33	35	20	12

Note: Unemployment (23%), international tensions (20%), and the federal budget deficit (13%) are named by the American public as the top problems facing the nation today. Although drug abuse is still far overshadowed by economic and foreign policy problems, it has grown dramatically as a key domestic concern of the American people, and today's figure of 8% is far higher than that found in all previous Gallup audits of the last four decades.

Further evidence of the growing concern over drug abuse is seen in a recent survey of Americans' attitudes toward public schools, conducted by the Gallup Poll and Phi Delta Kappa Inc., which revealed that, for the first time since these surveys were initiated almost two decades ago, a problem other than discipline was seen by the public as the most important problem facing public schools. Almost three in ten (28%) named drugs, a 10-point increase over a one-year period.

In addition, a recent Gallup Youth Survey reported that teen-agers name drug abuse far and away as the top problem facing the teen-age population. This problem was cited by 40% of teens, far ahead of alcohol abuse (14%), unemployment (8%), and peer pressures (8%).

The two major parties are now viewed as about equally qualified to deal with the nation's most pressing problems, representing a gain for Democrats since a January survey. Currently, 33% consider the Republican party and 36% the Democratic party as more qualified to deal with the major problems, with 21% seeing little difference and 10% undecided. In January, 33% credited the GOP but fewer, 28%, said the Democrats were better on the issues. Another 27% saw little difference and 12% were undecided.

After leading the Democrats on this political barometer in early 1981, the Republicans trailed throughout 1982 and 1983, a consequence of the recession. The two parties were neck and neck during 1984, but the GOP regained the lead in early 1985, holding it until the January 1986 survey.

AUGUST 28
JOGGING

Interviewing Date: 7/11–14/86
Survey #266-G

Do you happen to jog, or not?

		Yes
National	....	13%

Profile of Joggers

By Sex	1986	1984
Male	17%	22%
Female	9	14

By Education

College graduate	19%	22%
College incomplete	16	22
High-school graduate	10	15
Less than high-school graduate	9	13

By Region

East	15%	14%
Midwest	10	21
South	13	17
West	12	19

By Age

18–24 years	27%	33%
25–29 years	19	36
30–49 years	15	18
50–64 years	4	9
65 years and over	4	3

Selected National Trend

	Yes
1985	15%
1984	18
1982	14
1980	12
1977	11
1961	6

Asked of joggers: About how often do you jog?

Less than once a week	14%
Once or twice a week	28
Three or four times a week	37
Every day or almost every day	21
Not sure	*

*Less than 1%

Selected National Trend

	1985	1984
Less than once a week	18%	5%
Once or twice a week	31	25
Three or four times a week	28	35
Every day or almost every day	21	34
Not sure	2	1

Also asked of those who jog: On the average, how far do you usually jog, in terms of miles or fractions of miles?

Less than two miles	40%
Two to three miles	26
Three miles or more	34
Not sure	*

*Less than 1%

Selected National Trend

	1985	1984
Less than two miles	44%	32%
Two to three miles	24	29
Three miles or more	30	39
Not sure	2	*

*Less than 1%

Note: Among Americans jogging has declined in appeal since the peak year of 1984 when 18% engaged in this recreational activity. The latest figure is 13%, with the decline most pronounced among adults under 30. Prior to 1984 the percentage of joggers had grown steadily since the first measurement in 1961 when only 6% participated.

Frequency of jogging among participants also has declined since 1984 when 34% jogged every day or almost every day; the figure for both the 1986 and 1985 surveys is 21%. The average distance covered has changed only slightly in the last two years.

Sex, education, and age play important roles in the popularity of jogging. Twice the proportion of men as women are joggers, and persons who attended college are also far more likely to be joggers than those with less than a college education. The most important factor, however, is age. From the peak of 27% among 18 to 24 year olds, participation falls off to 4% among those 50 and older. Jogging at present tends to be more popular in the East than elsewhere.

The change since 1984 has been most pronounced among young adults in their late twenties (down 17 points); by region the decline has been greatest in the Midwest (down 11 points) and West (7 points). The last figure is of particular interest since the West tends to be a predictor of life-style trends.

AUGUST 31
PUBLIC SCHOOLS*

Interviewing Date: 4/11–20/86
Special Survey

Thinking about the future, would you like the federal government in Washington to have more influence or less influence in determining the educational program of the local public schools?

More influence 26%
Less influence 53
Same as now (volunteered) 12
No opinion 9

Public School Parents Only

More influence 23%
Less influence 62
Same as now (volunteered) 11
No opinion 4

How about the state government? Would you like the state government to have more influence or less influence in determining the educational program of the local public schools?

More influence 45%
Less influence 32
Same as now (volunteered) 16
No opinion 7

Public School Parents Only

More influence 45%
Less influence 38
Same as now (volunteered) 13
No opinion 4

How about the local school board? Would you like the local school board to have more

*This survey was conducted jointly by the Gallup Poll and Phi Delta Kappa Inc.

influence or less influence in determining the educational program of the local public schools?

More influence 57%
Less influence 17
Same as now (volunteered) 17
No opinion 9

Public School Parents Only

More influence 61%
Less influence 15
Same as now (volunteered) 19
No opinion 5

There is always a lot of discussion about the best way to finance the public schools. Which do you think is the best way to finance the public schools: by means of local property taxes, by state taxes, or by taxes from the federal government in Washington?

Local property taxes 24%
State taxes 33
Federal taxes 24
No opinion 19

By Education
College Graduate

Local property taxes 43%
State taxes 30
Federal taxes 14
No opinion 13

College Incomplete

Local property taxes 25%
State taxes 39
Federal taxes 23
No opinion 13

High-School Graduate

Local property taxes 21%
State taxes 33
Federal taxes 27
No opinion 19

Less Than High-School Graduate

Local property taxes 13%
State taxes 31
Federal taxes 33
No opinion 23

By Age
18–29 Years

Local property taxes 18%
State taxes 34
Federal taxes 31
No opinion 17

30–49 Years

Local property taxes 29%
State taxes 33
Federal taxes 24
No opinion 14

50 Years and Over

Local property taxes 24%
State taxes 32
Federal taxes 19
No opinion 25

Public School Parents Only

Local property taxes 28%
State taxes 32
Federal taxes 28
No opinion 12

Note: The American people clearly believe their local school boards and state governments, rather than the federal government, should bear most of the responsibility for determining their local schools' educational programs. Nevertheless, many look to Washington for financial assistance to help implement these programs. The latest Gallup/Phi Delta Kappa Poll on Americans' attitudes toward the public schools finds strong public support (57% to 17%) for giving local school boards more influence in setting school policy and moderate support (45% to 32%) for giving state governments more influence. However, the public, by a 2-to-1 ratio, opposes broadening the federal government's influence over the way local schools are run (53% to 26%).

Although the public overwhelmingly rejects greater federal influence over the content of the public schools' educational programs, many Americans expect Washington to help finance them. The slight weight of public opinion is that state taxes are the best way to finance the public schools, cited by 33%. Local property taxes and federal taxes are named by 24% each, while 19% are undecided. Among parents, roughly equal percentages name each of these three funding sources: state taxes, 32%; local and federal taxes, 28% each.

To a considerable degree, age and education affect public responses to this question, with persons over 30 and those who attended college more inclined to cite property taxes as the best source of school financing. Conversely, 18 to 29 year olds and persons with no college exposure are more likely to name state and federal taxes.

Regardless of the source of funding, American schools are at a crossroads, according to a recent report of the Carnegie Forum on Education and the Economy. The report, which cites a chronic shortage of teachers, poor quality of instruction, and dismal working conditions, calls for teacher certification, national proficiency testing, an advanced-degree requirement for new teachers, and large salary hikes for "master teachers." The Carnegie program would cost almost $50 billion over the next ten years.

SEPTEMBER 4
PRESIDENT REAGAN

Interviewing Date: 7/11–14; 8/8–11/86
Survey #266-G; 267-G

Do you approve or disapprove of the way Ronald Reagan is handling his job as president?

Approve 62%
Disapprove 28
No opinion 10

By Sex

Male

Approve 66%
Disapprove 27
No opinion 7

Female

Approve 59%
Disapprove 28
No opinion 13

By Ethnic Background

White

Approve 66%
Disapprove 24
No opinion 10

Black

Approve 31%
Disapprove 54
No opinion 15

Hispanic

Approve 62%
Disapprove 25
No opinion 13

By Education

College Graduate

Approve 63%
Disapprove 32
No opinion 5

College Incomplete

Approve 70%
Disapprove 22
No opinion 8

High-School Graduate

Approve 65%
Disapprove 23
No opinion 12

Less Than High-School Graduate

Approve 51%
Disapprove 34
No opinion 15

By Region

East

Approve 64%
Disapprove 27
No opinion 9

Midwest

Approve 63%
Disapprove 27
No opinion 10

South

Approve 63%
Disapprove 26
No opinion 11

West

Approve 60%
Disapprove 30
No opinion 10

By Age

18–29 Years

Approve 70%
Disapprove 20
No opinion 10

30–49 Years

Approve 65%
Disapprove 27
No opinion 8

50 Years and Over

Approve 54%
Disapprove 34
No opinion 12

By Income

$40,000 and Over

Approve 67%
Disapprove 26
No opinion 7

$25,000–$39,999

Approve 69%
Disapprove 24
No opinion 7

$15,000–$24,999

Approve 64%
Disapprove 26
No opinion 10

Under $15,000

Approve 51%
Disapprove 34
No opinion 15

By Politics

Republicans

Approve 87%
Disapprove 7
No opinion 6

Democrats

Approve 44%
Disapprove 45
No opinion 11

Independents

Approve 62%
Disapprove 26
No opinion 12

By Religion

Protestants

Approve 63%
Disapprove 27
No opinion 10

Catholics

Approve 68%
Disapprove 23
No opinion 9

By Occupation

Professional and Business

Approve 69%
Disapprove 25
No opinion 6

Other White Collar

Approve 62%
Disapprove 26
No opinion 12

Blue Collar—Total

Approve 63%
Disapprove 26
No opinion 11

Blue Collar—Skilled

Approve 69%
Disapprove 23
No opinion 8

Blue Collar—Unskilled

Approve 59%
Disapprove 28
No opinion 13

Selected National Trend

	Approve	Dis-approve	No opinion
1986			
August 8–11	61%	27%	12%
July 11–14	63	28	9
June 9–16	64	26	10
June 6–9	61	29	10
May 16–19	68	23	9
April 11–14	62	29	9
March 7–10	63	26	11
January 10–13	64	27	9
1985	61	30	9
1984	56	35	9

			Dis-	No
1983	44	46	10
1982	44	46	10
1981	58	28	14

The following table compares Reagan's current standing with those of his predecessors in August of the second year of their second or elective term:

Presidential Performance Ratings

Incumbent	Year	Approve	Dis-approve	No opinion
Reagan	1986	61%	27%	12%
Nixon*	1974	24	66	10
Johnson	1966	48	38	14
Eisenhower	1958	56	27	17
Truman	1950	43	32	25

*Final career measurement

Note: A solid majority of Americans continues to approve of President Ronald Reagan's overall handling of the duties of his office, despite growing economic, international, and other urgent problems. In a just completed Gallup Poll, 62% approve of Reagan's job performance, 28% disapprove, and 10% are undecided. These ratings, while not significantly different from those recorded last month, are below his peak of 68% approval in May.

Although Reagan's popularity has shown some slippage in recent months, it continues to defy historical precedent. Each of his postwar predecessors who won reelection (Nixon, Eisenhower), or who was elected to his own term after non-elective presidential service (Johnson, Truman), saw his popularity erode sharply as his tenure progressed.

Reagan's current job approval rating, on the other hand, matches his average score during 1985 and betters his averages for each of the preceding four years. Currently, he enjoys the virtually unanimous support of his fellow Republicans, as well as a majority of independents. Democrats are evenly divided between those who approve (44%) and disapprove (45%) of his performance in office.

As in every Gallup Poll conducted since Reagan took office, more men (66%) than women (59%)—the now familiar "gender gap"—approve of the way the president is handling his job. Fewer blacks (31%) than whites (66%) or Hispanics (62%) now approve of Reagan's job performance, as consistently has been the case throughout his tenure. However, his recent ratings among blacks surpass those during 1982–84 when his scores rarely topped the 20% approval mark. President Reagan is considerably more popular with 18 to 29 year olds (70% approve) than with persons 50 and older (54%).

Differences in Reagan's popularity profile by education, income, and occupation are surprisingly small, given the tendency of the less affluent, less well educated, and persons from households in which the chief wage-earner is employed in a blue collar position to align themselves with the Democratic party.

SEPTEMBER 7
CATHOLIC CHURCH

Interviewing Date: 3/7–10/86
Special Telephone Survey

Asked of Roman Catholics: What kind of job do you think the Catholic church in the United States is doing in handling the following— excellent, good, only fair, or poor:

Church's relations with non-Christians?

Excellent; good	54%
Only fair; poor	38
No opinion	8

Role of lay people in the church?

Excellent; good	52%
Only fair; poor	41
No opinion	7

Changes in the church since the Second Vatican Council?

Excellent; good	47%
Only fair; poor	46
No opinion	7

Role of women in the church?

Excellent; good 37%
Only fair; poor 60
No opinion 3

Church's involvement in politics and public policy?

Excellent; good 27%
Only fair; poor 63
No opinion 10

Church's marriage annulment system?

Excellent; good 26%
Only fair; poor 60
No opinion 14

Serving the needs of the elderly?

Excellent; good 54%
Only fair; poor 42
No opinion 4

Serving the needs of single people?

Excellent; good 30%
Only fair; poor 62
No opinion 8

Serving the needs of families?

Excellent; good 58%
Only fair; poor 39
No opinion 3

Serving the needs of minorities?

Excellent; good 41%
Only fair; poor 49
No opinion 10

Serving the needs of new immigrants?

Excellent; good 38%
Only fair; poor 47
No opinion 15

Serving the needs of separated, divorced, and remarried Catholics?

Excellent; good 30%
Only fair; poor 63
No opinion 7

Serving your own needs?

Excellent; good 50%
Only fair; poor 46
No opinion 4

Note: Catholics give their church high marks for its relations with non-Christians and for handling the role of the laity, such as encouraging greater participation on the part of rank-and-file Catholics. Opinions are more closely divided when it comes to "changes in the church since the Second Vatican Council" and are negative on three other policies or practices—the role of women, the church's involvement in politics and public policy, and its marriage annulment system.

A representative national sample of the nation's Catholics also was asked to rate the church on serving the needs of seven key population groups. The church is given high marks for the way it has served families and the elderly, while it receives mixed grades on serving one's own needs and those of minorities. Ratings shift to the negative side on the job the church is doing in serving the needs of new immigrants, single people, and separated, divorced, and remarried Catholics.

SEPTEMBER 11
PHYSICAL FITNESS

Interviewing Date: 7/11–14/86
Survey #266-G

Aside from any work you do here at home or at a job, do you do anything regularly—that is, on a daily basis—that helps keep you physically fit?

                                              Yes
National 51%

By Sex

Male	55%
Female	48

By Education

College graduate	65%
College incomplete	57
High-school graduate	48
Less than high-school graduate	40

By Region

East	47%
Midwest	51
South	48
West	63

By Age

18–24 years	67%
25–29 years	56
30–49 years	49
50–64 years	50
65 years and over	43

By Income

$35,000 and over	58%
$25,000–$34,999	55
$15,000–$24,999	49
Under $15,000	44

By Occupation

Professional and business	61%
Other white collar	53
Blue collar	52

Selected National Trend

1982	47%
1980	46
1977	47
1961	24

Do you, yourself, have a membership in a health club or fitness center?

	Yes
National	10%

By Sex

Male	11%
Female	10

By Education

College graduate	17%
College incomplete	16
High-school graduate	7
Less than high-school graduate	4

By Region

East	10%
Midwest	10
South	9
West	12

By Age

18–24 years	20%
25–29 years	12
30–49 years	12
50–64 years	5
65 years and over	2

By Income

$35,000 and over	19%
$25,000–$34,999	14
$15,000–$24,999	7
Under $15,000	5

By Occupation

Professional and business	19%
Other white collar	13
Blue collar	9

Note: Americans' preoccupation with physical fitness shows no sign of letting up, with a 51% majority of adults currently claiming to follow some kind of daily regimen that helps them stay in shape, aside from their jobs or housework. This is roughly the same proportion recorded in Gallup surveys over the last decade but twice the rate of a generation ago. In Gallup's first fitness audit (1961), only 24% exercised daily.

As a further sign of this country's obsession with physical fitness, one adult in ten belongs to a health club or fitness center, with this proportion rising to about two in ten among 18 to 24 year olds, persons who attended college, people employed in business or the professions, and those with household incomes of $35,000 or more per year. Equal percentages of men and women are members of health or fitness clubs.

Although daily exercise also is more prevalent among the young, well educated, and affluent, it enjoys wide popularity in all population groups. Half of 50 to 64 year olds and 43% of those 65 and older, for example, say they have some kind of fitness regimen. Similarly, 44% of persons with incomes under $15,000 per year and 40% of those whose formal education ended before graduation from high school exercise on a daily basis. Men are marginally more likely to follow a daily fitness routine than are women, 55% and 48%, respectively. Daily workouts are more common in the West than in other regions of the nation, consistent with earlier survey findings.

SEPTEMBER 14
DEMOCRATIC PRESIDENTIAL CANDIDATES

Interviewing Date: 1/10–13; 4/11–14; 7/11–14/86
Survey #261-G; 262-G; 266-G

Asked of Democrats and Democratic-leaning independents: Which of the persons on this list would you like to see nominated as the Democratic party's candidate for president in 1988? And who would be your second choice?*

Hart 40%
Cuomo 24
Iacocca 20
Jackson 16

*Results are based on first and second choices combined. Other candidates named and the "no opinion" vote have been eliminated from this study.

By Sex
Male

Hart 42%
Cuomo 28
Iacocca 24
Jackson 16

Female

Hart 39%
Cuomo 21
Iacocca 16
Jackson 16

By Ethnic Background
White

Hart 43%
Cuomo 25
Iacocca 21
Jackson 8

Black

Hart 27%
Cuomo 17
Iacocca 12
Jackson 57

By Region
East

Hart 38%
Cuomo 41
Iacocca 16
Jackson 14

Midwest

Hart 45%
Cuomo 21
Iacocca 28
Jackson 13

South

Hart	36%
Cuomo	12
Iacocca	16
Jackson	20

West

Hart	43%
Cuomo	25
Iacocca	19
Jackson	16

By Age

18–29 Years

Hart	42%
Cuomo	18
Iacocca	17
Jackson	23

30–49 Years

Hart	40%
Cuomo	23
Iacocca	21
Jackson	17

50 Years and Over

Hart	39%
Cuomo	28
Iacocca	20
Jackson	11

By Religion

Protestants

Hart	38%
Cuomo	17
Iacocca	19
Jackson	21

Catholics

Hart	45%
Cuomo	32
Iacocca	22
Jackson	9

Selected National Trend

1986	Hart	Cuomo	Iacocca	Jackson
January 10–13	46%	23%	17%	15%
April 11–14	40	26	16	16
July 11–14	34	22	26	17

Note: The first half of 1986 saw a perceptible shift in rank-and-file Democrats' early favorites for their party's 1988 presidential nominee. And, while further shifts are inevitable as the campaign progresses, patterns of potential candidates' strengths and weaknesses among various voter groups are beginning to emerge.

Senator Gary Hart of Colorado saw his 2-to-1 January nomination lead over runner-up New York Governor Mario Cuomo gradually erode. By July, Cuomo had been supplanted in the number two position by businessman Lee Iacocca, who then trailed Hart by a slim 8-point margin. The Reverend Jesse Jackson maintained a solid grip on fourth place throughout this six-month period. None of the other possible candidates included in these tests received more than 8% of Democrats' combined first- and second-place nomination votes.

In order to examine potential nominees' strong and weak points in detail, Gallup analysts combined the results of three national in-person surveys, conducted in January, April, and July. These surveys recorded the knowledge and opinions of over 2,000 self-described Democrats and Democratic-leaning independents regarding their familiarity with eighteen possible Democratic nominees and their favorites for the presidency in 1988.

With one and one-half years remaining before the early state primaries, name recognition plays a vital role in the potential candidates' standing with the rank and file. In the most recent survey, Jackson's name is familiar to 89% of Democrats and Democratic leaners, Hart's to 80%, Iacocca's to 70%, and Cuomo's to 53%. Since name recognition is strongly related to education and related factors, such as income and occupation, these are not included in the analysis.

Not surprisingly, Jackson is the overwhelming choice of black Democrats and Democratic sympathizers, winning 57% of their first- and second-place nomination votes to 27% for Hart, 17% for Cuomo, and 12% for Iacocca. Cuomo and Iacocca are slightly more popular nomination choices among men than women, while Hart fares about equally well with both sexes; Jackson draws the same proportion of male and female votes. Hart's preference profile by age is remarkably even, as is Iacocca's. Cuomo is chosen more frequently by older than younger Democrats, while the reverse is true of Jackson.

SEPTEMBER 18
DRUG ABUSE

Interviewing Date: 7/31–8/1/86
Special Telephone Survey

Do you think the possession of small amounts of marijuana should or should not be treated as a criminal offense?

Should 67%
Should not 27
No opinion 6

Selected National Trend

	Should	Should not	No opinion
1985	50%	46%	4%
1980	43	52	5
1977	41	53	6

Which one of the following do you think is the most serious problem for society today—marijuana, alcohol abuse, heroin, crack, other forms of cocaine, or other drugs?

Alcohol abuse 34%
Crack 22
Other cocaine 21
All others 14
No opinion 9

By Education
College Graduate

Alcohol abuse 42%
Crack 19
Other cocaine 21
All others 8
No opinion 10

College Incomplete

Alcohol abuse 42%
Crack 17
Other cocaine 26
All others 8
No opinion 7

High-School Graduate

Alcohol abuse 28%
Crack 23
Other cocaine 21
All others 18
No opinion 10

Less Than High-School Graduate

Alcohol abuse 33%
Crack 24
Other cocaine 15
All others 18
No opinion 10

By Region
East

Alcohol abuse 26%
Crack 32
Other cocaine 18
All others 13
No opinion 11

Midwest

Alcohol abuse 39%
Crack 18
Other cocaine 19
All others 15
No opinion 9

South

Alcohol abuse	34%
Crack	19
Other cocaine	22
All others	17
No opinion	8

West

Alcohol abuse	40%
Crack	17
Other cocaine	23
All others	9
No opinion	11

By Age

18–29 Years

Alcohol abuse	41%
Crack	19
Other cocaine	21
All others	17
No opinion	2

30–49 Years

Alcohol abuse	38%
Crack	16
Other cocaine	24
All others	13
No opinion	9

50 Years and Over

Alcohol abuse	26%
Crack	28
Other cocaine	17
All others	15
No opinion	14

There are many things that our government is doing to fight drug use. Which one of the following activities in the government's fight against drugs do you think deserves the most money and effort? And which is the next most important?

	Most important	Next most important
Teaching young people about dangers of drugs	42%	24%
Working with foreign governments to stop export of drugs	25	23
Arresting drug dealers	23	31
Helping drug users overcome addiction	4	12
Arresting drug users	3	5
No opinion	3	5

The following are the most cited responses by key socioeconomic groups:

By Sex

Male

Teaching young people about dangers of drugs	47%
Working with foreign governments to stop export of drugs	22
Arresting drug dealers	21
Others; no opinion	10

Female

Teaching young people about dangers of drugs	39%
Working with foreign governments to stop export of drugs	28
Arresting drug dealers	25
Others; no opinion	8

By Education

College Graduate

Teaching young people about dangers of drugs	56%
Working with foreign governments to stop export of drugs	16
Arresting drug dealers	19
Others; no opinion	9

College Incomplete

Teaching young people about
  dangers of drugs 45%
Working with foreign governments
  to stop export of drugs 25
Arresting drug dealers 22
Others; no opinion 8

High-School Graduate

Teaching young people about
  dangers of drugs 44%
Working with foreign governments
  to stop export of drugs 22
Arresting drug dealers 24
Others; no opinion 10

Less Than High-School Graduate

Teaching young people about
  dangers of drugs 24%
Working with foreign governments
  to stop export of drugs 40
Arresting drug dealers 26
Others; no opinion 10

*In general, do you think the government
spends too much money and effort fighting
drug abuse, too little money and effort fighting drug abuse, or is the government's
expenditure of money and effort just about
right?*

Too much 9%
Too little 56
About right 21
No opinion 14

Note: President and Mrs. Reagan's call for a
national crusade against illicit drugs came at a time
of mounting public concern about the problem.
Recent polls also suggest that Americans will be
highly receptive to effective government programs
to combat drug abuse. The rising tide of concern is
illustrated by the following national survey
findings:

1) In a *Newsweek* Poll conducted by the Gallup Organization, 56% say the government is
spending too little money and effort fighting drug
abuse; only 9% characterize it as too much, while
21% think the expenditures are adequate.

2) In the 1986 Gallup/Phi Delta Kappa Poll,
Americans cite students' use of drugs as the biggest problem facing the public schools. In sixteen
out of seventeen previous annual polls, lack of
discipline was named the schools' most serious
problem.

3) More Americans now than at any time in
the last four decades perceive drug abuse to be
the most important problem confronting the nation,
although drugs are still overshadowed by economic and international concerns.

4) Perhaps the best single indication of the
public's growing concern over drug abuse is the
extraordinary change in attitudes toward marijuana. As recently as 1980, only 43% favored
criminal penalties for the possession of small
amounts of "pot." Today, fully two-thirds (67%)
express this view.

Asked which of a number of substances constitutes the most serious problem for society today,
alcohol abuse is mentioned by 34%, followed by
crack (22%), and then other forms of cocaine
(21%). Fewer cite heroin and other drugs (5%
each) or marijuana (4%). Easterners (32%) are far
more likely to perceive crack as the most serious
drug problem than are residents of other areas of
the nation. Older people (28%) and the less well
educated (24%) also mention crack more often as
a source of concern. Alcohol abuse is more frequently cited by younger adults (41%) and the
college educated (42%).

When asked how the government should combat drug abuse, the public cites teaching young
people about the dangers of drugs (42%) and shut-
ting down sources, either by arresting dealers (23%)
or by working with foreign governments to stop
the export of drugs (25%). Few put their emphasis
on arresting abusers (3%) or helping them overcome their addiction (4%). Men, the better educated, and young people tend to put greater stock

in education, while women, older people, and the less well educated seem to place more emphasis on arrests and interdiction of drug exports.

SEPTEMBER 21
DEMOCRATIC PARTY—AN ANALYSIS

After suffering a setback in voter support in the months following President Ronald Reagan's landslide 1984 victory, the Democratic party appears to be on the rebound in several key respects:

1) Current national support for Democratic congressional candidates has increased 6 percentage points since the previous June survey, with growing public concern over the economy undoubtedly a major factor. In the current poll, registered voters pick Democratic candidates over Republicans, 54% to 40%, with 6% choosing other candidates or undecided. In June the figures were 49% Democrats, 43% Republicans, and 8% other or undecided.

2) A gain of 8 points since January is recorded in the percentage of persons who view the Democratic party as able to do a better job of handling the nation's top problems. Currently, 36% consider the Democratic party and 33% the Republican party as more qualified to deal with the major problems, while 21% see little difference and 10% are undecided. By comparison, 33% in January credited the GOP, but fewer, 28%, said the Democrats were better on the issues. Another 27% perceived little difference and 12% were undecided. The top problems named in the latest survey are unemployment (23%), international tensions (20%), the budget deficit (13%), and drug abuse (8%).

The political significance of these findings is that the views of voters on the relative ability of the parties to deal with the top problems in measurements taken close to elections have been an accurate barometer of the division of the popular vote in the congressional elections. In 1982, for example, an August measurement showed the Democrats holding a 55%-to-45% lead on this question, with the undecided vote allocated equally to each party. In the congressional elections in November, Democratic candidates won 56% of the popular vote to 44% for Republican candidates.

3) The proportion of adults giving their political preference as Democratic declined in the period immediately following President Reagan's 1984 victory, but increased in late 1985 and has stabilized in the 1986 surveys. Currently, 32% of adults identify themselves as Republicans, 39% as Democrats, and 29% as independents.

4) President Reagan's popularity has trended downward since May when it reached a high point of 68% approval. The latest figure is 61%. This 7-point decline could be good news for the Democrats since it could minimize the influence of Reagan's popularity on GOP candidates.

5) Although the GOP once could boast a higher proportion of registered voters, the two parties are statistically tied in the latest series of Gallup surveys, in which 79% of Republicans and 81% of Democrats say they are registered to vote. In 1984, 80% of Republicans registered to vote, compared to 78% of Democrats; in 1980 the figures were 78% and 74%, respectively.

SEPTEMBER 25
ECONOMIC SITUATION

Interviewing Date: 9/3–17/86
Special Telephone Survey

The economy is now in the fourth year of recovery from the recession of 1981–82. Of course, no one knows for sure, but what is your best guess about how long this recovery will last before the economy turns down again? Will the recovery end this year, early next year, late next year, or later than that?

This year 7%
Early next year 11
Late next year 21
Later than that 44
Never (volunteered) 2
No opinion 15

By Sex*

Male

This year	8%
Next year	30
Later; never	48
No opinion	14

Female

This year	6%
Next year	33
Later; never	45
No opinion	16

By Education

College Graduate

This year	12%
Next year	36
Later; never	42
No opinion	10

College Incomplete

This year	5%
Next year	38
Later; never	46
No opinion	11

High-School Graduate

This year	5%
Next year	27
Later; never	53
No opinion	15

Less Than High-School Graduate

This year	7%
Next year	27
Later; never	41
No opinion	25

By Region

East

This year	6%
Next year	38
Later; never	42
No opinion	14

Midwest

This year	3%
Next year	29
Later; never	51
No opinion	17

South

This year	6%
Next year	31
Later; never	49
No opinion	14

West

This year	12%
Next year	29
Later; never	43
No opinion	16

By Age

18–29 Years

This year	5%
Next year	33
Later; never	54
No opinion	8

30–49 Years

This year	8%
Next year	34
Later; never	46
No opinion	12

50 Years and Over

This year	7%
Next year	27
Later; never	42
No opinion	24

By Politics

Republicans

This year	3%
Next year	35
Later; never	46
No opinion	16

Democrats

This year 9%
Next year 31
Later; never 45
No opinion 15

Independents

This year 8%
Next year 30
Later; never 50
No opinion 12

*In the above responses, several categories were combined for simplicity.

Note: Although few Americans see an economic downturn on the immediate horizon, signs of doubt are starting to emerge after three years of steadily growing optimism. Four in ten (39%) in the most recent Gallup survey believe the recovery will start to run out of steam by next year, while 46% predict that a healthy economy will prevail into 1988 or beyond; 15% express no opinion. By contrast, in March, 32% thought the recovery might start to wind down by the end of 1987, 58% were more bullish than that, and 10% had no opinion. The latest figures, therefore, reflect a 12-percentage point decline in long-term optimism, with offsetting increases in the short-term perspective and uncertainty.

In the first Gallup measurement (September 1983), only 43% thought the recovery would last beyond the end of 1984. In May 1984 the proportion saying the recovery would extend into 1986 dropped to 37%, but optimism rose to 54% in August 1985. By last March, 58% were comparably bullish.

Conversely, in the 1983 survey, 38% believed the recovery would start to wind down by the end of 1984, while, in 1984, 47% thought it would last only until the end of 1985. By comparison, 32% in 1985 said it would turn down by the end of 1986, while last March the same percentage claimed it would run out of steam by the end of the year.

The prevailing view in most groups is that the recovery will last beyond the end of next year.

As in earlier surveys, however, young adults (18 to 29 years) tend to be more bullish than their elders about the duration of the economy. Conversely, the slight weight of opinion among college graduates is that the recovery will start to unwind by the end of next year. The views of Democrats, Republicans, and independents are statistically identical.

SEPTEMBER 28
TAX REFORM

Interviewing Date: 9/3–17/86
Special Telephone Survey

From what you've heard or read about it, would you say that you approve or disapprove of the tax reform bill passed by the House and Senate conference committee?

Approve 39%
Disapprove 33
No opinion 28

By Politics*
Republicans

Approve 50%
Disapprove 23
No opinion 27

Democrats

Approve 31%
Disapprove 43
No opinion 26

*Includes independents who lean toward each party

Selected National Trend

	Approve	Disapprove	No opinion
1986			
August	40%	34%	26%
June	38	36	26

If the new tax bill is passed, do you think the amount of taxes you now pay will go down a lot, go down a little, go up a little, go up a lot, or stay about the same?

Go down 18%
Go up 41
Stay the same 30
No opinion 11

Republicans

Go down 22%
Go up 37
Stay the same 31
No opinion 10

Democrats

Go down 17%
Go up 44
Stay the same 28
No opinion 11

*Includes independents who lean toward each party

Selected National Trend

	Go down	Go up	Stay the same	No opinion
1986				
August	25%	36%	29%	10%
June*	22	34	30	14
1985				
August**	11	46	30	13
June**	25	32	29	14

*Senate Finance Committee's proposal
**Administration's proposal

Do you think the new tax bill will make for a fairer distribution of the tax load among all taxpayers, one that's less fair, or won't it be much different from the present system?

Fairer than old 27%
Less fair 20
Not much different 36
No opinion 17

Republicans

Fairer than old 35%
Less fair 16
Not much different 35
No opinion 14

Democrats

Fairer than old 21%
Less fair 26
Not much different 36
No opinion 17

*Includes independents who lean toward each party

Selected National Trend

	Fairer than old	Less fair	Not much different	No opinion
1986				
August	33%	24%	30%	13%
June*	25	17	40	18
1985				
August**	25	20	40	15
June**	29	22	34	15

*Senate Finance Committee's proposal
**Administration's proposal

Do you think the new tax bill will make it less complicated for you to pay your taxes, more complicated, or about the same as the present system?

Less complicated 19%
More complicated 17
About the same 51
No opinion 13

By Politics*

Republicans

Less complicated 22%
More complicated 10
About the same 55
No opinion 13

NINETEEN HUNDRED EIGHTY-SIX   197

Democrats

Less complicated 18%
More complicated 22
About the same 48
No opinion 12

*Includes independents who lean toward each party

All things considered, do you think the new tax bill will have a positive effect on the nation's economy, a negative effect, or won't it make much difference one way or the other?

Positive 28%
Negative 15
Neutral 41
No opinion 16

By Politics*

Republicans

Positive 36%
Negative 11
Neutral 39
No opinion 14

Democrats

Positive 24%
Negative 18
Neutral 43
No opinion 15

*Includes independents who lean toward each party

Note: Despite assurances from Washington that the new tax reform bill now moving through Congress will bring tax relief to most Americans, the public remains highly skeptical that they will benefit. This, together with the widespread perception that the proposed tax program is no fairer than the old, undoubtedly is the major impediment to greater public acceptance of the new plan.

Overall, four in ten (39%) in a just completed Gallup survey express approval of the tax reform bill, while almost as many (33%) disapprove; a large 28% are undecided. Opinion is slightly more favorable, 48% to 35%, among the six in ten who say they have followed the tax reform discussions

very (16%) or fairly (43%) closely. Three surveys conducted since the broad outlines of the tax bill have been known have found almost identical overall assessments.

By shifting some of the present tax burden from individuals to corporations and by eliminating many preferential deductions, the new tax program is expected to remove some 6 million working poor from the federal income tax rolls altogether and to lower tax rates for the vast majority of other taxpayers. However, four in ten (41%) in the current survey say their taxes would increase—either a little (30%) or a lot (11%)—if the new plan were passed, and 30% believe theirs would stay about the same. Only one in six (18%) foresees lower taxes under the new system.

Similarly, only one in four (27%) in the current survey thinks the new tax plan would provide a more equitable distribution of the tax load among all taxpayers, while 36% say it would not be much different, and 20% believe the new tax code would not be as fair as the present one.

Tax simplification—an original goal of the reform movement—seems to have fallen by the wayside, a fact acknowledged by the public. A 51% majority believes the new tax bill will be about as complicated as the old, while roughly equal percentages say it will be less complex (19%) or more complex (17%). The prevailing opinion (cited by 41%) is that the new tax bill will not have much effect on the nation's economy. Those who disagree lean to the view that it will have a positive (28%), rather than a negative (15%), impact.

As expected, Americans' political convictions have a bearing on their assessments of the tax reform bill. Republicans and Republican-leaning independents, for example, approve of the bill by a 2-to-1 margin, while Democrats and Democratic leaners disapprove by a narrow 4-to-3 ratio. However, there is less political disagreement on specific aspects of the bill. Pluralities of both Democrats (44%) and Republicans (37%), for instance, say their taxes will increase; 62% of Democrats and 51% of Republicans think the new system will be less fair or not much different than the old; 70% of Democrats and 65% of Republicans claim the new plan will be more complicated or about the same as the present one; and 24% of Democrats and 36% of Republicans believe tax reform will have a positive effect on the economy.

OCTOBER 2
SPEED LIMIT

Interviewing Date: 9/3–17/86
Special Telephone Survey

Do you favor or oppose keeping the present 55-mile-per-hour speed limit on the highways of the nation?

Favor 62%
Oppose 37
No opinion 1

By Sex
Male

Favor 51%
Oppose 48
No opinion 1

Female

Favor 71%
Oppose 28
No opinion 1

By Region
East

Favor 66%
Oppose 33
No opinion 1

Midwest

Favor 67%
Oppose 32
No opinion 1

South

Favor 58%
Oppose 40
No opinion 2

West

Favor 54%
Oppose 46
No opinion .... *

By Age
18–29 Years

Favor 59%
Oppose 41
No opinion .... *

30–49 Years

Favor 60%
Oppose 39
No opinion 1

50 Years and Over

Favor 64%
Oppose 34
No opinion 2

*Less than 1%

Selected National Trend

	Favor	Oppose	No opinion
June 1986	66%	32%	2%
1984	71	25	4
1982	76	21	3
1981	75	23	2
1980	81	17	2
1979	71	26	3
1977	76	22	2
1974	73	24	3

Asked of those who are opposed to retaining the 55-mile-per-hour limit: Suppose there were a new national speed limit. What do you think the speed limit should be?

Under 55 mph	1%
60	5
65	22
70	6
75 or over	2
No opinion	1
	37%

Note: A strong public majority (62%) continues to favor the 55-mile-per-hour national speed limit, but support has reached its lowest point since the law's adoption in 1974. Even among the minority who oppose the current law (37%), however, few want the United States to emulate the many European countries that leave speed largely to drivers' discretion: only 6% of Americans prefer a maximum legal speed of over 65 mph. Others favor 60 mph (5%) or 65 mph (22%); 1% favors speeds lower than the present limit.

Last week the U.S. Senate, prodded by members from western states, voted to end the national limit on interstate highways in rural areas. Individual states would be free to set their own limits, up to 65 mph, on these roads. House opponents of repeal narrowly defeated a similar measure recently, but passage seems likely if strict compliance standards are mandated.

Americans' continued support of the 55-mph limit doubtless reflects their awareness of the law's effectiveness in reducing fuel consumption and auto fatalities. According to some estimates, as many as 4,000 lives have been saved each year the law has been in effect. As in earlier surveys, women are far more supportive than men of keeping the present speed limit—71% and 51%, respectively. Opposition is slightly greater in the South and West.

OCTOBER 5
SOUTH AFRICA

Interviewing Date: 9/3–17/86
Special Telephone Survey

How closely would you say you've followed the recent events in South Africa—very closely, fairly closely, or not very closely?

Very closely	12%
Fairly closely	46
Not very closely	42
Don't know	*

*Less than 1%

Asked of the 58% who said that they have followed the recent events in South Africa: Do you think the United States should put more pressure on the South African government to end its apartheid racial system, less pressure, or about the same amount of pressure as now?

More pressure	55%
Less pressure	14
Same as now	24
No opinion	7

By Sex
Male

More pressure	54%
Less pressure	14
Same as now	26
No opinion	6

Female

More pressure	56%
Less pressure	14
Same as now	22
No opinion	8

By Ethnic Background
White

More pressure	51%
Less pressure	15
Same as now	26
No opinion	8

Nonwhite

More pressure	77%
Less pressure	7
Same as now	12
No opinion	4

Black

More pressure	79%
Less pressure	7
Same as now	10
No opinion	4

By Education
College Graduate

More pressure	64%
Less pressure	12
Same as now	18
No opinion	6

College Incomplete

More pressure	49%
Less pressure	14
Same as now	33
No opinion	4

High-School Graduate

More pressure	53%
Less pressure	15
Same as now	21
No opinion	11

Less Than High-School Graduate

More pressure	52%
Less pressure	16
Same as now	24
No opinion	8

By Region
East

More pressure	62%
Less pressure	10
Same as now	21
No opinion	7

Midwest

More pressure	50%
Less pressure	17
Same as now	24
No opinion	9

South

More pressure	52%
Less pressure	17
Same as now	23
No opinion	8

West

More pressure	56%
Less pressure	11
Same as now	29
No opinion	4

By Age
18–29 Years

More pressure	63%
Less pressure	11
Same as now	22
No opinion	4

30–49 Years

More pressure	60%
Less pressure	10
Same as now	26
No opinion	4

50 Years and Over

More pressure	46%
Less pressure	18
Same as now	24
No opinion	12

By Politics
Republicans

More pressure	45%
Less pressure	17
Same as now	29
No opinion	9

Democrats

More pressure	61%
Less pressure	11
Same as now	22
No opinion	6

Independents

More pressure 59%
Less pressure 14
Same as now 22
No opinion 5

Also asked of the aware group (58% of the sample): Do you think the United States should or should not apply tough economic sanctions against South Africa, such as imposing a trade embargo and ending U.S. investments there?

Should 53%
Should not 34
No opinion 13

By Ethnic Background
White

Should 50%
Should not 37
No opinion 13

Nonwhite

Should 74%
Should not 18
No opinion 8

By Age
18–29 Years

Should 63%
Should not 30
No opinion 7

30–49 Years

Should 55%
Should not 37
No opinion 8

50 Years and Over

Should 46%
Should not 33
No opinion 21

By Politics
Republicans

Should 46%
Should not 41
No opinion 13

Democrats

Should 62%
Should not 26
No opinion 12

Independents

Should 52%
Should not 37
No opinion 11

Note: Congress proved last week to be more in tune than President Ronald Reagan with American public opinion on South Africa. In voting overwhelmingly to override the president's veto of tough economic sanctions, Congress clearly reflected the public's mood, which has become increasingly impatient with the administration's perceived failure to bring about meaningful changes in South Africa's repressive racial policies.

The latest Gallup Poll finds a 55% majority of aware Americans believing the United States should put more pressure on South Africa to end apartheid, while 24% think our present efforts are adequate, 14% would apply less pressure, and 7% express no opinion. (The aware group comprises the 58% of the total sample who say they have followed recent events in South Africa "very" or "fairly closely.") When this question was first asked one year ago, 47% called for more pressure, 15% for less, and 30% for no change.

A companion question, asked for the first time in the current survey, shows majority support for tough economic sanctions against South Africa, such as imposing a trade embargo and ending U.S. investments there. The aware group favors such measures by a 53%-to-34% margin, with 13% saying they have no opinion.

The intensity of public opinion on the issue is suggested by the fact that statistically equal proportions of aware Republicans favor (46%) and oppose (41%) imposing tough sanctions, despite President Reagan's insistence on less stringent measures. As expected, aware Democrats vote overwhelmingly in favor of tough sanctions, 62% to 26%, with independents also coming down strongly in favor, 52% to 37%.

The bill passed by Congress and vetoed by the president would ban new corporate investments in South Africa, prohibit imports of textiles, steel, coal, and other minerals as well as agricultural goods, gold coins, and other products. It also would end commercial air traffic between the two countries.

OCTOBER 6
SOUTH AFRICA

Interviewing Date: 9/3–17/86
Special Telephone Survey

Asked of the 58% who said that they have followed the recent events in South Africa: Do you think the South African government has or has not made significant progress during the last year in trying to resolve its racial problems?

Has	22%
Has not	72
No opinion	6

By Sex
Male

Has	25%
Has not	70
No opinion	5

Female

Has	17%
Has not	75
No opinion	8

By Ethnic Background
White

Has	22%
Has not	71
No opinion	7

Nonwhite

Has	18%
Has not	78
No opinion	4

Black

Has	18%
Has not	79
No opinion	3

By Education
College Graduate

Has	20%
Has not	75
No opinion	5

College Incomplete

Has	21%
Has not	73
No opinion	6

High-School Graduate

Has	23%
Has not	70
No opinion	7

Less Than High-School Graduate

Has	24%
Has not	70
No opinion	6

By Region
East

Has	23%
Has not	71
No opinion	6

Midwest

Has	23%
Has not	67
No opinion	10

South

Has 25%
Has not 69
No opinion 6

West

Has 13%
Has not 84
No opinion 3

By Age
18–29 Years

Has 20%
Has not 77
No opinion 3

30–49 Years

Has 15%
Has not 79
No opinion 6

50 Years and Over

Has 27%
Has not 64
No opinion 9

By Politics
Republicans

Has 32%
Has not 63
No opinion 5

Democrats

Has 17%
Has not 77
No opinion 6

Independents

Has 16%
Has not 78
No opinion 6

Also asked of the aware group (58% of the sample): Do you think the South African government will eventually grant full political power to the black majority by peaceful means, or that the blacks will only be able to achieve power by violent means?

Peaceful means 31%
Violent means 57
No opinion 12

By Sex
Male

Peaceful means 35%
Violent means 54
No opinion 11

Female

Peaceful means 27%
Violent means 59
No opinion 14

By Ethnic Background
White

Peaceful means 30%
Violent means 58
No opinion 12

Nonwhite

Peaceful means 37%
Violent means 48
No opinion 15

Black

Peaceful means 38%
Violent means 48
No opinion 14

By Education
College Graduate

Peaceful means 28%
Violent means 59
No opinion 13

College Incomplete

Peaceful means 34%
Violent means 53
No opinion 13

High-School Graduate

Peaceful means 30%
Violent means 59
No opinion 11

Less Than High-School Graduate

Peaceful means 36%
Violent means 52
No opinion 12

By Region
East

Peaceful means 28%
Violent means 57
No opinion 15

Midwest

Peaceful means 31%
Violent means 59
No opinion 10

South

Peaceful means 43%
Violent means 45
No opinion 12

West

Peaceful means 20%
Violent means 69
No opinion 11

By Age
18–29 Years

Peaceful means 31%
Violent means 57
No opinion 12

30–49 Years

Peaceful means 32%
Violent means 60
No opinion 8

50 Years and Over

Peaceful means 31%
Violent means 53
No opinion 16

By Politics
Republicans

Peaceful means 35%
Violent means 49
No opinion 16

Democrats

Peaceful means 32%
Violent means 59
No opinion 9

Independents

Peaceful means 28%
Violent means 61
No opinion 11

Those Who Say South Africa Has Made Progress

Peaceful means 49%
Violent means 39
No opinion 12

Those Who Say South Africa Has Not Made Progress

Peaceful means 25%
Violent means 64
No opinion 11

Also asked of the aware group (58% of the sample): In the South African situation, are your sympathies more with the black population or more with the South African government?

Black population 73%
South African government 12
Both; neither (volunteered) 9
Don't know 6

By Sex
Male

Black population 71%
South African government 14
Both; neither (volunteered) 10
Don't know 5

Female

Black population 75%
South African government 10
Both; neither (volunteered) 9
Don't know 6

By Ethnic Background
White

Black population 72%
South African government 13
Both; neither (volunteered) 9
Don't know 6

Nonwhite

Black population 76%
South African government 8
Both; neither (volunteered) 11
Don't know 5

Black

Black population 81%
South African government 7
Both; neither (volunteered) 8
Don't know 4

By Education
College Graduate

Black population 76%
South African government 9
Both; neither (volunteered) 10
Don't know 5

College Incomplete

Black population 74%
South African government 10
Both; neither (volunteered) 12
Don't know 4

High-School Graduate

Black population 75%
South African government 14
Both; neither (volunteered) 5
Don't know 6

Less Than High-School Graduate

Black population 62%
South African government 16
Both; neither (volunteered) 13
Don't know 9

By Region
East

Black population 75%
South African government 8
Both; neither (volunteered) 12
Don't know 5

Midwest

Black population 69%
South African government 15
Both; neither (volunteered) 9
Don't know 7

South

Black population 69%
South African government 17
Both; neither (volunteered) 9
Don't know 5

West

Black population 81%
South African government 8
Both; neither (volunteered) 5
Don't know 6

By Age
18–29 Years

Black population 81%
South African government 11
Both; neither (volunteered) 6
Don't know 2

30–49 Years

Black population 77%
South African government 13
Both; neither (volunteered) 6
Don't know 4

50 Years and Over

Black population 64%
South African government 13
Both; neither (volunteered) 14
Don't know 9

By Politics
Republicans

Black population 67%
South African government 18
Both; neither (volunteered) 9
Don't know 6

Democrats

Black population 80%
South African government 10
Both; neither (volunteered) 6
Don't know 4

Independents

Black population 73%
South African government 8
Both; neither (volunteered) 13
Don't know 6

Selected National Trend

	Black popu- lation	South African govern- ment	Both; neither	No opinion
1986				
March	73%	12%	10%	5%
1985				
October	63	13	18	6
August	67	11	8	14

Note: Americans' perceptions that the South African government has made little progress toward ending its apartheid racial system have led many to conclude that the black majority will only be able to achieve political power through the use of force. As reported, this dire conclusion has resulted in a growing popular demand for the United States to apply more pressure on South Africa to end apartheid. Specifically, Americans, by a 3-to-2 ratio, endorse tough economic sanctions.

In the latest Gallup Poll, fully 72% of aware Americans believe the South African government has not made any significant progress during the last year in trying to resolve its racial problems, while 22% think it has and 6% express no opinion. Large majorities in all major population groups concur with the national consensus, including 77% of Democrats, 78% of independents, and 63% of Republicans. (The aware group comprises the 58% of the total sample who say they have followed recent events in South Africa "very" or "fairly closely.")

By almost a 2-to-1 ratio, aware Americans believe that the black majority of South Africans will only be able to achieve full political power by the use of violence (57%), rather than by peaceful negotiations with their government (31%). Again, at least a plurality in every socioeconomic group agrees with the consensus. An exception is found among the one in five who believes South Africa has made progress toward solving its racial problems, 49% of whom think the government will grant full power to the blacks through peaceful negotiations. However, almost as many (39%) say the blacks will have to use violence to attain political power.

As in past surveys, Americans are strongly supportive of the black majority in South Africa, with 73% saying they sympathize. By comparison, 12% side with the South African government, and 9% are equally sympathetic to both sides.

OCTOBER 12
SATISFACTION INDEX

Interviewing Date: 9/3–17/86
Special Telephone Survey

In general, are you satisfied or dissatisfied with the way things are going in the United States at this time?

Satisfied 58%
Dissatisfied 38
No opinion 4

Selected National Trend

	Satisfied	Dis-satisfied	No opinion
1986			
March	66%	30%	4%
1985			
November	51	46	3
1984			
December	52	40	8
September	48	45	7
February	50	46	4
1983			
August	35	59	6
1982			
November	24	72	4
April	25	71	4
1981			
December	27	67	6
June	33	61	6
January	17	78	5
1979			
November	19	77	4
August	12	84	4
February	26	69	5

In general, are you satisfied or dissatisfied with the way things are going in your own personal life?

Satisfied 84%
Dissatisfied 14
No opinion 2

By Sex
Male

Satisfied 87%
Dissatisfied 11
No opinion 2

Female

Satisfied 82%
Dissatisfied 16
No opinion 2

By Ethnic Background
White

Satisfied 87%
Dissatisfied 12
No opinion 1

Nonwhite

Satisfied 67%
Dissatisfied 26
No opinion 7

Black

Satisfied 66%
Dissatisfied 28
No opinion 6

By Education
College Graduate

Satisfied 92%
Dissatisfied 6
No opinion 2

College Incomplete

Satisfied 90%
Dissatisfied 8
No opinion 2

High-School Graduate

Satisfied	80%
Dissatisfied	17
No opinion	3

Less Than High-School Graduate

Satisfied	76%
Dissatisfied	23
No opinion	1

By Region
East

Satisfied	87%
Dissatisfied	12
No opinion	1

Midwest

Satisfied	84%
Dissatisfied	14
No opinion	2

South

Satisfied	83%
Dissatisfied	15
No opinion	2

West

Satisfied	82%
Dissatisfied	14
No opinion	14

By Age
18–29 Years

Satisfied	87%
Dissatisfied	11
No opinion	2

30–49 Years

Satisfied	81%
Dissatisfied	16
No opinion	3

50 Years and Over

Satisfied	85%
Dissatisfied	13
No opinion	2

By Income
$40,000 and Over

Satisfied	92%
Dissatisfied	7
No opinion	1

$25,000–$39,999

Satisfied	87%
Dissatisfied	10
No opinion	3

$15,000–$24,999

Satisfied	86%
Dissatisfied	12
No opinion	2

Under $15,000

Satisfied	73%
Dissatisfied	25
No opinion	2

Selected National Trend

	Satisfied	Dis-satisfied	No opinion
1986			
March	84%	15%	1%
1985			
November	82	17	1
1984			
December	79	17	4
February	79	19	2
1983			
August	77	20	3
1982			
November	75	23	2
April	76	22	2
1981			
December	81	17	2
June	81	16	3
January	81	17	2

November	79	19	2
July	73	23	4
February	77	21	2

Note: The heady, ebullient mood of the American people last spring has subsided somewhat, according to the latest survey. Those satisfied with the way things are going in the country has declined from 66% in March—the highest percentage recorded in the seven years this measurement has been taken—to 58% today. The current figure, however, remains the next highest in the seven-year trend. In addition, the percentage of Americans who are satisfied with the way things are going in their own personal lives remains at a seven-year high point of 84%.

The slight downturn in satisfaction with national trends may be due in part to the growing number of people who believe the economy will start to run out of steam before the end of next year. Four in ten (39%) in the current Gallup survey say the recovery will turn down by next year, while 46% predict that a healthy economy will prevail into 1988 or beyond. By contrast, in March, 32% thought the recovery might start to wind down by the end of 1987, while 58% were more bullish.

The new tax reform bill apparently has done little to bolster sagging economic hopes, with the public skeptical that they themselves will benefit from this bill. Many Americans hold the widespread perception that the new program is no fairer than the old.

OCTOBER 16
PRESIDENTIAL TRIAL HEATS

Interviewing Date: 9/3–17/86
Special Telephone Survey

Asked of registered voters: Suppose the 1988 presidential election were being held today. If Vice President George Bush were the Republican candidate and Senator Gary Hart were the Democratic candidate, which would you like to see win? [Those who named other candidates or were undecided were then

asked: As of today, do you lean more to Bush, the Republican, or to Hart, the Democrat?]

Bush	46%
Hart	46
Other; undecided	8

By Politics*
Republicans

Bush	77%
Hart	16
Other; undecided	7

Democrats

Bush	17%
Hart	78
Other; undecided	5

*Includes independents who lean toward each party

Selected National Trend

	Bush	Hart	Other; undecided
1986			
July	45%	45%	10%
April	44	46	10
January	45	47	8
1985			
July	50	39	11

Asked of registered voters: Suppose the 1988 presidential election were being held today. If Vice President George Bush were the Republican candidate and New York Governor Mario Cuomo were the Democratic candidate, which would you like to see win? [Those who named other candidates or were undecided were then asked: As of today, do you lean more to Bush, the Republican, or to Cuomo, the Democrat?]

Bush	54%
Cuomo	34
Other; undecided	12

By Politics*

Republicans

Bush 81%
Cuomo 12
Other; undecided 7

Democrats

Bush 30%
Cuomo 56
Other; undecided 14

*Includes independents who lean toward each party

Selected National Trend

	Bush	Cuomo	Other; undecided
1986			
July	53%	37%	10%
April	51	36	13
January	54	34	12
1985			
July	55	31	14

Asked of registered voters: Suppose the 1988 presidential election were being held today. If Vice President George Bush were the Republican candidate and Chrysler Corporation Chairman Lee Iacocca were the Democratic candidate, which would you like to see win? [Those who named other candidates or were undecided were then asked: As of today, do you lean more to Bush, the Republican, or to Iacocca, the Democrat?]

Bush 47%
Iacocca 42
Other; undecided 11

By Politics*

Republicans

Bush 64%
Iacocca 30
Other; undecided 6

Democrats

Bush 33%
Iacocca 55
Other; undecided 12

*Includes independents who lean toward each party

Selected National Trend

	Bush	Iacocca	Other; undecided
July 1986	42%	48%	10%
July 1985	52	35	13

Note: If the 1988 presidential election were held now, Republican candidate George Bush and Democratic candidate Gary Hart would win about the same share of the popular vote, according to a Gallup test election. Both Vice President Bush and Senator Hart are selected by 46% of registered voters nationwide, with 8% naming other candidates or undecided. The current figures are statistically unchanged from those recorded in three trial heats conducted earlier this year.

Businessman Lee Iacocca, who held a narrow 48% to 42% lead over Bush in a test election conducted shortly after the July 4 weekend, has seen that lead disappear, as the publicity surrounding his role as chief fund-raiser for the restoration of the Statue of Liberty wore off. Nevertheless, Iacocca still has a strong following among the Democratic rank and file, losing to Bush in the current trial heat by a statistically inconclusive 42%-to-47% margin. Although Iacocca consistently has said he is not interested in the Democratic nomination, many supporters are urging him to make a run for it.

New York's Governor Mario Cuomo, the third potential Democratic nominee included in these early test elections, currently trails Bush 34% to 54%. This is exactly the same margin that separated the two possible rivals last January.

Republican voters stand solidly behind Bush in the test races against Hart and Cuomo, but three in ten desert the probable GOP nominee to vote for Iacocca. On the other hand, roughly the same proportion of Democrats cross party lines to cast their ballots for Bush in the Bush-Cuomo and Bush-Iacocca trial heats. Lack of familiarity with

Cuomo undoubtedly contributes to his relatively poor showing among Democrats. In a mid-July Gallup survey that measured name recognition, Cuomo was familiar to only 53% of Democrats, compared to 70% for Iacocca and 80% for Hart.

OCTOBER 19
DEMOCRATIC PRESIDENTIAL CANDIDATES

Interviewing Date: 9/3–17/86
Special Telephone Survey

Asked of Democrats and Democratic-leaning independents: Suppose the choice for president in the Democratic convention narrows down to Senator Gary Hart and New York Governor Mario Cuomo. Which one would you prefer to see the Democratic convention select?

Hart 54%
Cuomo 29
Undecided 17

Asked of Democrats and Democratic-leaning independents: Suppose the choice for president in the Democratic convention narrows down to Senator Gary Hart and the Reverend Jesse Jackson. Which one would you prefer to see the Democratic convention select?

Hart 74%
Jackson 15
Undecided 11

Asked of Democrats and Democratic-leaning independents: Suppose the choice for president in the Democratic convention narrows down to Senator Gary Hart and businessman Lee Iacocca. Which one would you prefer to see the Democratic convention select?

Hart 58%
Iacocca 29
Undecided 13

Note: Senator Gary Hart continues to be the leading contender for the 1988 Democratic presidential nomination, with no strong challengers apparent at this early stage in the selection process. In simulated head-to-head contests for the nomination, Democrats and Democratic-leaning independents choose Hart over his nearest rivals—Chrysler Corporation Chairman Lee Iacocca, New York Governor Mario Cuomo, and the Reverend Jesse Jackson—by convincing margins. Hart currently leads Iacocca by a 2-to-1 ratio, 58% to 29%, with 13% undecided. Iacocca, who has said he is not a candidate for the Democratic nomination, gained national prominence in July as the chief fundraiser for the Statue of Liberty restoration.

In a mid-July Gallup Poll, Iacocca was a strong runner-up to Hart on the basis of Democrats' combined first- and second-place nomination votes. Iacocca's popular appeal as a possible 1988 Democratic standard-bearer was demonstrated at that time when he beat Vice President George Bush, the leading Republican candidate, 48% to 42% in a presidential test election among registered voters nationwide. As reported recently, Iacocca has since lost some of his drawing power and loses to Bush, 42% to 47%, in a new trial heat. In a similar head-to-head nomination match, self-identified Democrats and Democratic sympathizers prefer Hart to Cuomo by a 54%-to-29% margin, with 17% undecided.

Cuomo is severely hampered by low name recognition outside his native East. In the July survey, his name was familiar to three-fourths of eastern Democrats, as was Iacocca's. Elsewhere in the nation, however, fewer than one-half (46%) had heard of Cuomo, while two-thirds (68%) were aware of Iacocca. In contrast, Hart was familiar to 70% or more in every area, averaging 80% nationwide. The importance of name recognition is illustrated by the fact that Hart and Cuomo are statistically tied as nomination favorites in the East, while Hart beats Cuomo by almost 3 to 1, on average, outside the East. Iacocca loses to Hart in all regions by roughly the same margin.

Despite Jackson's fourth-place ranking as Democrats' nomination favorite in July, Hart easily defeats him in the current nomination showdown, 74% to 15%, with 11% undecided. Perhaps surprisingly, blacks in the new survey, as in a similar test last June, split their votes evenly between Hart and Jackson.

OCTOBER 23
HOMOSEXUALITY

Interviewing Date: 9/3–17/86
Special Telephone Survey

Do you think homosexual relations between consenting adults should or should not be legal?

Should 33%
Should not 54
No opinion 13

By Sex
Male

Should 33%
Should not 54
No opinion 13

Female

Should 33%
Should not 54
No opinion 13

By Ethnic Background
White

Should 35%
Should not 53
No opinion 12

Nonwhite

Should 23%
Should not 58
No opinion 19

Black

Should 21%
Should not 59
No opinion 20

By Education
College Graduate

Should 42%
Should not 42
No opinion 16

College Incomplete

Should 36%
Should not 48
No opinion 16

High-School Graduate

Should 31%
Should not 59
No opinion 10

Less Than High-School Graduate

Should 22%
Should not 64
No opinion 14

By Region
East

Should 39%
Should not 45
No opinion 16

Midwest

Should 33%
Should not 52
No opinion 15

South

Should 24%
Should not 67
No opinion 9

West

Should 38%
Should not 47
No opinion 15

By Age

18–29 Years

Should 40%
Should not 49
No opinion 11

30–49 Years

Should 37%
Should not 52
No opinion 11

50 Years and Over

Should 24%
Should not 59
No opinion 17

By Religion

Protestants

Should 27%
Should not 60
No opinion 13

Catholics

Should 39%
Should not 48
No opinion 13

Evangelicals

Should 19%
Should not 69
No opinion 12

Nonevangelicals

Should 41%
Should not 45
No opinion 14

Selected National Trend

	Should	Should not	No opinion
1985	44%	47%	9%
1982	45	39	16
1977	43	43	14

Interviewing Date: 7/11–14/86
Survey #266-G

The Supreme Court recently ruled that the Constitution does not give consenting adults the right to have private homosexual relations. Do you approve or disapprove of this ruling?

Approve 51%
Disapprove 41
No opinion 8

By Sex

Male

Approve 54%
Disapprove 38
No opinion 8

Female

Approve 47%
Disapprove 44
No opinion 9

By Ethnic Background

White

Approve 50%
Disapprove 42
No opinion 8

Nonwhite

Approve 53%
Disapprove 33
No opinion 14

Black

Approve 53%
Disapprove 36
No opinion 11

By Education
College Graduate

Approve 34%
Disapprove 60
No opinion 6

College Incomplete

Approve 47%
Disapprove 45
No opinion 8

High-School Graduate

Approve 58%
Disapprove 35
No opinion 7

Less Than High-School Graduate

Approve 57%
Disapprove 28
No opinion 15

By Region
East

Approve 43%
Disapprove 45
No opinion 12

Midwest

Approve 52%
Disapprove 40
No opinion 8

South

Approve 60%
Disapprove 32
No opinion 8

West

Approve 45%
Disapprove 49
No opinion 6

By Age
18–29 Years

Approve 50%
Disapprove 45
No opinion 5

30–49 Years

Approve 47%
Disapprove 45
No opinion 8

50 Years and Over

Approve 55%
Disapprove 34
No opinion 11

By Religion
Protestants

Approve 59%
Disapprove 34
No opinion 7

Catholics

Approve 44%
Disapprove 47
No opinion 9

Evangelicals

Approve 70%
Disapprove 25
No opinion 5

Nonevangelicals

Approve 43%
Disapprove 47
No opinion 9

Note: Public support for the legalization of homosexual relations has declined sharply during the last year, with 33% in the latest survey favoring legalization and 54% opposed. This is the first time a majority has opposed legalization since Gallup began assessing public opinion on the issue nine years ago, thus reflecting growing concern about the AIDS epidemic. Paralleling the latest findings, a July Gallup Poll found majority approval of the recent Supreme Court ruling that the Constitution does not give consenting adults the right to have homosexual relations in private.

In the Gallup Poll's first (1977) sounding of public opinion, equal proportions said homosexual relations between consenting adults should and should not be legal. In 1982, a 45% plurality favored legislation, while 39% were opposed. The 1985 survey found no significant decline in those approving legalization, a slight upturn in opposition, and a decline in the undecided vote.

The latest findings doubtless reflect growing public antipathy toward the gay community. Although six in ten in last year's survey claimed the AIDS epidemic had not made any difference in the way they felt about homosexuals, more than one-third (37%) said their opinions had changed for the worse, while only 2% claimed theirs had changed for the better.

Public opinion on the issue is strongly influenced by age, education, and religious affiliation, with young adults (18 to 29 years), the college educated, Catholics, and nonevangelicals holding more liberal views than their opposite numbers. Southerners, on the other hand, are opposed to legalization by almost a 3-to-1 ratio, reflecting the large evangelical population there.

OCTOBER 26
REPUBLICAN PRESIDENTIAL CANDIDATES

Interviewing Date: 9/3–17/86
Special Telephone Survey

Asked of Republicans and Republican-leaning independents: Suppose the choice in the Republican convention narrows down to Vice President George Bush and Senator Bob Dole. Which one would you prefer to see the Republican convention select?

Bush 54%
Dole 24
Undecided 22

Asked of Republicans and Republican-leaning independents: Suppose the choice in the Republican convention narrows down to Vice President George Bush and former Senator Howard Baker. Which one would you prefer to see the Republican convention select?

Bush 62%
Baker 21
Undecided 17

Asked of Republicans and Republican-leaning independents: Suppose the choice for president in the Republican convention narrows down to Vice President George Bush and Representative Jack Kemp. Which one would you prefer to see the Republican convention select?

Bush 69%
Kemp 12
Undecided 19

Note: Vice President George Bush remains the overwhelming popular favorite for the 1988 Republican presidential nomination, with no serious challengers yet in sight. In simulated head-to-head contests for the nomination among Republicans and Republican-leaning independents, Bush easily defeats his nearest rivals—Senator Robert Dole, former Senator Howard Baker, and Representative Jack Kemp. Bush also currently holds better than a 2-to-1 lead over Dole, 54% to 24%, with 22% undecided. The vice president beats Baker by almost 3 to 1, 62% to 21%, with 17% undecided, and defeats Kemp by a huge 69%-to-12% margin, with 19% undecided.

Name recognition plays a vital role at this early stage in the nomination process. In a July survey, Bush's name was familiar to 93% of Republicans and Republican sympathizers, Dole's to 67%, Baker's to 58%, and Kemp's to only 39%. In a more stringent test of familiarity—the proportion of party loyalists who claim to "know something about" each of the potential nominees—a similar imbalance was found. Eight in ten (82%) said this about Bush, 45% about Dole, 38% about Baker, and 25% about Kemp.

Baker, who decided not to seek reelection to the Senate in 1984 in order to pursue his presidential ambitions, has been losing popular recognition. In a mid-1985 survey, 71% of Republicans and GOP leaners were aware of Baker, and 50% said they knew something about him. In July, those figures had dropped to 58% and 38%, as noted above.

OCTOBER 30
PRESIDENTIAL TENURE

Interviewing Date: 9/3–17/86
Special Telephone Survey

> *Would you favor or oppose changing the term of office of the president of the United States to one six-year term with no reelection?*

Favor 25%
Oppose 70
No opinion 5

By Education
College Graduate

Favor 27%
Oppose 69
No opinion 4

College Incomplete

Favor 18%
Oppose 79
No opinion 3

High-School Graduate

Favor 24%
Oppose 72
No opinion 4

Less Than High-School Graduate

Favor 32%
Oppose 58
No opinion 10

By Politics
Republicans

Favor 22%
Oppose 70
No opinion 8

Democrats

Favor 25%
Oppose 72
No opinion 3

Independents

Favor 28%
Oppose 69
No opinion 3

Selected National Trend

	Favor	Oppose	No opinion
1979	30%	62%	8%
1971	20	73	7
1945	25	68	7
1936	26	74	*

*Not recorded

> *As you may know, the 22d Amendment to the Constitution limits presidents to two terms of four years each. Would you like to see this amendment repealed so that presidents could run for more than two terms, or not?*

Favor 33%
Oppose 64
No opinion 3

By Education
College Graduate

Favor 27%
Oppose 73
No opinion .... *

College Incomplete

Favor 35%
Oppose 64
No opinion 1

High-School Graduate

Favor 39%
Oppose 58
No opinion 3

Less Than High-School Graduate

Favor 32%
Oppose 64
No opinion 4

By Politics
Republicans

Favor 47%
Oppose 51
No opinion 2

Democrats

Favor 22%
Oppose 76
No opinion 2

Independents

Favor 33%
Oppose 64
No opinion 3

*Less than 1%

If the amendment were repealed, do you think President Reagan would run for a third term, or not?

Would 59%
Would not 33
No opinion 8

By Education
College Graduate

Would 60%
Would not 36
No opinion 4

College Incomplete

Would 59%
Would not 35
No opinion 6

High-School Graduate

Would 64%
Would not 28
No opinion 8

Less Than High-School Graduate

Would 53%
Would not 35
No opinion 12

By Politics
Republicans

Would 54%
Would not 37
No opinion 9

Democrats

Would 62%
Would not 32
No opinion 6

Independents

Would 64%
Would not 30
No opinion 6

If this amendment were repealed and presidents could run for more than two terms, would you like to see President Reagan run for a third term, or not?

Would 39%
Would not 58
No opinion 3

By Sex
Male

Would 42%
Would not 56
No opinion 2

Female

Would 36%
Would not 60
No opinion 4

By Ethnic Background
White

Would 40%
Would not 57
No opinion 3

Nonwhite

Would 27%
Would not 70
No opinion 3

Black

Would 16%
Would not 82
No opinion 2

By Education
College Graduate

Would 35%
Would not 63
No opinion 2

College Incomplete

Would 40%
Would not 57
No opinion 3

High-School Graduate

Would 42%
Would not 54
No opinion 4

Less Than High-School Graduate

Would 35%
Would not 52
No opinion 3

By Region
East

Would 36%
Would not 61
No opinion 3

Midwest

Would 38%
Would not 61
No opinion 1

South

Would 40%
Would not 55
No opinion 5

West

Would 40%
Would not 57
No opinion 3

By Age
18–29 Years

Would 51%
Would not 44
No opinion 5

30–49 Years

Would 41%
Would not 56
No opinion 3

50 Years and Over

Would 28%
Would not 69
No opinion 3

By Politics
Republicans

Would 60%
Would not 37
No opinion 3

Democrats

Would 19%
Would not 80
No opinion 1

Would 39%
Would not 57
No opinion 4

Note: Two proposals for changing the tenure of U.S. presidents are voted down by a large majority in the latest Gallup Poll. First, limiting presidents to a single six-year term in office meets with almost 3-to-1 public resistance, with 25% in favor and 70% opposed. Gallup surveys over the last half century consistently have found about the same level of public opposition to this idea.

A second proposal, removing the constitutional restraint on the number of terms presidents can serve, is favored by 33% and opposed by 64%. This proposal, which would require repeal of the 22d Amendment limiting presidents to two four-year terms, is far more popular among Republicans—many of whom would like to see President Ronald Reagan run for a third term—than among Democrats and independents. In fact, majorities of Americans of all political persuasions believe Reagan would try for a third term, if the law allowed.

The six-year term for presidents was one of several alternatives considered at the Constitutional Convention in 1787. In the last century many proposals for such a term have been introduced in Congress, and in 1913 the Senate, but not the House, passed a resolution. More recently, President Jimmy Carter espoused limiting presidents to a single six-year term, claiming that the public saw a political motivation in everything he did. The most common argument advanced by advocates of the six-year term is that presidents could attend to their duties without having to expend enormous amounts of time and money trying to get reelected. Those opposed generally believe that such a term would be "too long for a bad president, too short for a good one."

Although the public as a whole opposed repeal of the 22d Amendment by a 2-to-1 ratio, self-described Republicans are evenly divided between those who oppose (51%) and favor (47%) revoking the two-term limitation. Democrats, on the other hand, vigorously oppose the idea by a

3-to-1 margin. Among independents, opposition outweighs support by 2 to 1.

Republicans, by a 54%-to-37% margin, would like to see President Reagan run for a third term, while Democrats overwhelmingly oppose such a move. Independents reflect the national consensus, with 3-to-2 opposition.

Perhaps surprisingly, in view of his age (he would be eighty-one at the end of his third term), almost six in ten Americans believe Reagan would run again if permitted by the Constitution. Voters of all political stripes share this opinion to about the same extent.

NOVEMBER 1
ATTITUDES TOWARD PUBLIC SCHOOLS

Interviewing Date: 4/11–20/86
Special Survey*

Do you have any children in the local public schools—that is, kindergarten, elementary, junior, or high school?

	Yes
National	27%

By Sex

Male	27%
Female	28

By Ethnic Background

White	26%
Nonwhite	37

*The 1986 survey, which measures the attitudes of Americans toward their public schools, is the eighteenth annual survey in the series funded by Phi Delta Kappa. A great effort is made each year to deal with issues of major concern to both educators and the public. New questions, as well as trend questions, are included in this and every survey. To be sure that the survey would cover the most important issues, Phi Delta Kappa solicited from various leaders in the field of education their ideas, responses to proposed questions, and suggestions for new questions.

By Education

College graduate	23%
College incomplete	30
High-school graduate	30
Less than high-school graduate	24

By Region

East	22%
Midwest	30
South	30
West	27

By Age

18–29 years	15%
30–49 years	56
50 years and over	6

By Income

$40,000 and over	30%
$30,000–$39,999	35
$20,000–$29,999	32
$10,000–$19,999	24
Under $10,000	20

By Religion

Protestant	28%
Catholic	26

By Occupation

Professional and business	31%
Clerical and sales	28
Manual workers	34

By Community Size

One million and over	26%
500,000–999,999	23
50,000–499,999	23
2,500–49,999	26
Under 2,500; rural	34

Do you have any children in parochial or private schools—that is, nonpublic kindergarten, elementary, junior, or high school?

	Yes
National	5%

By Sex

Male	6%
Female	5

By Ethnic Background

White	5%
Nonwhite	5

By Education

College graduate	8%
College incomplete	5
High-school graduate	6
Less than high-school graduate	2

By Region

East	5%
Midwest	5
South	6
West	5

By Age

18–29 years	2%
30–49 years	11
50 years and over	2

By Income

$40,000 and over	8%
$30,000–$39,999	4
$20,000–$29,999	6
$10,000–$19,999	3
Under $10,000	2

By Religion

Protestant	4%
Catholic	8

By Occupation

Professional and business	8%
Clerical and sales	6
Manual workers	4

One million and over 7%
500,000–999,999 5
50,000–499,999 3
2,500–49,999 5
Under 2,500; rural 4

Major Problems Confronting Public Schools

*What do you think are the biggest problems with which the public schools in this community must deal?**

	National	No children in school	Public school parents	Non-public school parents
Use of drugs	28%	28%	27%	22%
Lack of discipline	24	24	23	26
Lack of proper financial support	11	9	15	14
Poor curriculum/ poor standards	8	7	10	11
Difficulty getting good teachers	6	6	6	5
Moral standards/ dress code	5	5	5	11
Drinking/ alcoholism	5	4	5	8
Large schools/ overcrowding	5	4	6	5
Teachers' lack of interest	4	4	6	7
Lack of respect for teachers/ other students	4	4	4	3
Parents' lack of interest	4	3	5	4
Low teacher pay	3	2	4	3
Integration/ busing	3	4	3	3
Crime/vandalism	3	3	3	1
Pupils' lack of interest/ truancy	3	3	2	1
Problems with administration	2	2	3	5
Other problems	14	16	15	18
There are no problems	2	2	4	3
Don't know	11	13	4	5

*Totals add to more than 100% due to multiple responses.

*Asked of public school parents: What do you think are the biggest problems with which the school your oldest child attends must deal?**

Use of drugs 16%
Lack of discipline 15
Lack of proper financial support 9
Large schools/overcrowding 9
Poor curriculum/poor standards 7
Parents' lack of interest 4
Teachers' lack of interest 4
Moral standards/dress code 4
Difficulty getting good teachers 3
Pupils' lack of interest/truancy 3
Drinking/alcoholism 3
Lack of needed teachers 3
Lack of respect for teachers/
  other students 3
Fighting 3
Other problems 27
There are no problems 8
Don't know 12

*Total adds to more than 100% due to multiple responses.

Support for Antidrug Measures in Local Schools

This card lists various ways to deal with the problem of drugs in the public schools. As I read off each one of these plans, would you tell me whether you would favor or oppose its use in the public schools in your community:

Requiring instruction for all students in the dangers of drug abuse?

	National	No children in school	Public school parents	Non-public school parents
Favor	90%	90%	91%	92%
Oppose	6	6	6	5
Don't know	4	4	3	3

Permitting expulsion of students who are caught using drugs in school buildings or on school grounds?

	National	No children in school	Public school parents	Non-public school parents
Favor	78%	77%	81%	82%
Oppose	16	16	14	17
Don't know	6	7	5	1

Using school funds to provide counseling and treatment for students who use drugs?

	National	No children in school	Public school parents	Non-public school parents
Favor	69%	68%	70%	83%
Oppose	25	26	24	16
Don't know	6	6	6	1

Allowing teachers or school authorities to search lockers or personal property if they suspect drugs, without obtaining a court-issued search warrant?

	National	No children in school	Public school parents	Non-public school parents
Favor	67%	67%	67%	77%
Oppose	28	28	30	22
Don't know	5	5	3	1

Testing students for drug use by urinalysis?

	National	No children in school	Public school parents	Non-public school parents
Favor	49%	49%	49%	49%
Oppose	44	44	43	46
Don't know	7	7	8	5

Public Grades Public Schools, Principals, and Administrators

Students are often given the grades A, B, C, D, and Fail to denote the quality of their work. Suppose the public schools themselves, in this community, were graded in the same way. What grade would you give the public schools here—A, B, C, D, or Fail?

	National	No children in school	Public school parents	Non-public school parents
A	11%	8%	18%	11%
B	30	28	37	29
C	28	27	29	29
D	11	11	11	16
Fail	5	5	4	11
Don't know	15	21	1	4

Now, what grade would you give the teachers in the public schools in this community?

	National	No children in school	Public school parents	Non-public school parents
A	15%	11%	24%	16%
B	33	32	36	34
C	26	26	26	26
D	7	6	9	8
Fail	2	3	2	7
Don't know	17	22	3	9

Now, what grade would you give the principals and administrators in this community?

	National	No chil- dren in school	Public school parents	Non- public school parents
A	14%	11%	24%	17%
B	28	27	32	29
C	24	23	25	25
D	9	9	8	8
Fail	5	4	6	12
Don't know	20	26	5	9

How about the public schools in the nation as a whole? What grade would you give the public schools nationally—A, B, C, D, or Fail?

	National	No chil- dren in school	Public school parents	Non- public school parents
A	3%	3%	2%	3%
B	25	25	26	23
C	41	40	43	46
D	10	9	12	10
Fail	5	6	4	7
Don't know	16	17	13	11

Asked of public school parents: Using the A, B, C, D, and Fail scale again, what grade would you give the school your oldest child attends?

A	28%
B	37
C	26
D	4
Fail	2
Don't know	3

Asked of public school parents: Using the A, B, C, D, and Fail scale again, what grade would you give the teachers in the school your oldest child attends?

A	26%
B	39
C	24
D	5
Fail	1
Don't know	5

Asked of public school parents: Using the A, B, C, D, and Fail scale again, what grade would you give the principals and adminis- trators in the school your oldest child attends?

A	30%
B	33
C	19
D	7
Fail	3
Don't know	8

Public School Parents Describe Their Children's Schools

Asked of public school parents: Would you tell me how accurately you feel the state- ment—the school's environment is safe and orderly—describes the school your oldest child attends—very accurately, fairly accu- rately, not very accurately, not at all accurately?

Very accurately	40%
Fairly accurately	44
Not very accurately	10
Not at all accurately	2
Don't know	4

Asked of public school parents: Would you tell me how accurately you feel the state- ment—student progress toward school goals is regularly measured and reported— describes the school your oldest child attends—very accurately, fairly accurately, not very accurately, not at all accurately?

Very accurately	41%
Fairly accurately	39
Not very accurately	9
Not at all accurately	5
Don't know	6

Asked of public school parents: Would you tell me how accurately you feel the statement—the teachers and administrators have high expectations of the students and demand high achievement—describes the school your oldest child attends—very accurately, fairly accurately, not very accurately, not at all accurately?

Very accurately	33%
Fairly accurately	41
Not very accurately	16
Not at all accurately	3
Don't know	7

Asked of public school parents: Would you tell me how accurately you feel the statement—there is general agreement among administrators, teachers, and parents about school goals—describes the school your oldest child attends—very accurately, fairly accurately, not very accurately, not at all accurately?

Very accurately	31%
Fairly accurately	39
Not very accurately	14
Not at all accurately	6
Don't know	10

Asked of public school parents: Would you tell me how accurately you feel the statement—the school's principal spends most of his or her time helping teachers improve their teaching—describes the school your oldest child attends—very accurately, fairly accurately, not very accurately, not at all accurately?

Very accurately	17%
Fairly accurately	37
Not very accurately	18
Not at all accurately	8
Don't know	20

Educational Goals

People have different reasons why they want their children to receive an education. What are the chief reasons that come to your mind?*

	National	No children in school	Public school parents	Non-public school parents
Increases job opportunities	34%	35%	33%	18%
Prepares for better life	23	22	25	33
Education is a necessity of life	12	12	12	10
Learn more knowledge	10	10	10	11
Obtain financial security/economic stability	9	8	11	13
Find better paying job	8	9	5	2
Become better citizens	6	6	6	5
Gain success	5	4	7	6
Learn to get along with people	4	4	3	1
Have better/easier life than parents	4	2	7	3
Provides specialized training	4	3	4	9
Teaches person to think/learn/understand	3	3	3	8
Make a contribution to society	3	3	4	4
Promotes personal development/self-realization	3	3	4	3
Develops self-sufficiency	3	3	4	3
Learn basic skills	3	3	3	1

Develops ability
to deal with
adult
responsibilities 2 2 3 5
Attain happier
life 2 2 2 5
Creates oppor-
tunities/opens
doors 2 2 2 2
Develops appre-
ciation for
culture 1 2 1 2
Helps keep chil-
dren out of
trouble 1 1 1 3
Obtain social
status 1 1 1 2
Develops self-
discipline 1 1 1 1
Acquire basic
individual
values 1 ** 1 1
Learn critical
thinking skills 1 1 ** 1
Other 2 2 1 3
Don't know 4 5 3 3

*Totals add to more than 100% due to multiple responses.
**Less than 1%

Attitudes on Increased Federal, State, and Local Influence on Public Education

Thinking about the future, would you like the federal government in Washington to have more influence or less influence in determining the educational program of the local public schools?

	National	No children in school	Public school parents	Non-public school parents
More influence	26%	28%	23%	21%
Less influence	53	49	62	56
Same as now	12	12	11	14
Don't know	9	11	4	9

How about the state government? Would you like the state government to have more influence or less influence in determining the educational program of the local public schools?

	National	No children in school	Public school parents	Non-public school parents
More influence	45%	46%	45%	35%
Less influence	32	29	38	38
Same as now	16	16	13	20
Don't know	7	9	4	7

How about the local school board? Would you like the local school board to have more influence or less influence in determining the educational program of the local public schools?

	National	No children in school	Public school parents	Non-public school parents
More influence	57%	56%	61%	55%
Less influence	17	17	15	19
Same as now	17	16	19	19
Don't know	9	11	5	7

Financing Public Schools

There is always a lot of discussion about the best way to finance the public schools. Which do you think is the best way to finance the public schools: by means of local property taxes, by state taxes, or by taxes from the federal government in Washington?

	National	No children in school	Public school parents	Non-public school parents
Local property taxes	24%	22%	28%	22%
State taxes	33	34	32	36
Taxes from federal government	24	23	28	22
Don't know	19	21	12	20

Suppose the local public schools said they needed much more money. As you feel at this time, would you vote to raise taxes for this purpose, or would you vote against raising taxes for this purpose?

	National	No chil- dren in school	Public school parents	Non- public school parents
Raise taxes	37%	34%	45%	38%
Against raise	52	54	46	51
No opinion	11	12	9	11

Now, where do you think most of the funds to finance the public schools come from— local property taxes, state taxes, or the federal government in Washington?

	National	No chil- dren in school	Public school parents	Non- public school parents
Local property taxes	45%	44%	44%	46%
State taxes	30	30	31	36
Taxes from federal government	11	10	14	4
Don't know	14	16	11	14

Many states recently have passed school improvements legislation that requires additional financial expenditures. If your state needed to raise more money for the public schools, would you favor or oppose the following proposals:

Increasing alcoholic beverage taxes?

	National	No chil- dren in school	Public school parents	Non- public school parents
Favor	79%	78%	82%	79%
Oppose	18	18	17	20
Don't know	3	4	1	1

Increasing percentage of state lottery money that goes to support public schools in those states with a state lottery?

	National	No chil- dren in school	Public school parents	Non- public school parents
Favor	78%	77%	81%	69%
Oppose	10	9	12	22
Don't know	12	14	7	9

Increasing cigarette and tobacco taxes?

	National	No chil- dren in school	Public school parents	Non- public school parents
Favor	74%	74%	74%	79%
Oppose	22	21	25	20
Don't know	4	5	1	1

Increasing local property taxes?

	National	No chil- dren in school	Public school parents	Non- public school parents
Favor	33%	31%	39%	31%
Oppose	60	61	56	63
Don't know	7	8	5	6

Increasing gasoline taxes?

	National	No chil- dren in school	Public school parents	Non- public school parents
Favor	28%	28%	29%	29%
Oppose	67	67	68	70
Don't know	5	5	3	1

Increasing income taxes?

	National	No chil- dren in school	Public school parents	Non- public school parents
Favor	27%	25%	31%	26%
Oppose	66	67	65	68
Don't know	7	8	4	6

Support for Stricter Requirements for Grade Promotion/High-School Graduation

In your opinion, should promotion from grade to grade in the public schools be made more strict than it is now, or less strict?

	National	No chil- dren in school	Public school parents	Non- public school parents
More strict	72%	72%	70%	73%
Less strict	6	5	7	6
Same as now	16	15	20	16
Don't know	6	8	3	5

Asked of public school parents: In your opinion, should promotion from grade to grade in the public schools be made more strict than it is now, or less strict?

More strict	70%
Less strict	7
Same as now	20
Don't know	3

In your opinion, should the requirements for graduation from the public high schools be made more strict than they are now, or less strict?

	National	No chil- dren in school	Public school parents	Non- public school parents
More strict	70%	71%	68%	75%
Less strict	5	5	7	*
Same as now	19	17	23	20
Don't know	6	7	2	5

*Less than 1%

Would you favor or oppose stricter requirements for high-school graduation even if it meant that significantly fewer students would graduate than is now the case?

	National	No chil- dren in school	Public school parents	Non- public school parents
Favor	68%	68%	68%	77%
Oppose	23	22	26	18
Don't know	9	10	6	5

This card lists several ways to deal with those students who do not meet the requirements for public high-school graduation. Which one of these plans would you prefer?

	National	No chil- dren in school	Public school parents	Non- public school parents
Have high schools set up a remedial program for students who initially failed to meet the requirements for graduation (supported by taxes)	45%	44%	45%	53%
Have high schools set up a remedial program for students who initially failed to meet the requirements for graduation (supported by tuition)	27	27	30	23

Have high
schools award
lesser diploma
to students
who cannot
meet require-
ments for
standard

	National	No children in school	Public school parents	Non-public school parents
diploma	19	19	19	16
Don't know	9	10	6	8

Support for National Public School Testing

Would you like to see the students in the local schools be given national tests so that their educational achievement could be compared with students in other communities?

	National	No children in school	Public school parents	Non-public school parents
Would	77%	76%	78%	82%
Would not	16	15	19	17
Don't know	7	9	3	1

Time Spent Helping on Homework

Asked of public school parents: During the school year, on average, about how many hours per week do you help your oldest child with his or her homework?

None	34%
Up to 1 hour	13
1–1:59 hours	17
2–2:59 hours	10
3–3:59 hours	7
4–4:59	5
5–5:59	4
6 hours or more	5
Undesignated	5

Average: 1½ hours per week

Competency Testing for Teachers

In your opinion, should experienced teachers periodically be required to pass a statewide basic competency test in their subject area(s) or not?

	National	No children in school	Public school parents	Non-public school parents
Should	85%	84%	87%	87%
Should not	11	11	11	13
Don't know	4	5	2	*

*Less than 1%

Teachers' Salaries

What do you think the annual salary should be for a beginning public school teacher, with a bachelor's degree and teaching certificate, in this community?

Less than $10,000	3%
$10,000–$11,999	4
$12,000–$13,999	6
$14,000–$15,999	13
$16,000–$17,999	12
$18,000–$19,999	16
$20,000–$24,999	19
$25,000–$29,999	8
$30,000 and over	6
Don't know	13

Average salary: $21,300
Median salary: $19,500

Now, what do you think the salary actually is for a beginning public school teacher, with a bachelor's degree and teaching certificate, in this community?

Less than $10,000	3%
$10,000–$11,999	7
$12,000–$13,999	12
$14,000–$15,999	15
$16,000–$17,999	16
$18,000–$19,999	11
$20,000–$24,999	6
$25,000–$29,999	3
$30,000 and over	2
Don't know	25

Average salary: $16,500
Median salary: $17,600

	National	No children in school	Public school parents	Non-public school parents
Deserve higher salary than perceived	49%	47%	55%	56%
Deserve lower salary than perceived	14	14	15	8
Deserve same salary as perceived	10	9	10	13
Don't know	27	30	20	23

Attracting Teachers in Shortage Areas

Today there is a shortage of teachers in science, math, technical subjects, and vocational subjects. If your local schools needed teachers in these subjects, would you favor or oppose paying them higher wages than teachers of other subjects?

	National	No children in school	Public school parents	Non-public school parents
Favor	48%	48%	48%	54%
Oppose	44	43	47	43
Don't know	8	9	5	3

If your local schools needed teachers in science, math, technical subjects, and vocational subjects, would you favor or oppose these proposals:

Increasing the number of scholarships to college students who agree to enter teacher training programs in these subjects?

	National	No children in school	Public school parents	Non-public school parents
Favor	83%	81%	88%	89%
Oppose	11	11	9	11
Don't know	6	8	3	*

*Less than 1%

Relaxing teacher education and certification plans so more people could qualify to teach these subjects?

	National	No children in school	Public school parents	Non-public school parents
Favor	18%	18%	19%	31%
Oppose	74	73	77	67
Don't know	8	9	4	2

When Children Should Begin Public School

A proposal has been made to make kindergarten available for all those who wish it as part of the public school system. The program would be supported by taxes. Would you favor or oppose such a program in your school district?

	National	No children in school	Public school parents	Non-public school parents
Favor	80%	77%	86%	78%
Oppose	13	14	10	12
Don't know	7	9	4	10

Some educators have proposed that kindergarten be made compulsory for all children before entering first grade. Would you favor or oppose such a program in your school district?

	National	No children in school	Public school parents	Non-public school parents
Favor	71%	68%	80%	80%
Oppose	22	24	16	17
Don't know	7	8	4	3

Some educators have proposed that young children start school one year earlier, at the age of 4. Does this sound like a good idea or not?

	National	No children in school	Public school parents	Non-public school parents
Good idea	29%	29%	27%	29%
Not a good idea	64	62	70	67
Don't know	7	9	3	4

Asked of those who responded in the negative: At what age do you think children should start school?

	National	No children in school	Public school parents	Non-public school parents
5 years	41%	40%	44%	42%
6 years	18	18	20	23
7 years or over	2	1	2	*
No opinion	10	12	7	6
	71%	71%	73%	71%

*Less than 1%

Selecting Children's Schools

Asked of public school parents: Do you wish you had the right to choose which public schools your children attend in this community?

Yes 68%
No 25
Don't know 7

Asked of public school parents: If you could choose your children's schools among any of the public schools in this community, would you choose the ones they now attend, or different ones?

Same as now 65%
Different ones 24
Don't know 11

Asked of public school parents: If you had the means, would you send any of your children to a private or church-related school?

Would 49%
Would not 46
Don't know 5

Private and Parochial Schools

It has been proposed that some government tax money be used to help parochial (church-related) schools make ends meet. How do you feel about this? Do you favor or oppose giving some government tax money to help parochial schools?

	National	No children in school	Public school parents	Non-public school parents
Favor	42%	42%	40%	57%
Oppose	50	48	54	41
No opinion	8	10	6	2

How do you feel about private schools? Do you favor or oppose giving some government tax money to help private schools?

	National	No children in school	Public school parents	Non-public school parents
Favor	27%	26%	26%	48%
Oppose	65	66	67	50
No opinion	8	8	7	2

In some nations the government allots a certain amount of money for each child for his education. The parents can send the child to any public, parochial, or private school they choose. This is called the voucher system. Would you like to see such an idea adopted in this country?

	National	No children in school	Public school parents	Non-public school parents
Yes	46%	44%	51%	64%
No	41	41	41	28
No opinion	13	15	8	8

Asked of public school parents: Suppose the federal government gave you a voucher worth $600 which you could use to enroll your oldest child in any school, public, private, or church-related. Would you use the voucher to enroll the child in another public school, in a private school, a church-related school, or would you keep the child in the same school?

Another public school	6%
Private school	13
Church-related school	14
Keep child in same school	61
Don't know	6

NOVEMBER 2
CATHOLIC CHURCH'S VIEWS ON SEXUAL MORALITY

Interviewing Date: 9/3–17/86
Special Telephone Survey

Asked of Catholics: Some people say that the official position of the Catholic Church on sexual morals should not be changed. Others say that this position should be changed to reflect trends in the modern world. Which point of view more closely reflects your own opinion?

Should change	57%
Should not	36
No opinion	7

Practicing Catholics Only

Should change	46%
Should not	45
No opinion	9

Nonpracticing Catholics Only

Should change	68%
Should not	26
No opinion	6

Asked of Catholics: A Roman Catholic priest and professor of theology has been forbidden by the Vatican to teach theology on the basis that his teachings on sexual morals varied from the Vatican's official position. Have you heard or read about this?

	Yes
All Catholics	54%
Practicing Catholics	69
Nonpracticing Catholics	39

Asked of Catholics: Do you agree or disagree with the Vatican's decision?

Agree	32%
Disagree	45
No opinion	23

Practicing Catholics Only

Agree	47%
Disagree	30
No opinion	23

Nonpracticing Catholics Only

Agree	16%
Disagree	61
No opinion	23

Note: In a climate of widely publicized conflicts between liberal U.S. Catholic theologians and the Vatican, a majority of American Catholic laity would like their church to adopt more flexible policies on sexual morality to reflect trends in the modern world. In the latest Gallup Poll, 57% of Roman Catholics say their church should change its official position, while 36% believe it should adhere to its present policies on sexual morals.

The impetus for change comes mainly from Catholics who are less active in religious activities than from "practicing" Catholics, defined as church members who attend Mass weekly and who describe religion as very important in their lives. Among practicing Catholics, who comprise about one-half the total Catholic sample, public opinion is evenly divided between those who believe the church should (46%) and should not (45%) change its position on sexual morality. Among "nonpracticing" Catholics, the heavy weight of opinion favors the church changing its stance to reflect trends in the modern world, 68% to 26%.

This survey was conducted shortly after the Vatican revoked the license of the Reverend Charles Curran, a Roman Catholic priest and university professor of theology, because his teachings on homosexuality, abortion, contraception, and other moral issues were at variance with Catholic dogma. Among all Catholics in the survey, those who disagree with the Vatican's decision to censure Curran (45%) slightly outnumber those who agree (32%), with a large 23% saying they have no opinion.

Attitudes toward the Curran case, as on the broader issue of the church's position on sexual morality, reveal a dichotomy between the views of practicing and nonpracticing Catholics. Among practicing Catholics, 47% agree with the Vatican's decision, while only 16% agree among the nonpracticing group.

NOVEMBER 6
RELIGION

Interviewing Date: 9/3–17/86
Special Telephone Survey

At the present time, do you think religion as a whole is increasing its influence on American life, or losing its influence?

Increasing influence 48%
Losing influence 39
Same (volunteered) 6
Don't know 7

By Sex
Male

Increasing influence 50%
Losing influence 35
Same (volunteered) 7
Don't know 8

Female

Increasing influence 47%
Losing influence 42
Same (volunteered) 5
Don't know 6

By Ethnic Background
White

Increasing influence 48%
Losing influence 38
Same (volunteered) 7
Don't know 7

Nonwhite

Increasing influence 48%
Losing influence 43
Same (volunteered) 2
Don't know 7

Black

Increasing influence 48%
Losing influence 44
Same (volunteered) 2
Don't know 6

By Education
College Graduate

Increasing influence 51%
Losing influence 33
Same (volunteered) 8
Don't know 8

College Incomplete

Increasing influence 55%
Losing influence 36
Same (volunteered) 5
Don't know 4

High-School Graduate

Increasing influence 45%
Losing influence 42
Same (volunteered) 5
Don't know 8

Less Than High-School Graduate

Increasing influence 42%
Losing influence 42
Same (volunteered) 9
Don't know 7

By Region

East

Increasing influence 45%
Losing influence 40
Same (volunteered) 7
Don't know 8

Midwest

Increasing influence 43%
Losing influence 43
Same (volunteered) 8
Don't know 6

South

Increasing influence 51%
Losing influence 39
Same (volunteered) 5
Don't know 5

West

Increasing influence 54%
Losing influence 31
Same (volunteered) 5
Don't know 10

By Age

18–29 Years

Increasing influence 53%
Losing influence 38
Same (volunteered) 6
Don't know 3

30–49 Years

Increasing influence 48%
Losing influence 41
Same (volunteered) 5
Don't know 6

50 Years and Over

Increasing influence 45%
Losing influence 36
Same (volunteered) 8
Don't know 11

By Religion

Protestants

Increasing influence 51%
Losing influence 37
Same (volunteered) 7
Don't know 5

Catholics

Increasing influence 41%
Losing influence 45
Same (volunteered) 7
Don't know 7

Selected National Trend

	Increasing influence	Losing influence	Same; don't know
1985	49%	39%	12%
1983	44	42	14
1981	38	46	16
1978	37	48	15
1976	44	45	11
1970	14	75	11
1968	18	67	15
1965	33	45	22
1962	45	31	24
1957	69	14	17

Do you believe that religion can answer all or most of today's problems, or that religion is largely old-fashioned and out of date?

Can answer today's problems 57%
Old-fashioned/out of date 23
No opinion 20

By Sex

Male

Can answer today's problems 50%
Old-fashioned/out of date 26
No opinion 4

Female

Can answer today's problems 65%
Old-fashioned/out of date 20
No opinion 15

By Ethnic Background

White

Can answer today's problems 55%
Old-fashioned/out of date 24
No opinion 21

Nonwhite

Can answer today's problems 72%
Old-fashioned/out of date 17
No opinion 11

Black

Can answer today's problems 77%
Old-fashioned/out of date 15
No opinion 8

By Education

College Graduate

Can answer today's problems 47%
Old-fashioned/out of date 24
No opinion 29

College Incomplete

Can answer today's problems 61%
Old-fashioned/out of date 23
No opinion 16

High-School Graduate

Can answer today's problems 61%
Old-fashioned/out of date 21
No opinion 18

Less Than High-School Graduate

Can answer today's problems 59%
Old-fashioned/out of date 25
No opinion 16

By Region

East

Can answer today's problems 49%
Old-fashioned/out of date 29
No opinion 22

Midwest

Can answer today's problems 52%
Old-fashioned/out of date 27
No opinion 21

South

Can answer today's problems 73%
Old-fashioned/out of date 12
No opinion 15

West

Can answer today's problems 51%
Old-fashioned/out of date 26
No opinion 23

By Age

18–29 Years

Can answer today's problems 54%
Old-fashioned/out of date 28
No opinion 18

30–49 Years

Can answer today's problems 56%
Old-fashioned/out of date 23
No opinion 21

50 Years and Over

Can answer today's problems 61%
Old-fashioned/out of date 19
No opinion 20

By Religion

Protestants

Can answer today's problems 65%
Old-fashioned/out of date 18
No opinion 17

Catholics

Can answer today's problems 50%
Old-fashioned/out of date 27
No opinion 23

	Can answer today's problems	Old-fashioned/ out of date	No opinion
1985	61%	22%	17%
1984	56	21	23
1982	60	22	18
1981	65	15	20
1974	62	20	18
1957	81	7	12

Note: The number of Americans who believe religion is increasing in influence on U.S. life continues at the highest level recorded in almost three decades of measurements. Nearly one-half, 48%, say religion is gaining in impact, while 39% hold the opposite view, 6% say it is staying the same, and 7% do not express an opinion.

The percentage expressing that religion is on the rise is more than three times the proportion recorded in 1969 when 14% said religion was increasing its influence and 70% said losing. When this index was started in 1957, 69% saw religion gaining influence on American life, while far fewer, 14%, said losing. Most likely to say religion's influence is growing are young adults (18 to 29 years), persons with a college background, southerners and westerners, and Evangelicals.

Comparison of the current findings with those in 1970 shows the change to have occurred more or less equally among all major population groups. The survey reveals a 57% majority holding the belief that religion can answer all or most of today's problems, while 23% disagree and another 20% are undecided. The current percentage saying religion can answer problems is marginally down from last year's 61%, and is far below the peak figure in 1957 when 81% said religion could answer the problems of the world.

NOVEMBER 9
VIEWS OF EVANGELICALS

Interviewing Date: 7/11–14; 9/3–17/86
Survey #266-G; Special Telephone Survey

> *Would you describe yourself as a "born-again" or evangelical Christian, or not?*

	Yes
National	32%

By Sex

Male	29%
Female	36

By Ethnic Background

White	31%
Black	44

By Education

College graduate	17%
College incomplete	32
High-school graduate	34
Less than high-school graduate	38

By Region

East	19%
Midwest	31
South	48
West	28

By Age

18–29 years	29%
30–49 years	32
50 years and over	35

By Income

$40,000 and over	24%
$25,000–$39,999	31
$15,000–$24,999	36
Under $15,000	37

By Religion

Protestants	45%
Catholics	16

In general, are you satisfied or dissatisfied with the way things are going in the United States at this time?

	Total U.S.	Evan-gelicals	Non-Evan-gelicals
Satisfied	58%	57%	57%
Dissatisfied	38	37	39
No opinion	4	6	4

In general, are you satisfied or dissatisfied with the way things are going in your own personal life?

	Total U.S.	Evan-gelicals	Non-Evan-gelicals
Satisfied	84%	81%	86%
Dissatisfied	14	17	12
No opinion	2	2	2

What do you think is the most important problem facing this country today?

	Total U.S.	Evan-gelicals	Non-Evan-gelicals
Unemployment; recession	23%	28%	21%
International tensions; fear of war	22	15	24
Budget deficit	13	12	13
Drug abuse	8	9	7
Economy (general)	7	5	8
Poverty; hunger	6	8	6
High cost of living; taxes	4	4	4
Crime	3	3	3
Moral, religious decline in society	3	8	1
All others	23	21	22
No opinion	3	2	3
	115%*	115%*	112%*

*Total adds to more than 100% due to multiple responses.

Asked of registered voters: In politics, as of today, do you consider yourself a Republican, a Democrat, or an independent?*

	Total U.S.	Evan-gelicals	Non-Evan-gelicals
Republican	34%	38%	32%
Democrat	41	43	40
Independent	25	19	28

*Those saying they have no party preference, or who named other parties (3% in the latest surveys), are excluded.

Asked of registered voters: Suppose the 1988 presidential election were being held today. If Vice President George Bush were the Republican candidate and Senator Gary Hart were the Democratic candidate, which would you like to see win? [Those who named other candidates or were undecided were then asked: As of today, do you lean more to Bush, the Republican, or to Hart, the Democrat?]

	Total U.S.	Evan-gelicals	Non-Evan-gelicals
Bush	45%	50%	43%
Hart	45	40	48
Other; undecided	10	10	9

Asked of registered voters: Suppose the 1988 presidential election were being held today. If Vice President George Bush were the Republican candidate and New York Governor Mario Cuomo were the Democratic candidate, which would you like to see win? [Those who named other candidates or were undecided were then asked: As of today, do you lean more to Bush, the Republican, or to Cuomo, the Democrat?]

	Total U.S.	Evan-gelicals	Non-Evan-gelicals
Bush	53%	59%	50%
Cuomo	36	29	39
Other; undecided	11	12	11

Note: The vote of the one-third of the electorate who describe themselves as "born-again" or evangelical Christians provides a crucial margin of support for Vice President George Bush in early test elections against the leading Democratic challenger for the presidency in 1988, Senator Gary Hart. In the latest Gallup surveys, Bush is the choice of 50% of registered Evangelicals to 40% for Hart, with 10% undecided. In parallel contests the vice president leads New York Governor Mario Cuomo, 59% to 29%. Among non-Evangelicals, however, Hart holds a 48%-to-43% edge over Bush. Cuomo also fares better with this group, but he still lags behind Bush, 39% to 50%.

At least some of Bush's stronger showing among Evangelicals than non-Evangelicals against both potential Democratic rivals can be attributed to Evangelicals' relatively greater identification with the Republican party. Similar proportions of both groups describe themselves as Democrats, but Evangelicals are slightly more inclined to identify with the GOP and fewer say they are independents.

In assessing the findings, however, it is important to bear in mind that Evangelicals include a high proportion of blacks, who are overwhelmingly Democratic in their political affiliation. Evangelicals also include a disproportionately high percentage of Protestants and southerners. Since the views of the large bloc of evangelical voters likely will be a major factor in the 1988 presidential election, the Gallup Poll regularly will report the vote of both Evangelicals and non-Evangelicals in three key dimensions: candidate popularity, basic party strength, and issues.

Evangelicals are twice as likely as non-Evangelicals to say that religion is "very important" in their lives. Furthermore, both groups differ markedly on personal and moral issues. For example, Evangelicals are nearly 4 to 1 of the opinion that homosexual relations between consenting adults should not be legal, while non-Evangelicals are evenly divided on the issue.

Despite these differences, Evangelicals and non-Evangelicals are in general agreement on the top issues facing the nation, with economic and international issues rating high with both groups. Also, they both express about the same degree of satisfaction with trends in the nation as a whole and in their own personal lives.

NOVEMBER 13
PARTY BETTER FOR PEACE AND PROSPERITY

Interviewing Date: 10/24–27/86
Survey #269-G

Looking ahead for the next few years, which political party do you think would be more likely to keep the United States out of World War III—the Republican party or the Democratic party?

Republican 34%
Democratic 29
No difference (volunteered) 23
No opinion 14

By Politics
Republicans

Republican 64%
Democratic 11
No difference (volunteered) 17
No opinion 8

Democrats

Republican 14%
Democratic 52
No difference (volunteered) 21
No opinion 13

Independents

Republican 29%
Democratic 21
No difference (volunteered) 28
No opinion 22

Selected National Trend

	Republican party	Democratic party	No difference; no opinion
1986			
March	39%	36%	25%
1985			
June	35	37	28
March	39	33	28
1984			
September	38	38	24
August	36	40	24
April	30	42	28
1983	26	39	35
1982	29	38	33
1981	29	34	37
1980	25	42	33

Selected National Trend

	Republican party	Democratic party	No difference; no opinion
1986			
March	51%	33%	16%
1985			
June	44	35	21
March	48	32	20
1984			
September	49	33	18
August	48	36	16
April	44	36	20
1983	33	40	27
1982	34	43	23
1981	40	31	29
1980	35	36	29

Which political party—the Republican party or the Democratic party—do you think will do a better job of keeping the country prosperous?

Republican	41%
Democratic	30
No difference (volunteered)	18
No opinion	11

By Politics

Republicans

Republican	75%
Democratic	8
No difference (volunteered)	12
No opinion	5

Democrats

Republican	19%
Democratic	55
No difference (volunteered)	16
No opinion	10

Independents

Republican	35%
Democratic	23
No difference (volunteered)	25
No opinion	17

Note: Americans' declining perception of the Republican party as better able than the Democratic party to keep the nation prosperous may have contributed to the GOP's losses in the recent House and Senate elections. In a late October Gallup Poll, 41% cite the Republicans as the party of prosperity, while 30% name the Democratic party, and 29% see little difference between the two or are undecided.

Although the GOP continues to lead the Democratic party on this barometer of political sentiment, the latest findings represent a sharp decline since last spring in the proportion viewing the GOP as superior in this respect. In a March survey, 51% named the Republican party, 33% the Democratic party, and only 16% said neither was better able to sustain the economy. Thus, the current findings represent a 10-percentage point loss for the GOP, a 3-point drop for the Democrats, and a sharp 13-point increase in those expressing little confidence in either party.

The March findings marked the first time a majority of Americans had singled out the Republican party over the Democratic party in a Gallup trend that began in 1951. The Republicans have held a significant advantage over the Democrats on the prosperity issue only since 1984 and during President Ronald Reagan's first year in office. Prior to 1981 the Democrats enjoyed a near monopoly, at times by ratios of 3 to 1 or better.

As expected, in the current poll self-described Republicans and Democrats name their respective parties as better able to keep the country prosperous, although more Democrats than Republicans concede the advantage to the rival party. The growing perception that neither is more effective in this regard is found among members of both parties and, especially, political independents.

In the March survey, independents overwhelmingly named the Republican party (51%) as better able than the Democrats (28%) to maintain prosperity, with 21% saying neither party was more qualified. Today, 35% of independents cite the GOP, 23% the Democratic party, and 42% perceive no difference or are undecided. Thus independents, who comprise almost one-third of the electorate, account for most of the GOP's overall decline as the party of prosperity.

A shift also has occurred on the issue of which party is better able to keep the nation at peace, with a 12-point increase recorded since March in the percentage who think neither party enjoys an advantage. Unlike the prosperity issue, however, both the Democratic party (down 7 points) and the GOP (down 5) declined about equally. As in March, neither party currently enjoys a clear-cut advantage as better able to keep the nation at peace, with the GOP now named by 34%, the Democratic party by 29%, and 37% seeing no difference or undecided.

With only a few exceptions, the Democrats have led on this issue for the last decade, with the lead changing hands periodically before then. The last time the GOP held an outright advantage as better able to keep the nation out of war was during the closing months of President Richard Nixon's 1972 reelection campaign.

NOVEMBER 16
REPUBLICAN PRESIDENTIAL CANDIDATES

Interviewing Date: 10/24–27/86
Survey #269-G

Asked of Republicans and Republican-leaning independents: Will you please look over this list and tell me which of these persons, if any, you have heard of?

George Bush	94%
Alexander Haig	71
Robert Dole	70
Pat Robertson	62
Howard Baker	61
Elizabeth Dole	60
Jeane Kirkpatrick	58
Jesse Helms	57
James Baker	53
Jack Kemp	49
William Brock	30
Paul Laxalt	30
Robert Packwood	29
Donald Rumsfeld	28
Richard Lugar	28
Pierre du Pont	24
James Thompson	20
Pete Domenici	19
William Armstrong	19
Richard Thornburgh	16
Thomas Kean	15

Asked of Republicans and Republican-leaning independents: Which one would you like to see nominated as the Republican party's candidate for president in 1988? And who would be your second choice?

The following results are based on first and second choices combined:

Bush	57%
Dole, R.	20
Baker, H.	14
Kemp	12
Haig	9
Robertson	8
Kirkpatrick	6
Dole, E.	4
Helms	4
Baker, J.	3
Lugar	3
Others	*

*All others on the list were chosen by 2% or fewer.

Selected National Trend

	July 1986	April 1986
Bush	53%	51%
Dole, R.	16	19
Baker, H.	12	18
Kemp	9	10
Haig	10	8
Robertson	8	6
Kirkpatrick	9	7
Dole, E.	3	2
Helms	3	3
Baker, J.	2	4
Lugar	2	3
Others	*	*

*All others on the list were chosen by 2% or fewer.

Note: With the 1988 presidential campaign ready to begin in earnest, Vice President George Bush holds a large early lead for the Republican nomination. In a just completed Gallup Poll, he receives 57% of Republicans' and Republican-leaning independents' combined first- and second-place nomination votes. Bush has been the nomination choice of a majority of potential GOP voters in each of five Gallup nomination tests conducted this year and last.

Runners-up in the new survey are Senator Robert Dole, with 20% of the votes; former Senator Howard Baker, with 14%; and Representative Jack Kemp, with 12%. Further down the list are former Secretary of State Alexander Haig (9%), television evangelist Pat Robertson (8%), former U.S. Ambassador to the United Nations Jeane Kirkpatrick (6%), Transportation Secretary Elizabeth Dole and Senator Jesse Helms (4% each), and Treasury Secretary James Baker and Senator Richard Lugar (3% each). None of the ten others on a list of twenty-one people mentioned as possible nominees receives more than 2% of the votes.

Some of the runners-up, however, exhibit pockets of comparative strength that, while insufficient now to put them into real contention with Bush, may represent areas of opportunity as the campaign progresses. The most obvious of these is Robertson's relatively strong standing with the three in ten Republicans and Republican-leaning independents who describe themselves as "born-again" or evangelical Christians. Robertson receives 18% of Evangelicals' nomination votes, which puts him in third place, behind Bush with 61% and Senator Dole with 22%. Bush is the choice of 54% of non-Evangelicals to 19% for Dole and 3% for Robertson.

Dole exhibits somewhat greater strength in his native Midwest than he does elsewhere in the nation, as does Howard Baker in the South. Also, nomination support for Dole and Baker is slightly stronger among older Republican partisans, while Bush's backing is skewed toward younger voters (18 to 29 year olds).

With more than one year remaining before the early state primaries, name recognition plays a vital role in determining potential candidates' standing with the rank and file. At present only nine of the twenty-one names on the list are familiar to 50% or more of Republican sympathizers; all nine are among the leading GOP nomination choices.

NOVEMBER 20
DEMOCRATIC PRESIDENTIAL CANDIDATES

Interviewing Date: 10/24–27/86
Survey #269-G

Asked of Democrats and Democratic-leaning independents: Will you please look over this list and tell me which of these persons, if any, you have heard of?

Jesse Jackson	92%
Gary Hart	81
Lee Iacocca	73
Mario Cuomo	58
Tom Bradley	53
Jay Rockefeller	49
Dianne Feinstein	43
Bill Bradley	39
Charles Robb	29
Sam Nunn	26
Mark White	24
Patricia Schroeder	20

Dale Bumpers 18
Michael Dukakis 17
Richard Gephardt 17
Bruce Babbitt 14
Bill Clinton 11
Tony Coelho 11
Joseph Biden 10

Robb	3	3	4
White	3	3	5
Others	**	**	**

*Not asked
**All others on the list were chosen by 2% or fewer.

Note: Although Gary Hart remains the popular favorite for the 1988 Democratic presidential nomination, the wide gap that separated Hart and runners-up Mario Cuomo and Lee Iacocca earlier this year has narrowed sharply. Hart currently receives 32% of Democrats' and Democratic-leaning independents' combined first- and second-place nomination votes. Governor Cuomo and businessman Iacocca statistically are tied as runners-up, receiving 27% and 26% of the votes, respectively.

In Gallup's first nomination test of the year in January, Hart enjoyed a 2-to-1 advantage over Cuomo, his closest rival, and nearly a 3-to-1 margin over Iacocca. Since then Hart's lead has progressively declined—to 14 percentage points over Cuomo in April, to 8 points over Iacocca in July, and to his current slim (and statistically inconclusive) edge over both men.

Next on the current list of nineteen possible Democratic nominees is the Reverend Jesse Jackson, with 14% of the votes, followed by Senator Bill Bradley with 8%, Los Angeles Mayor Tom Bradley with 7%, and Senator Jay Rockefeller with 6%. Governors Michael Dukakis and Mark White and former Governor Charles Robb are the choices of 3% each. None of the nine other people on the list receives more than 2% of the votes. These include San Francisco Mayor Dianne Feinstein; Governors Bruce Babbitt and Bill Clinton; Senators Joseph Biden, Dale Bumpers, and Sam Nunn; and Representatives Tony Coelho, Richard Gephardt, and Patricia Schroeder.

With more than one year remaining before the early state primaries, name recognition plays a key role in determining potential candidates' standing with the rank and file. At present, only five of the nineteen names on the list are familiar to 50% or more of Democratic partisans, and all five are among the leading nomination choices.

Asked of Democrats and Democratic-leaning independents: Which one would you like to see nominated as the Democratic party's candidate for president in 1988? And who would be your second choice?

The following results are based on first and second choices combined:

Hart 32%
Cuomo 27
Iacocca 26
Jackson 14
Bradley, B. 8
Bradley, T. 7
Rockefeller 6
Dukakis 3
Robb 3
White 3
Others .... *

*All others on the list were chosen by 2% or fewer.

Selected National Trend

	July 1986	April 1986	January 1986
Hart	34%	40%	46%
Cuomo	22	26	23
Iacocca	26	16	17
Jackson	17	16	15
Bradley, B.	7	6	7
Bradley, T.	7	7	8
Rockefeller	6	6	6
Dukakis	*	*	*

The importance of name recognition is illustrated by the fact that Cuomo is the 2-to-1 nomination favorite in his native East, where he, Hart, and Iacocca are about equally well known. Outside the East, however, Cuomo, with 18% of the nomination votes, runs well behind both Hart, with 35%, and Iacocca, with 27%. In these areas, Cuomo's name is familiar to only half the prospective voters, while eight in ten are aware of Hart and seven in ten have heard of Iacocca.

NOVEMBER 23
THE BIBLE*

Interviewing Date: 10/24–27/86
Survey #269-G

Here are some questions about the Bible, including both the Old and New Testaments. Please tell me whether you would or would not object to the public schools:

Teaching about the major religions of the world?

Would object 16%
Would not object 79
No opinion 5

Using the Bible in literature, history, and social studies classes?

Would object 20%
Would not object 75
No opinion 5

Making facilities available after school hours for use by student religious groups or organizations?

Would object 21%
Would not object 74
No opinion 5

*This survey was conducted by the Gallup Poll as a public service, in conjunction with the Laymen's National Bible Committee.

Offering elective courses in Bible studies?

Would object 20%
Would not object 75
No opinion 5

How often do you read the Bible?

More than once a day 1%
Daily 10
Two or three times a week 9
Weekly 13
Two or three times a month 6
Once a month 8
Less than once a month 26
Never read 22
Can't say 5

By Sex
Male

Daily 8%
Weekly 18
Monthly 12
Less than monthly 30
Never 27
Can't say 5

Female

Daily 15%
Weekly 25
Monthly 16
Less than monthly 22
Never 17
Can't say 5

By Ethnic Background
White

Daily 11%
Weekly 21
Monthly 14
Less than monthly 26
Never 23
Can't say 5

Black

Daily	17%
Weekly	31
Monthly	12
Less than monthly	21
Never	15
Can't say	4

By Education

College Graduate

Daily	8%
Weekly	21
Monthly	11
Less than monthly	32
Never	23
Can't say	5

College Incomplete

Daily	8%
Weekly	21
Monthly	17
Less than monthly	25
Never	25
Can't say	4

High-School Graduate

Daily	14%
Weekly	20
Monthly	14
Less than monthly	25
Never	23
Can't say	4

Less Than High-School Graduate

Daily	15%
Weekly	25
Monthly	12
Less than monthly	23
Never	18
Can't say	7

By Region

East

Daily	10%
Weekly	17
Monthly	12
Less than monthly	28
Never	30
Can't say	3

Midwest

Daily	10%
Weekly	20
Monthly	13
Less than monthly	31
Never	18
Can't say	8

South

Daily	16%
Weekly	27
Monthly	18
Less than monthly	20
Never	15
Can't say	4

West

Daily	8%
Weekly	21
Monthly	12
Less than monthly	26
Never	28
Can't say	5

By Age

18–29 Years

Daily	8%
Weekly	17
Monthly	16
Less than monthly	28
Never	27
Can't say	4

30–49 Years

Daily	9%
Weekly	21
Monthly	15
Less than monthly	29
Never	21
Can't say	5

50 Years and Over

Daily	17%
Weekly	26
Monthly	11
Less than monthly	21
Never	20
Can't say	5

By Religion

Protestants

Daily	18%
Weekly	27
Monthly	15
Less than monthly	23
Never	12
Can't say	5

Catholics

Daily	4%
Weekly	16
Monthly	13
Less than monthly	32
Never	31
Can't say	4

Evangelicals

Daily	28%
Weekly	37
Monthly	15
Less than monthly	15
Never	4
Can't say	1

Non-Evangelicals

Daily	4%
Weekly	15
Monthly	13
Less than monthly	31
Never	30
Can't say	7

Selected National Trend

	1982	1978
Daily	15%	12%
Weekly	18	18
Monthly	12	11
Less than monthly	25	28
Never	24	24
Can't say	6	7

Note: By overwhelming margins, the American people favor having the public schools offer a variety of religious studies. These include elective Bible study courses; use of the Bible in literature, history, and social studies classes; and comparative religion courses. In addition, a large majority favors making school facilities available for use by student religious groups after school hours. Unlike prayer, which the Supreme Court has prohibited on constitutional grounds, these activities are all permissible under the First Amendment.

The current Gallup survey found no significant difference in public opinion about the schools' participation in each activity, with 79% expressing no objection to teaching about the world's major religions, 75% (each) to using the Bible in conjunction with secular studies and offering Bible study courses, and 74% to making school facilities available for use by student religious organizations. Similarly, the percentage objecting to each of these actions ranges only between 16% and 21% nationwide. Heavy public support for each of the activities studied is found in all regions of the nation and among all major population groups.

With the exception of comparative religion courses, to which no more than one in six in any group objects, college graduates are slightly more likely than those with less formal education to resist having the schools pursue the activities studied. However, support heavily outweighs opposition among college graduates as well as nongraduates.

The survey also found that one-third of adult Americans (33%) reads the Bible at least once a week, with one in ten a daily reader. In addition, 14% read the Bible at least once a month, 26% are less frequent readers, 22% never read it, and 5% are uncommitted. These figures virtually are unchanged from earlier surveys.

NOVEMBER 27
HONESTY IN POLITICS

Interviewing Date: 10/13–11/4/86
Special Telephone Survey

Do you think the overall level of ethics and honesty in politics has risen, fallen, or stayed the same during the past ten years?

Risen	17%
Fallen	42
Stayed the same	33
No opinion	8

By Politics
Republicans

Risen	28%
Fallen	24
Stayed the same	38
No opinion	10

Democrats

Risen	12%
Fallen	57
Stayed the same	25
No opinion	6

Independents

Risen	12%
Fallen	44
Stayed the same	37
No opinion	7

Just your best guess: How many people running the government of this state do you think are dishonest or crooked—almost all, quite a few, not very many, or none at all?

Almost all	9%
Quite a few	42
Not very many	39
None at all	4
No opinion	6

By Politics
Republicans

Almost all	8%
Quite a few	42
Not very many	42
None at all	3
No opinion	5

Democrats

Almost all	7%
Quite a few	42
Not very many	40
None at all	6
No opinion	5

Independents

Almost all	10%
Quite a few	46
Not very many	35
None at all	3
No opinion	6

And how many people running your local government would you say are dishonest or crooked—almost all, quite a few, not very many, or none at all?

Almost all	9%
Quite a few	29
Not very many	45
None at all	10
No opinion	7

By Politics

Republicans

Almost all	6%
Quite a few	24
Not very many	48
None at all	12
No opinion	10

Democrats

Almost all	5%
Quite a few	30
Not very many	48
None at all	13
No opinion	4

Independents

Almost all	14%
Quite a few	34
Not very many	40
None at all	6
No opinion	6

Note: Although some political observers have characterized this year's congressional campaign as among the dirtiest in recent history, the ethical image of politics and politicians has improved markedly over the last three years. In a 1983 Gallup survey for the *Wall Street Journal*, six in ten said the general level of ethics and honesty in politics had fallen during the previous decade; today, in a Gallup poll conducted at the height of the current campaign, only four in ten do so.

Evidence from other Gallup surveys points in the same direction. Small increases were recorded between 1977 and 1985 in the percentages of Americans giving senators, congressmen, and local and state political officeholders very high or high ratings for their honesty and ethical standing.

That is the good news, from the point of view of politicians. The bad news is that Americans continue to hold national, state, and local officeholders in relatively low esteem. For example, majorities in the 1985 survey assigned very high or high ratings to clergymen, pharmacists, doctors, dentists, college teachers, and engineers. By contrast, senators (23%), congressmen (20%), local officeholders (18%), and state officeholders (15%) ranked near the bottom of the list of twenty-five occupations tested.

Furthermore, the stereotype of the crooked politician is far from dead. In the current survey, about half of those questioned say that quite a few (42%) or almost all (9%) of the people running their state government are dishonest or crooked. Fewer, but over one-third (38%), hold these views about their local government officials.

There are strong political overtones to the public's perceptions of the overall trend in political ethics, with Republicans twice as apt as Democrats and independents to say the level has risen and about half as likely to say it has fallen. The political slant to the public's view of their state and local officeholders is less extreme, with independents slightly more inclined than either Republicans or Democrats to hold cynical opinions about these officials.

NOVEMBER 30
PRESIDENTIAL TRIAL HEATS

Interviewing Date: 10/24–27/86
Survey #269-G

Asked of registered voters: Suppose the 1988 presidential election were being held today. If Vice President George Bush were the Republican candidate and Senator Gary Hart were the Democratic candidate, which would you like to see win? [Those who named other candidates or were undecided were then asked: As of today, do you lean more to Bush, the Republican, or to Hart, the Democrat?]

Bush	43%
Hart	45
Other; undecided	12

Selected National Trend

	Bush	Hart	Other; undecided
1986			
September	46%	46%	8%
July	45	45	10
April	44	46	10
January	45	47	8
1985			
July	50	39	11

Asked of registered voters: Suppose the 1988 presidential election were being held today. If Vice President George Bush were the Republican candidate and New York Governor Mario Cuomo were the Democratic candidate, which would you like to see win? [Those who named other candidates or were undecided were then asked: As of today, do you lean more to Bush, the Republican, or to Cuomo, the Democrat?]

Bush 51%
Cuomo 37
Other; undecided 12

Selected National Trend

	Bush	Cuomo	Other; undecided
1986			
September	54%	34%	12%
July	53	37	10
April	51	36	13
January	54	34	12
1985			
July	55	31	14

Asked of registered voters: Suppose the 1988 presidential election were being held today. If Vice President George Bush were the Republican candidate and Chrysler Corporation Chairman Lee Iacocca were the Democratic candidate, which would you like to see win? [Those who named other candidates or were undecided were then asked: As of today, do you lean more to Bush, the Republican, or to Iacocca, the Democrat?]

Bush 41%
Iacocca 47
Other; undecided 12

Selected National Trend

	Bush	Iacocca	Other; undecided
1986			
September	47%	42%	11%
July	42	48	10
1985			
July	52	35	13

Note: Chrysler Chairman Lee Iacocca demonstrates his broad popular appeal as a potential 1988 Democratic presidential candidate by leading Vice President George Bush, the Republican front-runner, 47% to 41% in a new Gallup test election. Iacocca now runs a better race against Bush than does either Senator Gary Hart or Governor Mario Cuomo. Bush and Hart are in a statistical 43%-to-45% tie, while Bush holds a 51%-to-37% lead over Cuomo. Although Iacocca has denied interest in the Democratic nomination, his supporters are urging him to make a run for it.

The latest Bush-Iacocca trial heat results virtually are identical to those recorded in July, when Iacocca gained widespread publicity as chief fundraiser for the Statue of Liberty restoration. In a September survey, however, Bush led Iacocca by a slim 47%-to-42% margin.

Such volatility is not unusual at this early stage in presidential campaigns, especially when one of the candidates exhibits broad popular appeal, as does nonpolitician Iacocca. However, volatility usually is a sign that voters are not committed firmly to their choice of candidates. A striking parallel occurred in early 1967—long before incumbent Lyndon Johnson decided not to run for reelection—when Johnson and Republican hopeful George Romney, chairman of American Motors, alternately held the lead in presidential test elections for 1968.

Iacocca's strong current showing against Bush can be traced to his popular appeal. First, independents indicate a greater preference for Iacocca than for either Hart or Cuomo in their respective trial heats against Bush. Second, Iacocca exhibits almost as much strength as Hart among Democrats and is tied with mainline Democrat Cuomo in this respect. Finally, Republicans overwhelmingly choose Bush over both Hart and Cuomo, but one-fourth deserts Bush to vote for Iacocca.

DECEMBER 4
SPORTS

Interviewing Date: 7/11–14; 10/24–27/86
Survey #266-G; #269-G

Which of these sports and activities have you, yourself, participated in within the last twelve months? [Respondents were handed a card listing fifty sports and activities.]

	Percent participating	Number of participants (millions)
Swimming	43%	75
Bicycling	35	60
Fishing	33	56
Jogging, running	28	49
Pool, billiards	26	44
Camping	25	44
Hiking	25	44
Bowling	22	39
Softball	22	39
Weight training*	21	37
Calisthenics	20	35
Volleyball	20	34
Basketball	19	34
Weight lifting	18	31
Table tennis	18	31
Body building	14	24
Hunting	14	24
Frisbee	13	22
Golf	12	21
Tennis	12	21
Canoeing, rowing	11	19
Target shooting	11	19
Roller skating	10	17

*Any form of weight training, including weight lifting, body building, or Nautilus

Men's Top Activities

Swimming	46%
Fishing	44
Bicycling	36
Pool, billiards	35
Jogging, running	31
Basketball	29
Camping	29
Softball	28
Weight training	27
Bowling	24

Women's Top Activities

Swimming	41%
Bicycling	33
Aerobics, dancercize	26
Jogging, running	26
Camping	22
Fishing	22
Bowling	21
Calisthenics	19
Pool, billiards	17
Softball	17
Volleyball	17

Selected National Trend

	1972	1966	1959
Swimming	42%	33%	33%
Fishing	24	*	32
Bowling	28	27	18
Softball	13	15	*
Volleyball	12	12	4
Motorboating	20	16	*
Golf	14	11	8
Tennis	12	9	4

*Not asked

Note: Swimming continues to be Americans' favorite sports activity, as it has for more than a quarter of a century. About four in ten adults (43%) went swimming one or more times during the last twelve months. Next most popular are bicycling and fishing, in which 35% and 33%, respectively, participated. Swimming, bicycling, and fishing have been among the leading activities since these surveys were begun in 1959.

Running or jogging, engaged in by about one adult in four (28%), is the next most popular. Interestingly, substantially fewer (15%) actually describe themselves as joggers, as reported earlier this year. Rounding out the top ten activities are pool or billiards (26%), camping (25%), hiking (25%), bowling (22%), softball (22%), and weight training (21%). These findings are based on in-person interviews with a national sample of adults who were shown a list of more than fifty sports and recreational activities and were asked to name those they had participated in within the previous twelve months.

The following sports and activities are reported by 5% to 9% of adults: touch football, horseback riding, racquetball, waterskiing, snow skiing, badminton, soccer, sailing, and ice skating. Named by 4% or less are martial arts, snorkeling, skeet and trap shooting, archery, handball, paddle and platform tennis, skateboarding, yoga, distance running, scuba diving, windsurfing, surfing, hang gliding, squash, and sky diving.

Men are slightly more likely than women to have engaged in each of the recreational activities listed, with the exception of aerobics and roller skating, in which higher levels of female participation are found. Eight of men's ten favorites, however, also are among women's top ten, although not always in the same order of preference. They are swimming, bicycling, jogging and running, camping, fishing, bowling, pool and billiards, and softball.

Basketball and weight training are favorites of men but not of women. In addition to aerobics, calisthenics and volleyball are among women's top ten but not men's.

DECEMBER 7
AMERICA'S FUTURE STRENGTH

Interviewing Date: 10/24–27/86
Survey #269-G

In determining America's strength in the future—say, twenty-five years from now—how important do you feel each of the following factors will be: very important, fairly important, not too important, or not at all important:

Developing the most efficient industrial production system in the world?

Very important 65%
Fairly important 29
Not too important 4
Not at all important . . . . *
No opinion 2

By Education
College Graduate

Very important 63%
Fairly important 33
Not too important 4
Not at all important . . . . *
No opinion . . . . *

College Incomplete

Very important 61%
Fairly important 31
Not too important 5
Not at all important 1
No opinion 2

High-School Graduate

Very important 71%
Fairly important 23
Not too important 3
Not at all important 1
No opinion 2

Less Than High-School Graduate

Very important 64%
Fairly important 30
Not too important 3
Not at all important . . . . *
No opinion 3

By Age
18–29 Years

Very important 52%
Fairly important 38
Not too important 7
Not at all important 1
No opinion 2

30–49 Years

Very important 65%
Fairly important .32
Not too important 2
Not at all important . . . . *
No opinion 1

50 Years and Over

Very important 76%
Fairly important .19
Not too important 2
Not at all important 1
No opinion 2

By Politics
Republicans

Very important 66%
Fairly important .29
Not too important 4
Not at all important . . . . *
No opinion 1

Democrats

Very important 65%
Fairly important .29
Not too important 3
Not at all important 1
No opinion 2

Independents

Very important 66%
Fairly important .28
Not too important 3
Not at all important 1
No opinion 2

*Less than 1%

Selected National Trend

	Percent responding "very important"
1984	70%
1982	66

Building the strongest military force in the world?

Very important 51%
Fairly important .34
Not too important 11
Not at all important 3
No opinion 1

By Education
College Graduate

Very important 30%
Fairly important .44
Not too important 22
Not at all important 4
No opinion . . . . *

College Incomplete

Very important 49%
Fairly important .37
Not too important 9
Not at all important 4
No opinion 1

High-School Graduate

Very important 55%
Fairly important .33
Not too important 9
Not at all important 2
No opinion 1

Less Than High-School Graduate

Very important 61%
Fairly important .26
Not too important 8
Not at all important 3
No opinion 2

By Age
18–29 Years

Very important 46%
Fairly important .37
Not too important 13
Not at all important 3
No opinion 1

30–49 Years

Very important	50%
Fairly important	34
Not too important	12
Not at all important	3
No opinion	1

50 Years and Over

Very important	55%
Fairly important	32
Not too important	9
Not at all important	2
No opinion	2

By Politics
Republicans

Very important	61%
Fairly important	32
Not too important	6
Not at all important	*
No opinion	1

Democrats

Very important	46%
Fairly important	35
Not too important	14
Not at all important	4
No opinion	1

Independents

Very important	46%
Fairly important	34
Not too important	14
Not at all important	4
No opinion	2

*Less than 1%

Selected National Trend

	Percent responding "very important"
1984	45%
1982	47

Developing the best educational system in the world?

Very important	89%
Fairly important	9
Not too important	1
Not at all important	*
No opinion	1

By Education
College Graduate

Very important	92%
Fairly important	8
Not too important	*
Not at all important	*
No opinion	*

College Incomplete

Very important	88%
Fairly important	10
Not too important	2
Not at all important	*
No opinion	*

High-School Graduate

Very important	90%
Fairly important	8
Not too important	1
Not at all important	1
No opinion	*

Less Than High-School Graduate

Very important	87%
Fairly important	11
Not too important	1
Not at all important	*
No opinion	1

By Age
18–29 Years

Very important	88%
Fairly important	9
Not too important	2
Not at all important	*
No opinion	1

30–49 Years

Very important	89%
Fairly important	10
Not too important	*
Not at all important	*
No opinion	1

50 Years and Over

Very important	90%
Fairly important	8
Not too important	1
Not at all important	*
No opinion	1

By Politics
Republicans

Very important	89%
Fairly important	10
Not too important	1
Not at all important	*
No opinion	*

Democrats

Very important	89%
Fairly important	10
Not too important	*
Not at all important	*
No opinion	1

Independents

Very important	91%
Fairly important	7
Not too important	1
Not at all important	*
No opinion	1

*Less than 1%

Selected National Trend

	Percent responding "very important"
1984	82%
1982	84

Note: Developing the best educational system in the world is the key to America's future strength, according to a large and growing number of citizens—more important than having the most efficient industrial production system or the strongest military force. Nine in ten Americans (89%) currently cite education as "very important" to the nation's strength twenty-five years from now, while 65% hold this view about industrial productivity and 51% about military power.

The same sequence of national priorities is found among all key population groups, but the relative importance of each varies considerably in some groups. Among Republicans, for example, nearly as many name the military as very important to the nation's future as name industrial productivity, although education is the top choice. Democrats and independents are closer to the national norms. Young adults are somewhat less likely than their elders to assign the highest level of importance to military power and much less apt to describe industrial efficiency in these terms. Least likely to stress the military are college graduates, at 30%.

Comparison of the latest findings with those from a 1984 poll shows modest increases in the perceived importance of education and military might and a slight decline for productivity. The percentage describing education as very important rose from 82% to 89% during the two-year span, while military power grew from 45% in 1984 to 51% today. In the earlier survey, 70% cited productivity, compared to 65% at present.

DECEMBER 8
PRESIDENT REAGAN

Interviewing Date: 12/4–5/86
Special Telephone Survey*

Do you approve or disapprove of the way Ronald Reagan is handling his job as president?

Approve	47%
Disapprove	44
No opinion	9

*This survey was conducted by the Gallup Organization for *Newsweek*.

By Sex

Male

Approve	53%
Disapprove	41
No opinion	6

Female

Approve	43%
Disapprove	46
No opinion	11

By Ethnic Background

White

Approve	50%
Disapprove	41
No opinion	9

Nonwhite

Approve	31%
Disapprove	63
No opinion	6

By Education

College Graduate

Approve	51%
Disapprove	44
No opinion	5

College Incomplete

Approve	49%
Disapprove	44
No opinion	7

High-School Graduate

Approve	49%
Disapprove	42
No opinion	9

Less Than High-School Graduate

Approve	38%
Disapprove	47
No opinion	15

By Region

East

Approve	45%
Disapprove	49
No opinion	6

Midwest

Approve	48%
Disapprove	43
No opinion	9

South

Approve	47%
Disapprove	41
No opinion	12

West

Approve	50%
Disapprove	42
No opinion	8

By Age

18–29 Years

Approve	53%
Disapprove	39
No opinion	8

30–49 Years

Approve	52%
Disapprove	41
No opinion	7

50 Years and Over

Approve	52%
Disapprove	41
No opinion	7

By Politics

Republicans

Approve	74%
Disapprove	17
No opinion	9

Democrats

Approve 24%
Disapprove 68
No opinion 6

Independents

Approve 45%
Disapprove 44
No opinion 11

Selected National Trend

1986	Approve	Dis-approve	No opinion
October 24–27	63%	29%	8%
September 12–15	61	25	14
August 8–11	61	27	12
July 11–14	63	28	9
June 9–16	64	26	10
June 6–9	61	29	10
May 16–19	68	23	9
April 11–14	62	29	9
March 7–10	63	26	11
January 10–13	64	27	9

Apart from whether you approve or disapprove of the way Reagan is handling his job as president, what do you think of Reagan as a person? Would you say you approve or disapprove of him?

Approve 75%
Disapprove 18
No opinion 7

By Sex
Male

Approve 78%
Disapprove 17
No opinion 5

Female

Approve 73%
Disapprove 20
No opinion 7

By Ethnic Background
White

Approve 79%
Disapprove 15
No opinion 6

Nonwhite

Approve 53%
Disapprove 36
No opinion 11

By Education
College Graduate

Approve 73%
Disapprove 22
No opinion 5

College Incomplete

Approve 78%
Disapprove 13
No opinion 9

High-School Graduate

Approve 80%
Disapprove 14
No opinion 6

Less Than High-School Graduate

Approve 67%
Disapprove 27
No opinion 6

By Region
East

Approve 73%
Disapprove 21
No opinion 6

Midwest

Approve 76%
Disapprove 14
No opinion 10

South

Approve 75%
Disapprove 21
No opinion 4

West

Approve 75%
Disapprove 18
No opinion 7

By Age
18–29 Years

Approve 79%
Disapprove 15
No opinion 6

30–49 Years

Approve 76%
Disapprove 17
No opinion 7

50 Years and Over

Approve 71%
Disapprove 22
No opinion 7

By Politics
Republicans

Approve 90%
Disapprove 7
No opinion 3

Democrats

Approve 63%
Disapprove 29
No opinion 8

Independents

Approve 74%
Disapprove 19
No opinion 7

Selected National Trend

	Approve	Dis-approve	No opinion
September 1986	80%	12%	8%
November 1985	81	10	9
August 1983	67	21	12
February 1982	70	20	10
July 1981	78	13	9

Now let me ask you about some specific foreign and domestic problems. As I read off each problem, would you tell me whether you approve or disapprove of the way President Reagan is handling that problem:

Economic conditions in this country?

Approve 50%
Disapprove 45
No opinion 5

By Sex
Male

Approve 54%
Disapprove 41
No opinion 5

Female

Approve 46%
Disapprove 50
No opinion 4

By Ethnic Background
White

Approve 53%
Disapprove 43
No opinion 4

Nonwhite

Approve 29%
Disapprove 65
No opinion 6

By Education

College Graduate

Approve 59%
Disapprove 39
No opinion 2

College Incomplete

Approve 48%
Disapprove 50
No opinion 2

High-School Graduate

Approve 52%
Disapprove 42
No opinion 6

Less Than High-School Graduate

Approve 38%
Disapprove 56
No opinion 6

By Region

East

Approve 48%
Disapprove 49
No opinion 3

Midwest

Approve 53%
Disapprove 42
No opinion 5

South

Approve 49%
Disapprove 47
No opinion 4

West

Approve 51%
Disapprove 44
No opinion 5

By Age

18–29 Years

Approve 55%
Disapprove 41
No opinion 4

30–49 Years

Approve 52%
Disapprove 44
No opinion 4

50 Years and Over

Approve 44%
Disapprove 50
No opinion 6

By Politics

Republicans

Approve 74%
Disapprove 24
No opinion 2

Democrats

Approve 28%
Disapprove 68
No opinion 4

Independents

Approve 51%
Disapprove 42
No opinion 7

Selected National Trend

	Percent approving
July 1986	49%
January 1986	53
July 1985	53

Foreign policy?

Approve 34%
Disapprove 57
No opinion 9

By Sex

Male

Approve 39%
Disapprove 53
No opinion 8

Female

Approve 29%
Disapprove 61
No opinion 10

By Ethnic Background

White

Approve 36%
Disapprove 55
No opinion 9

Nonwhite

Approve 21%
Disapprove 71
No opinion 8

By Education

College Graduate

Approve 37%
Disapprove 58
No opinion 5

College Incomplete

Approve 32%
Disapprove 55
No opinion 13

High-School Graduate

Approve 35%
Disapprove 57
No opinion 8

Less Than High-School Graduate

Approve 28%
Disapprove 61
No opinion 11

By Region

East

Approve 33%
Disapprove 63
No opinion 4

Midwest

Approve 32%
Disapprove 55
No opinion 13

South

Approve 36%
Disapprove 56
No opinion 8

West

Approve 34%
Disapprove 55
No opinion 11

By Age

18–29 Years

Approve 37%
Disapprove 56
No opinion 7

30–49 Years

Approve 36%
Disapprove 55
No opinion 9

50 Years and Over

Approve 28%
Disapprove 61
No opinion 11

By Politics

Republicans

Approve 53%
Disapprove 36
No opinion 11

Democrats

Approve 21%
Disapprove 73
No opinion 6

Independents

Approve 29%
Disapprove 60
No opinion 11

Selected National Trend

	Percent approving
July 1986	51%
January 1986	50
July 1985	50

Relations with the Soviet Union?

Approve 53%
Disapprove 36
No opinion 11

By Sex
Male

Approve 59%
Disapprove 31
No opinion 10

Female

Approve 48%
Disapprove 41
No opinion 11

By Ethnic Background
White

Approve 57%
Disapprove 33
No opinion 10

Nonwhite

Approve 32%
Disapprove 57
No opinion 11

By Education
College Graduate

Approve 59%
Disapprove 34
No opinion 7

College Incomplete

Approve 56%
Disapprove 32
No opinion 12

High-School Graduate

Approve 55%
Disapprove 37
No opinion 8

Less Than High-School Graduate

Approve 41%
Disapprove 40
No opinion 19

By Region
East

Approve 53%
Disapprove 39
No opinion 8

Midwest

Approve 54%
Disapprove 36
No opinion 10

South

Approve 49%
Disapprove 38
No opinion 13

West

Approve 58%
Disapprove 31
No opinion 11

By Age
18–29 Years

Approve 58%
Disapprove 35
No opinion 7

30–49 Years

Approve 57%
Disapprove 35
No opinion 8

50 Years and Over

Approve 45%
Disapprove 39
No opinion 16

By Politics
Republicans

Approve 69%
Disapprove 20
No opinion 11

Democrats

Approve 39%
Disapprove 53
No opinion 8

Independents

Approve 53%
Disapprove 34
No opinion 13

Selected National Trend

	Percent approving
July 1986	60%
January 1986	65
July 1985	52

Situation in the Middle East?

Approve 27%
Disapprove 59
No opinion 14

By Sex
Male

Approve 33%
Disapprove 57
No opinion 10

Female

Approve 22%
Disapprove 60
No opinion 18

By Ethnic Background
White

Approve 29%
Disapprove 56
No opinion 15

Nonwhite

Approve 19%
Disapprove 73
No opinion 8

By Education
College Graduate

Approve 32%
Disapprove 60
No opinion 8

College Incomplete

Approve 27%
Disapprove 57
No opinion 16

High-School Graduate

Approve 28%
Disapprove 58
No opinion 14

Less Than High-School Graduate

Approve 21%
Disapprove 59
No opinion 20

By Region
East
Approve 27%
Disapprove 64
No opinion 9

Midwest
Approve 30%
Disapprove 58
No opinion 12

South
Approve 29%
Disapprove 51
No opinion 20

West
Approve 21%
Disapprove 64
No opinion 15

By Age
18–29 Years
Approve 31%
Disapprove 57
No opinion 12

30–49 Years
Approve 29%
Disapprove 61
No opinion 10

50 Years and Over
Approve 22%
Disapprove 58
No opinion 20

By Politics
Republicans
Approve 42%
Disapprove 43
No opinion 15

Democrats
Approve 16%
Disapprove 73
No opinion 11

Independents
Approve 26%
Disapprove 59
No opinion 15

Selected National Trend

	Percent approving
1986	
July	47%
January	43

Situation in Nicaragua?
Approve 23%
Disapprove 64
No opinion 13

By Sex
Male
Approve 29%
Disapprove 60
No opinion 11

Female
Approve 17%
Disapprove 68
No opinion 15

By Ethnic Background
White
Approve 24%
Disapprove 63
No opinion 13

Nonwhite
Approve 17%
Disapprove 73
No opinion 10

By Education
College Graduate

Approve 27%
Disapprove 64
No opinion 9

College Incomplete

Approve 24%
Disapprove 62
No opinion 14

High-School Graduate

Approve 22%
Disapprove 67
No opinion 11

Less Than High-School Graduate

Approve 22%
Disapprove 67
No opinion 11

By Region
East

Approve 24%
Disapprove 68
No opinion 8

Midwest

Approve 19%
Disapprove 66
No opinion 15

South

Approve 23%
Disapprove 63
No opinion 14

West

Approve 24%
Disapprove 59
No opinion 17

By Age
18–29 Years

Approve 25%
Disapprove 64
No opinion 11

30–49 Years

Approve 24%
Disapprove 65
No opinion 11

50 Years and Over

Approve 20%
Disapprove 63
No opinion 17

By Politics
Republicans

Approve 37%
Disapprove 47
No opinion 16

Democrats

Approve 12%
Disapprove 78
No opinion 10

Independents

Approve 21%
Disapprove 66
No opinion 13

Selected National Trend

	Percent approving
July 1986	34%
July 1985	29

Note: Although President Ronald Reagan's over-all job performance rating has plunged in the wake of the Iran-*contra* affair, his personal popularity with the American people has declined only slightly and remains at a very high level. In a special Gallup survey, public approval of Reagan as a person outweighs disapproval by a 4-to-1 ratio, with 75% offering positive and 18% negative appraisals. The president's current personal rating represents only a 5-percentage point decline since mid-September, when 80% approved and 12% disapproved. The latest personal approval figure also is marginally higher than those accorded Reagan for 1982 and 1983, during and soon after the recession. In contrast, the current survey found a sharp drop in Reagan's job performance rating, from 63% approval in a late October Gallup Poll to 47% at present.

The strength of President Reagan's personal popularity is attested to by the fact that among persons who disapprove of his overall performance in office—44% of the total sample—a 54% majority nevertheless approves of him as a person. Among those who give the president a favorable job performance rating, his personal approval rating is a virtually unanimous 93%.

The Iran-*contra* affair has caused the sharpest declines in Reagan's ratings for his handling of foreign policy (from 51% approval in July to 34% today), the Middle East situation (from 47% to 27%), and the situation in Nicaragua (from 34% to 23%). However, the new survey revealed a comparatively modest drop in approval of the president's handling of relations with the Soviet Union, from 60% in July to 53% at present. As for domestic issues, 50% of Americans currently approve of Reagan's handling of economic conditions, statistically unchanged from the favorable ratings the president received in Gallup surveys earlier this year.

DECEMBER 9
U.S. INFLUENCE IN WORLD AFFAIRS

Interviewing Date: 12/4–5/86
Special Telephone Survey*

In general, are you satisfied or dissatisfied with the way things are going in the United States at this time?

*This survey was conducted by the Gallup Organization for *Newsweek*.

Satisfied 47%
Dissatisfied 49
No opinion 4

By Sex
Male

Satisfied 52%
Dissatisfied 45
No opinion 3

Female

Satisfied 42%
Dissatisfied 53
No opinion 5

By Ethnic Background
White

Satisfied 50%
Dissatisfied 46
No opinion 4

Nonwhite

Satisfied 21%
Dissatisfied 76
No opinion 3

By Education
College Graduate

Satisfied 53%
Dissatisfied 44
No opinion 3

College Incomplete

Satisfied 49%
Dissatisfied 46
No opinion 5

High-School Graduate

Satisfied 45%
Dissatisfied 52
No opinion 3

Less Than High-School Graduate

Satisfied 39%
Dissatisfied 55
No opinion 6

By Region

East

Satisfied 45%
Dissatisfied 52
No opinion 3

Midwest

Satisfied 53%
Dissatisfied 43
No opinion 4

South

Satisfied 43%
Dissatisfied 54
No opinion 3

West

Satisfied 46%
Dissatisfied 48
No opinion 6

By Age

18–29 Years

Satisfied 58%
Dissatisfied 39
No opinion 3

30–49 Years

Satisfied 49%
Dissatisfied 48
No opinion 3

50 Years and Over

Satisfied 35%
Dissatisfied 59
No opinion 6

By Politics

Republicans

Satisfied 67%
Dissatisfied 28
No opinion 5

Democrats

Satisfied 27%
Dissatisfied 70
No opinion 3

Independents

Satisfied 47%
Dissatisfied 49
No opinion 4

Selected National Trend

	Satisfied	Dis-satisfied	No opinion
September 1986	58%	38%	4%
March 1986	66	30	4
May 1985	51	46	3

How seriously do you feel the Iran-contra affair has damaged America's influence in world affairs—very seriously, fairly seriously, or not seriously?

Very seriously 36%
Fairly seriously 40
Not seriously 22
No opinion 2

By Sex

Male

Very seriously 32%
Fairly seriously 39
Not seriously 28
No opinion 1

Female

Very seriously 39%
Fairly seriously 42
Not seriously 16
No opinion 3

By Ethnic Background

White

Very seriously 34%
Fairly seriously 40
Not seriously 23
No opinion 3

Nonwhite

Very seriously 49%
Fairly seriously 38
Not seriously 12
No opinion 1

By Education

College Graduate

Very seriously 29%
Fairly seriously 43
Not seriously 27
No opinion 1

College Incomplete

Very seriously 29%
Fairly seriously 43
Not seriously 27
No opinion 1

High-School Graduate

Very seriously 39%
Fairly seriously 43
Not seriously 16
No opinion 2

Less Than High-School Graduate

Very seriously 43%
Fairly seriously 29
Not seriously 23
No opinion 5

By Region

East

Very seriously 34%
Fairly seriously 41
Not seriously 23
No opinion 2

Midwest

Very seriously 32%
Fairly seriously 43
Not seriously 23
No opinion 2

South

Very seriously 38%
Fairly seriously 37
Not seriously 23
No opinion 2

West

Very seriously 38%
Fairly seriously 41
Not seriously 18
No opinion 3

By Age

18–29 Years

Very seriously 30%
Fairly seriously 47
Not seriously 23
No opinion ....*

30–49 Years

Very seriously 31%
Fairly seriously 46
Not seriously 23
No opinion ....*

50 Years and Over

Very seriously 45%
Fairly seriously 30
Not seriously 19
No opinion 6

By Politics

Republicans

Very seriously 24%
Fairly seriously 42
Not seriously 31
No opinion 3

Democrats

Very seriously	47%
Fairly seriously	39
Not seriously	12
No opinion	2

Independents

Very seriously	36%
Fairly seriously	40
Not seriously	23
No opinion	1

*Less than 1%

Do you feel that Ronald Reagan is handling the Iran-contra affair better, worse, or about the same as Richard Nixon handled Watergate in its early stages?

Better than Nixon	45%
Worse than Nixon	8
About the same	35
No opinion	12

By Sex
Male

Better than Nixon	49%
Worse than Nixon	9
About the same	30
No opinion	12

Female

Better than Nixon	41%
Worse than Nixon	7
About the same	39
No opinion	12

By Ethnic Background
White

Better than Nixon	47%
Worse than Nixon	6
About the same	34
No opinion	13

Nonwhite

Better than Nixon	30%
Worse than Nixon	17
About the same	46
No opinion	7

By Education
College Graduate

Better than Nixon	56%
Worse than Nixon	6
About the same	31
No opinion	7

College Incomplete

Better than Nixon	50%
Worse than Nixon	5
About the same	32
No opinion	13

High-School Graduate

Better than Nixon	42%
Worse than Nixon	8
About the same	39
No opinion	11

Less Than High-School Graduate

Better than Nixon	34%
Worse than Nixon	13
About the same	34
No opinion	19

By Region
East

Better than Nixon	42%
Worse than Nixon	5
About the same	44
No opinion	9

Midwest

Better than Nixon	45%
Worse than Nixon	8
About the same	31
No opinion	16

South

Better than Nixon	48%
Worse than Nixon	10
About the same	30
No opinion	12

West

Better than Nixon	44%
Worse than Nixon	8
About the same	36
No opinion	12

By Age
18–29 Years

Better than Nixon	37%
Worse than Nixon	12
About the same	39
No opinion	12

30–49 Years

Better than Nixon	50%
Worse than Nixon	7
About the same	33
No opinion	10

50 Years and Over

Better than Nixon	45%
Worse than Nixon	6
About the same	34
No opinion	15

By Politics
Republicans

Better than Nixon	57%
Worse than Nixon	2
About the same	29
No opinion	12

Democrats

Better than Nixon	35%
Worse than Nixon	12
About the same	42
No opinion	11

Independents

Better than Nixon	44%
Worse than Nixon	9
About the same	33
No opinion	14

In your opinion, should the U.S. government be giving assistance to the guerrilla forces now opposing the Marxist government in Nicaragua?

Should	29%
Should not	58
No opinion	13

By Sex
Male

Should	43%
Should not	48
No opinion	9

Female

Should	16%
Should not	67
No opinion	17

By Ethnic Background
White

Should	30%
Should not	56
No opinion	14

Nonwhite

Should	21%
Should not	70
No opinion	9

By Education
College Graduate

Should	37%
Should not	56
No opinion	7

College Incomplete

Should 31%
Should not 58
No opinion 11

High-School Graduate

Should 26%
Should not 60
No opinion 14

Less Than High-School Graduate

Should 25%
Should not 56
No opinion 19

By Region
East

Should 28%
Should not 58
No opinion 14

Midwest

Should 30%
Should not 55
No opinion 15

South

Should 31%
Should not 59
No opinion 10

West

Should 24%
Should not 60
No opinion 16

By Age
18–29 Years

Should 27%
Should not 63
No opinion 10

30–49 Years

Should 30%
Should not 59
No opinion 11

50 Years and Over

Should 30%
Should not 53
No opinion 17

By Politics
Republicans

Should 42%
Should not 46
No opinion 12

Democrats

Should 18%
Should not 68
No opinion 14

Independents

Should 27%
Should not 59
No opinion 14

Some people feel the United States should try to develop a space-based "Star Wars" system to protect the United States from nuclear attack. Others oppose such an effort because they say it would be too costly and further escalate the arms race. Which comes closer to your view?

Favor 52%
Oppose 40
No opinion 8

By Sex
Male

Favor 62%
Oppose 32
No opinion 6

Female

Favor 43%
Oppose 47
No opinion 10

By Ethnic Background
White

Favor 54%
Oppose 38
No opinion 8

Nonwhite

Favor 38%
Oppose 55
No opinion 7

By Education
College Graduate

Favor 55%
Oppose 38
No opinion 7

College Incomplete

Favor 52%
Oppose 42
No opinion 6

High-School Graduate

Favor 49%
Oppose 45
No opinion 6

Less Than High-School Graduate

Favor 53%
Oppose 33
No opinion 14

By Region
East

Favor 52%
Oppose 39
No opinion 9

Midwest

Favor 48%
Oppose 44
No opinion 8

South

Favor 54%
Oppose 39
No opinion 7

West

Favor 53%
Oppose 38
No opinion 9

By Age
18–29 Years

Favor 44%
Oppose 49
No opinion 7

30–49 Years

Favor 54%
Oppose 42
No opinion 4

50 Years and Over

Favor 56%
Oppose 31
No opinion 13

By Politics
Republicans

Favor 64%
Oppose 27
No opinion 9

Democrats

Favor 42%
Oppose 49
No opinion 9

Independents

Favor 51%
Oppose 43
No opinion 6

Selected National Trend

	Favor	Oppose	No opinion
January 1986	47%	44%	9%
August 1985	45	47	8
September 1984	41	47	12

Note: Three-fourths of Americans think that U.S. influence in world affairs has been either very seriously (36%) or fairly seriously (40%) damaged by the Iran-*contra* affair. Less than one-fourth (22%) believes the damage has not been serious. The current Gallup survey also found a sharp decline in the percentage of Americans expressing satisfaction with the way things are going in the United States, from 58% in a September poll to 47% today.

In addition, survey participants were asked to compare President Ronald Reagan's handling of the Iran-*contra* affair with Richard Nixon's conduct of the Watergate affair in its early stages. The popular consensus is that Reagan is doing a better job than Nixon (45%), with slightly fewer (35%) perceiving about the same performance from each man.

One of the major questions being asked during the Iran-*contra* crisis is: To what extent has public support for the *contras* been affected? In the new survey, opposition to aid for the *contras* outweighs support by a 2-to-1 ratio, 58% to 29%, with 13% expressing no opinion, identical to the results of a *Newsweek* Poll conducted by the Gallup Organization in August 1985.

Perhaps surprisingly, Reagan's declining overall job and foreign policy ratings appear to have had little negative impact on the Strategic Defense Initiative, which the president has vigorously advanced. In fact, the latest survey found a slight increase, from 47% in January to 52% today, in those favoring development of the SDI, popularly called "Star Wars."

DECEMBER 18
ALCOHOL AND DRUG ABUSE

Interviewing Date: 10/24–27/86
Survey #269-G

Please tell me whether you favor or oppose each of the following proposals:

A federal law that would require television and radio stations carrying beer and wine commercials to provide equal time for health and safety warning messages about drinking?

Favor 75%
Oppose 20
No opinion 5

By Sex
Male

Favor 71%
Oppose 23
No opinion 6

Female

Favor 78%
Oppose 17
No opinion 5

By Education
College Graduate

Favor 65%
Oppose 29
No opinion 6

College Incomplete

Favor 75%
Oppose 20
No opinion 5

High-School Graduate

Favor 78%
Oppose 17
No opinion 5

Less Than High-School Graduate

Favor 78%
Oppose 16
No opinion 6

By Age
18–29 Years

Favor 81%
Oppose 13
No opinion 6

30–49 Years

Favor 73%
Oppose 23
No opinion 4

50 Years and Over

Favor 73%
Oppose 21
No opinion 6

A federal law that would require health and safety warning labels on alcoholic beverage containers like those now required on cigarette packages?

Favor 79%
Oppose 18
No opinion 3

By Sex
Male

Favor 74%
Oppose 23
No opinion 3

Female

Favor 84%
Oppose 13
No opinion 3

By Education
College Graduate

Favor 71%
Oppose 25
No opinion 4

College Incomplete

Favor 75%
Oppose 22
No opinion 3

High-School Graduate

Favor 81%
Oppose 15
No opinion 4

Less Than High-School Graduate

Favor 86%
Oppose 12
No opinion 2

By Age
18–29 Years

Favor 82%
Oppose 14
No opinion 4

30–49 Years

Favor 77%
Oppose 20
No opinion 3

50 Years and Over

Favor 79%
Oppose 18
No opinion 3

Doubling the federal excise taxes on alcoholic beverages to raise revenues to fight drug and alcohol abuse?

Favor 66%
Oppose 29
No opinion 5

By Sex

Male

Favor 61%
Oppose 36
No opinion 6

Female

Favor 70%
Oppose 24
No opinion 6

By Education

College Graduate

Favor 60%
Oppose 35
No opinion 5

College Incomplete

Favor 61%
Oppose 36
No opinion 3

High-School Graduate

Favor 67%
Oppose 27
No opinion 6

Less Than High-School Graduate

Favor 73%
Oppose 22
No opinion 5

By Age

18–29 Years

Favor 58%
Oppose 36
No opinion 6

30–49 Years

Favor 65%
Oppose 30
No opinion 5

50 Years and Over

Favor 73%
Oppose 23
No opinion 4

Note: Heavy public support is found for three far-reaching measures to help fight alcohol and drug abuse:

1) Eight persons in ten (79%) in a recent Gallup Poll favor a federal law mandating health and safety warnings on alcoholic beverage containers like those now required on cigarette packages.

2) Almost as many (75%) favor a law that would require television and radio stations that run beer and wine commercials to provide equal time for health and safety warning messages about drinking.

3) Two-thirds (66%) approve of doubling the federal excise taxes on alcoholic beverages to raise funds to combat drug and alcohol abuse.

Slightly greater opposition to these measures is expressed by persons from population groups in which drinking is more prevalent—men, younger adults of both sexes, the better educated, and the more affluent. Nevertheless, large majorities in these groups, as well as their opposite numbers, approve of each of the three measures.

Proposals for equal broadcast time and alcohol warning label legislation were introduced in Congress earlier this year. Although no definitive action was taken, the 100th Congress is expected to consider these and similar measures next year. Alcohol-related problems are believed to be responsible for 100,000 deaths, and economic loss of over $100 billion, each year.

DECEMBER 21
CONFIDENCE IN INSTITUTIONS

Interviewing Date: 7/11–14/86
Survey #266-G

I am going to read you a list of institutions in American society. Would you please tell me how much confidence you, yourself, have in each one—a great deal, quite a lot, some, or very little:

The military?

	Great deal or quite a lot
National	63%

By Sex

Male	64%
Female	60

By Ethnic Background

White	65%
Nonwhite	47
Black	47

By Education

College graduate	53%
College incomplete	67
High-school graduate	66
Less than high-school graduate	62

By Region

East	59%
Midwest	61
South	69
West	62

By Age

18–29 years	59%
30–49 years	60
50 years and over	68

By Income

$40,000 and over	62%
$25,000–$39,999	63
$15,000–$24,999	65
Under $15,000	63

By Politics

Republicans	73%
Democrats	60
Independents	56

Selected National Trend

1985	61%
1983	53
1979	54

Church or organized religion?

	Great deal or quite a lot
National	57%

By Sex

Male	52%
Female	62

By Ethnic Background

White	57%
Nonwhite	62
Black	65

By Education

College graduate	52%
College incomplete	54
High-school graduate	60
Less than high-school graduate	61

By Region

East	53%
Midwest	58
South	67
West	47

By Age

18–29 years	51%
30–49 years	56
50 years and over	62

By Income

$40,000 and over	51%
$25,000–$39,999	55
$15,000–$24,999	64
Under $15,000	58

By Politics

Republicans 60%
Democrats 62
Independents 48

By Religion

Protestants 63%
Catholics 58

Selected National Trend

1985 ....66%
1983 62
1979 65
1973 66

Banks?

	Great deal or quite a lot
National	49%

By Sex

Male 48%
Female 50

By Ethnic Background

White 50%
Nonwhite 40
Black 43

By Education

College graduate 50%
College incomplete 50
High-school graduate 52
Less than high-school graduate 44

By Region

East 47%
Midwest 52
South 52
West 44

By Age

18–29 years 44%
30–49 years 48
50 years and over 54

By Income

$40,000 and over 50%
$25,000–$39,999 51
$15,000–$24,999 49
Under $15,000 49

By Politics

Republicans 55%
Democrats 50
Independents 44

Selected National Trend

1985 ....51%
1983 51
1979 60

Public schools?

	Great deal or quite a lot
National	49%

By Sex

Male 48%
Female 50

By Ethnic Background

White 50%
Nonwhite 41
Black 41

By Education

College graduate 49%
College incomplete 52
High-school graduate 51
Less than high-school graduate 43

By Region

East 45%
Midwest 46
South 56
West 46

By Age

18–29 years	48%
30–49 years	47
50 years and over	51

By Income

$40,000 and over	51%
$25,000–$39,999	50
$15,000–$24,999	54
Under $15,000	44

By Politics

Republicans	49%
Democrats	52
Independents	44

Selected National Trend

1985	48%
1983	39
1979	53
1973	58

U.S. Supreme Court?

	Great deal or quite a lot
National	53%

By Sex

Male	56%
Female	51

By Ethnic Background

White	55%
Nonwhite	42
Black	39

By Education

College graduate	64%
College incomplete	58
High-school graduate	53
Less than high-school graduate	41

By Region

East	58%
Midwest	51
South	52
West	52

By Age

18–29 years	56%
30–49 years	55
50 years and over	50

By Income

$40,000 and over	64%
$25,000–$39,999	56
$15,000–$24,999	53
Under $15,000	45

By Politics

Republicans	57%
Democrats	53
Independents	51

Selected National Trend

1985	56%
1983	42
1979	45
1973	44

Newspapers?

	Great deal or quite a lot
National	37%

By Sex

Male	37%
Female	36

By Ethnic Background

White	37%
Nonwhite	32
Black	30

By Education

College graduate	36%
College incomplete	39
High-school graduate	39
Less than high-school graduate	31

By Region

East	37%
Midwest	34
South	38
West	38

By Age

18–29 years	44%
30–49 years	34
50 years and over	33

By Income

$40,000 and over	33%
$25,000–$39,999	39
$15,000–$24,999	39
Under $15,000	35

By Politics

Republicans	35%
Democrats	40
Independents	34

Selected National Trend

1985	35%
1983	38
1979	51
1973	39

Television?

	Great deal or quite a lot
National	27%

By Sex

Male	27%
Female	27

By Ethnic Background

White	27%
Nonwhite	27
Black	28

By Education

College graduate	17%
College incomplete	20
High-school graduate	31
Less than high-school graduate	36

By Region

East	28%
Midwest	30
South	25
West	28

By Age

18–29 years	31%
30–49 years	24
50 years and over	28

By Income

$40,000 and over	18%
$25,000–$39,999	23
$15,000–$24,999	30
Under $15,000	33

By Politics

Republicans	26%
Democrats	34
Independents	19

Selected National Trend

1985	29%
1983	25
1979	38
1973	37

Organized labor?

	Great deal or quite a lot
National	29%

By Sex

Male 32%
Female 26

National 41%

By Ethnic Background

White 30%
Nonwhite 22
Black 23

By Sex

Male 43%
Female 39

By Education

College graduate 19%
College incomplete 25
High-school graduate 34
Less than high-school graduate 34

By Ethnic Background

White 43%
Nonwhite 28
Black 31

By Education

College graduate 42%
College incomplete 46
High-school graduate 42
Less than high-school graduate 35

By Region

East 29%
Midwest 28
South 31
West 27

By Region

East 43%
Midwest 37
South 44
West 39

By Age

18–29 years 33%
30–49 years 27
50 years and over 28

By Age

18–29 years 43%
30–49 years 40
50 years and over 41

By Income

$40,000 and over 22%
$25,000–$39,999 32
$15,000–$24,999 31
Under $15,000 27

By Income

$40,000 and over 41%
$25,000–$39,999 47
$15,000–$24,999 43
Under $15,000 37

By Politics

Republicans 21%
Democrats 40
Independents 22

By Politics

Republicans 41%
Democrats 45
Independents 36

Selected National Trend

1985 ....28%
1983 26
1979 36
1973 30

By Politics

Republicans	36%
Democrats	25
Independents	25

Selected National Trend

1985	39%
1983	28
1979	34
1973	42

Big business?

	Great deal or quite a lot
National	28%

By Sex

Male	32%
Female	24

By Ethnic Background

White	30%
Nonwhite	16
Black	15

By Education

College graduate	31%
College incomplete	35
High-school graduate	25
Less than high-school graduate	23

By Region

East	27%
Midwest	28
South	30
West	28

By Age

18–29 years	36%
30–49 years	26
50 years and over	26

By Income

$40,000 and over	38%
$25,000–$39,999	29
$15,000–$24,999	24
Under $15,000	27

Selected National Trend

1985	31%
1983	28
1979	32
1973	26

Note: For the first time in over a decade, the church or organized religion has lost its primacy as the institution in which the American people have the greatest confidence. That distinction went to the military in a July Gallup Poll, the latest to assess the public's trust. In surveys conducted periodically since 1975, the military had been the second or third highest rated institution.

In the current survey, 63% said they had a great deal or quite a lot of confidence in the military, statistically unchanged from the 61% recorded in last year's poll. Organized religion, in which 66% indicated a high degree of confidence in 1985, fell to 57% in the 1986 survey. In seven previous surveys, the percentage expressing a great deal or quite a lot of confidence in the church had ranged from a high of 68% (in 1975) to a low of 62% (in 1983).

Consistent with the results of earlier surveys, Protestants, women, blacks, older Americans, southerners, and the less well educated and less affluent currently express greater confidence in the church than do people from different socioeconomic backgrounds. Comparison of the results of the 1986 and 1985 polls, however, shows the recent decline in confidence to have occurred among all population groups, including those mentioned above.

The U.S. Supreme Court is the third highest rated institution, with 53% currently expressing confidence. Tied for fourth are banks and public schools, each with 49%. The other institutions studied and the percentages saying they have a great deal or quite a lot of confidence in each are Congress (41%), newspapers (37%), organized labor (29%), big business (28%), and television (27%).

Aside from the 9-percentage point drop for organized religion, the current figures for the other institutions are not statistically different from those obtained in the 1985 poll.

DECEMBER 25
FAMILY LIFE

Interviewing Date: 10/10–11/10/86
Special Telephone Survey

How satisfied would you say you are with your own family life at this time—would you say you are very satisfied, mostly satisfied, mostly dissatisfied, or very dissatisfied with your family life at this time?*

	1986	1980
Very satisfied	45%	47%
Mostly satisfied	48	44
Mostly dissatisfied	3	6
Very dissatisfied	2	2
No opinion	2	1

To what extent, if at all, has religion in your home strengthened family relationships—a great deal, somewhat, hardly at all, or not at all?

	1986	1980
A great deal	35%	39%
Somewhat	37	35
Hardly at all	16	12
Not at all	10	11
No opinion	2	3

As a general rule, would you say that the family life of most of the people you know has gotten better or gotten worse in the last fifteen years or so?

*The 1980 findings are from a survey conducted by the Gallup Organization for the White House Conference on Families.

	1986	1980
Better	53%	37%
Worse	33	45
Same	8	12
No opinion	6	6

Note: Despite the high divorce rate, alcohol and drug use, poverty, and other problems that are undermining the U.S. family, as high a proportion of Americans today (45%) as in 1980 (47%) say they are very satisfied with their family life. In the current survey, as in 1980, about equal proportions say they are very or mostly satisfied; few in either survey express dissatisfaction. Younger persons and survey respondents with relatively little formal education are less likely than their counterparts to be very satisfied with their family life.

Religion is seen by a large majority of Americans (72%) as strengthening family relationships either a great deal or somewhat. Only about one person in four (26%) says hardly at all or not at all. Little change in the perceptions of religion's impact is noted since the 1980 survey.

Undoubtedly reflecting in considerable measure the improved overall economic climate, a higher proportion of Americans today (53%) than in 1980 think the family life of most of the people they know has gotten better. The comparable figure in the earlier survey was 37%.

DECEMBER 28
CHURCH/SYNAGOGUE ATTENDANCE

Interviewing Date: Five Selected Weeks during 1986
Various Surveys

Did you, yourself, happen to attend church or synagogue in the last seven days?

	Yes
National	40%

By Sex

Male	33%
Female	46

By Ethnic Background

White 40%
Black 43
Hispanic 46

By Education

College graduate 42%
College incomplete 41
High-school graduate 40
Less than high-school graduate 38

By Region

East 39%
Midwest 42
South 43
West 35

By Age

18–24 years 33%
25–29 years 33
30–49 years 39
50–64 years 47
65 years and over 49

By Religion

Protestants 41%
Catholics 49
Jews 20

Selected National Trend

	Yes
1985	42%
1984	40

1983	40
1982	41
1981	41
1980	40
1979	40
1978	41
1977	41
1972	40
1969	42
1967	43
1962	46
1958	49
1957	47
1955	49
1954	46
1950	39
1940	37
1939	41

Note: Four adults in every ten (40%) attended church or synagogue in a typical week in 1986. Churchgoing has remained remarkably constant since 1969, after having declined from the high point of 49% recorded in 1955 and 1958.

The level of churchgoing in 1986 was higher among women (46% attended in a typical week) than men (33%), and among older persons than younger. Nationally, 49% of Catholics, 41% of Protestants, and 20% of Jews attended. Southerners and midwesterners were most apt to attend church weekly, while westerners had the lowest level of attendance. Blacks and Hispanics are slightly more likely than whites to attend church in a typical week.

INDEX

A

Abortion
    in instructional program in elementary school, 28
    in instructional program in high school, 28
    Supreme Court ruling to end pregnancy during first
        three months, 49-51
Aerobics and dancercize
    participated in by women, 249
AIDS (Acquired Immune Deficiency Syndrome)
    heard or read about, 79
    permit your children to attend classes with a child
        who had AIDS, 80-82
    person can get, by being in crowded place, 79-80
Airlines
    quality of service received from, 60
Alcohol abuse
    alcohol as most serious among other drugs, 191-92
    drinking/alcoholism, as biggest problem with which
        public schools must deal, 29, 222
    drinking/alcoholism, as biggest problem with which
        school your oldest child attends must deal, 222
    require television and radio stations carrying beer and
        wine commercials to provide equal time about
        drinking, 270-71
Alcoholic beverages
    anyone had too much to drink to drive safely, 19
    double federal excise taxes on, to raise revenues to
        fight drug and alcohol abuse, 271-72
    drinking as cause of trouble in your family, 19
    increasing taxes on, for public schools, 227
    require warning labels on containers for, 271
    your use of, 18
    you sometimes drink more than you should, 18-19
    j*see also* Drinking age
Aquino, Corazon. *See* Philippines
Arab states
    military action against Libya, and peace between
        Israel and, 86
Argentina, questions asked in
    arms control talks between United States and Soviet

Union have increased chance of nuclear war,
    130
    chances of world war breaking out, 2
    heard about resumption of arms control talks between
        Soviet Union and United States, 130
    how often do you talk about chances of nuclear war,
        131
    important for United States and Soviet Union to sign
        arms control treaty, 129
    most people feel that chance of nuclear war has
        increased as consequence of arms control talks,
        130
    1986 as peaceful or troubled year, 3
    predictions for 1986, 1
    strikes will increase in 1986, 5
    your sources of information about problems of rear-
        mament and disarmament, 131
Arms control
    heard about resumption of talks between Soviet
        Union and United States, in opinion of twenty-
        one nations, 130
    important for United States and Soviet Union to sign
        treaty, in opinion of twenty-one nations, 129-30
    most people feel that chance of nuclear war has
        increased as consequence of talks, in opinion of
        twenty-one nations, 130
    talks between United States and Soviet Union have
        increased chance of nuclear war, in opinion of
        twenty-one nations, 130
    your sources of information about problems of rear-
        mament and disarmament, in opinion of twenty-
        one nations, 131
    see also SALT II
Arms sales ban
    arms trade would be reduced by UN resolution, 88-
        89
    UN resolution to request all nations not to sell arms
        to other nations, 87-88
Armstrong, William
    have heard of, 156, 240
Australia, questions asked in
    chances of world war breaking out, 2
    1986 as peaceful or troubled year, 3
    predictions for 1986, 1
    strikes will increase in 1986, 4
Austria, questions asked in
    1986 as peaceful or troubled year, 3
    predictions for 1986, 2
    strikes will increase in 1986, 4
Auto repair
    quality of service received in, 61

B

Babbitt, Bruce
    have heard of, 41, 91, 155, 242
    as nominee for Democratic presidential candidate,
        41, 91

Baker, Howard
  have heard of, 89, 156, 240
  as nominee for Republican presidential candidate, 89,
      90, 157, 240
    national trend, 157, 241
  as Republican convention choice vs. Bush, 157, 216
Baker, James
  have heard of, 89, 156, 240
  as nominee for Republican presidential candidate, 90,
      240
    national trend, 241
Banks
  confidence in, 274
    national trend, 274
  quality of service received in, 60
Baptists
  religious preference, by national trend, 15
Baseball
  boys and girls allowed on same school teams, 28
Basketball
  boys and girls allowed on same school teams, 28
  participated in, 249
    by men, 249
Behavior
  satisfied with honesty and standards of behavior of
      people today, 105-06
    national trend, 106
Belgium, questions asked in
  arms control talks between United States and Soviet
      Union have increased chance of nuclear war,
      130
  chances of world war breaking out, 3
  heard about resumption of arms control talks between
      Soviet Union and United States, 130
  how often do you talk about chances of nuclear war,
      131
  important for United States and Soviet Union to sign
      arms control treaty, 129
  most people feel that chance of nuclear war has in-
      creased as consequence of arms control talks, 130
  1986 as peaceful or troubled year, 3
  predictions for 1986, 2
  strikes will increase in 1986, 4
  your sources of information about problems of rear-
      mament and disarmament, 131
Bible
  how often do you read, 243-45
    national trend, 245
  and public schools offering elective courses in Bible
      studies, 243
  and public schools using, in literature and other
      classes, 243
  read by Catholics, within last thirty days, 62
Bicycling
  participated in, 249
    by men and women, 249
Biden, Joseph
  have heard of, 41, 91, 155, 242

  as nominee for Democratic presidential candidate,
      41, 91
Big business
  confidence in, 278
    national trend, 278
Billiards
  participated in, 249
    by men and women, 249
Birth control
  in instructional program in elementary school, 28
  in instructional program in high school, 27
Body building
  participated in, 249
Bolivia, questions asked in
  chances of world war breaking out, 2
  1986 as peaceful or troubled year, 3
  predictions for 1986, 1
  strikes will increase in 1986, 5
Books
  as source of information about problems of rearma-
      ment and disarmament, 131
  standard in determining whether book is obscene,
      176
    national trend, 176
"Born-again" Christians. See Evangelicals
Bowling
  participated in, 249
    by men and women, 249
    national trend, 249
Bradley, Bill
  have heard of, 41, 91, 154, 241
  as nominee for Democratic presidential candidate,
      41, 91, 155, 242
    national trend, 155, 242
Bradley, Tom
  have heard of, 40, 91, 154, 241
  as nominee for Democratic presidential candidate,
      41, 91, 155, 242
    national trend, 155, 242
Brazil, questions asked in
  arms control talks between United States and Soviet
      Union have increased chance of nuclear war,
      130
  chances of world war breaking out, 2
  heard about resumption of arms control talks between
      Soviet Union and United States, 130
  how often do you talk about chances of nuclear war,
      131
  important for United States and Soviet Union to sign
      arms control treaty, 129
  most people feel that chance of nuclear war has
      increased as consequence of arms control talks,
      130
  1986 as peaceful or troubled year, 3
  predictions for 1986, 1
  strikes will increase in 1986, 5
  your sources of information about problems of rear-
      mament and disarmament, 131

Brock, William
  have heard of, 89, 156, 240
  as nominee for Republican presidential candidate, 90
Budget deficit (federal)
  and Gramm-Rudman-Hollings Act, 47
  handled by Reagan, 153
  as most important problem, 48, 179, 237
    national trend, 48
  reduce by making cuts in defense spending, 45
  reduce by making cuts in "entitlement" programs, 45
  reduce by making cuts in social programs, 43-45
    national trend, 45
  reduce by raising income taxes, 43
Bumpers, Dale
  have heard of, 41, 91, 155, 242
  as nominee for Democratic presidential candidate,
    41, 91
Bush, George
  have heard of, 89, 156, 240
  as nominee for Republican presidential candidate, 89,
    90, 157, 240
    national trend, 157, 241
  as Republican convention choice vs. Baker, 157, 216
  as Republican convention choice vs. Dole, 157, 216
  as Republican convention choice vs. Kemp, 157, 216
  in trial heats vs. Cuomo, 42, 92, 177-78, 210-11,
    237, 248
    national trend, 92, 178, 211, 248
    viewed by Evangelicals, 237
  in trial heats vs. Hart, 41-42, 92, 177, 210, 237, 247
    national trend, 92, 177, 210
    viewed by Evangelicals, 237, 248
  in trial heats vs. Iacocca, 178, 211, 248
    national trend, 211, 248

C

Calisthenics
  participated in, 249
  by women, 249
Camping
  participated in, 249
  by men and women, 249
Canada, questions asked in
  arms control talks between United States and Soviet
    Union have increased chance of nuclear war,
    130
  chances of world war breaking out, 2
  heard about resumption of arms control talks between
    Soviet Union and United States, 130
  how often do you talk about chances of nuclear war,
    131
  important for United States and Soviet Union to sign
    arms control treaty, 129
  most people feel that chance of nuclear war has
    increased as consequence of arms control talks,
    130

1986 as peaceful or troubled year, 3
predictions for 1986, 1
strikes will increase in 1986, 4
your sources of information about problems of rearmament and disarmament, 131
Canoeing
  participated in, 249
Cards and games
  as favorite pastime, 104
Carter, Jimmy
  as outstanding president, 71
Catholic Church
  and changes since Second Vatican Council, 186
  involvement in politics and public policy, 187
  and marriage annulment system, 187
  official position whether sexual morals should be
    changed or not, 232
  priest/professor forbidden by Vatican to teach on sex-
    ual morals, 232
  relations with non-Christians, 186
  role of lay people in, 186
  role of women in, 187
  serving the needs of the elderly, 187
  serving the needs of families, 187
  serving the needs of minorities, 187
  serving the needs of new immigrants, 187
  serving the needs of separated, divorced, and remar-
    ried Catholics, 187
  serving the needs of single people, 187
  serving your own needs, 187
Catholics (Roman Catholics)
  approval of Vatican decision forbidding priest/
    professor to teach on sexual morals, 232
  heard about priest/professor forbidden by Vatican to
    teach on sexual morals, 232
  religious activities you have done within last thirty
    days, 62
  religious preference, 15
    increase in, 16
    national trend, 15
Child care centers
  make available for all preschool children, 30-31
Chile, questions asked in
  chances of world war breaking out, 2
  1986 as peaceful or troubled year, 3
  predictions for 1986, 1
  strikes will increase in 1986, 5
Church
  confidence in, 273-74
    national trend, 274
  did you attend, in last seven days, 279-80
    national trend, 280
Church-related schools. See Parochial schools
Cigarette smoking
  increase cigarette and tobacco taxes, to raise money
    for public schools, 227
  in past week, 118
    national trend, 118

Clinton, Bill
  have heard of, 155, 242
Coelho, Tony
  have heard of, 41, 91, 155, 242
  as nominee for Democratic presidential candidate,
    41, 91
College education
  advantages of, listed, 32
  importance of, 32
Colombia, questions asked in
  chances of world war breaking out, 2
  1986 as peaceful or troubled year, 3
  predictions for 1986, 1
  strikes will increase in 1986, 5
Congress
  confidence in, 277
    national trend, 278
  heard about debate in, over interstate sale of hand-
    guns, 96
  role in deciding about future military retaliation
    against terrorism, 86
Congressional elections
  party preference in, 62-64, 65, 179
    national trend, 179
Conservatives
  and your political position, 114-16
    national trend, 116
    by party affiliation, 117
Constitution
  does not give consenting adults right to private homo-
    sexual relations, 214-15
  repeal 22d Amendment limiting presidents to two
    terms, 217-18
Contras. See Iran-contra affair; Nicaragua
Costa Rica, questions asked in
  chances of world war breaking out, 2
  1986 as peaceful or troubled year, 3
  predictions for 1986, 1
  strikes will increase in 1986, 5
Cost of living
  amount needed each week for family of four, 117
    national trend, 117
  amount needed each week by your family, 117
  amount spent by your family on food each week, 103
    national trend, 104
  as most important problem, 48, 237
    national trend, 48
Crime
  as most important problem, 48, 179, 237
    national trend, 48
  and vandalism, as biggest problem with which public
    schools must deal, 29, 222
Cuomo, Mario
  as Democratic convention choice vs. Hart, 155, 212
  have heard of, 41, 91, 154, 241
  as nominee for Democratic presidential candidate,
    41, 91, 92, 155, 189-90, 242
    national trend, 155, 190, 242

in trial heats vs. Bush, 42, 92, 177-78, 210-11, 237,
  248
  national trend, 92, 178, 211, 248
  viewed by Evangelicals, 237

D

Dancing
  as favorite pastime, 104
Daylight saving time
  extending another three or four weeks each year,
    127-28
Death penalty
  acts as deterrent, 58
  approval, if death penalty does not act as deterrent,
    58
  approval rating by 65-and-older age group, 14
  or life imprisonment, for murder, 57
  opposing, if death penalty acts as deterrent, 59
  for persons convicted of murder, 55-57
    how strongly you favor, 57
    jnational trend, 57
Defense
  amount government should spend for, 78, 79
    national trend, 78
  building strongest military force, 251-52
    national trend, 252
  how many cents are wasted of tax dollar spent for,
    78
  United States or Soviet Union stronger in nuclear
    weapons, 78, 79, 120
    national trend, 78
  see also Nuclear weapons
Defense spending
  make cuts in, to reduce federal budget deficit, 45
Democratic party
  affiliation with, 16-18, 145- 47, 237
    by Evangelicals, 237
    national trend, 18, 147
  better for handling most important problem, 48, 180
    national trend, 48, 180
  better for keeping country prosperous, 100, 239
    national trend, 100, 239
  degree of liberals, moderates, and conservatives in,
    117
  Gallup analysis of, 194
  more likely to keep United States out of war, 100,
    238
    national trend, 100, 239
  nominees for presidential candidate, 40-41, 90-92,
    154-55, 189-90, 241-42
    national trend, 155, 190, 242
  preference for, in congressional elections, 62-64, 65,
    179
    national trend, 179

Denmark, questions asked in
arms control talks between United States and Soviet Union have increased chance of nuclear war, 130
chances of world war breaking out, 3
heard about resumption of arms control talks between Soviet Union and United States, 130
how often do you talk about chances of nuclear war, 131
important for United States and Soviet Union to sign arms control treaty, 129
most people feel that chance of nuclear war has increased as consequence of arms control talks, 130
1986 as peaceful or troubled year, 3
predictions for 1986, 1
strikes will increase in 1986, 4
your sources of information about problems of rearmament and disarmament, 131
Department stores
quality of service received in, 60
Dining out
as favorite pastime, 104
Dole, Elizabeth
have heard of, 89, 156, 240
as nominee for Republican presidential candidate, 90, 157, 240
national trend, 157, 241
Dole, Robert
have heard of, 89, 156, 240
as nominee for Republican presidential candidate, 89, 90, 157, 240
national trend, 157, 241
as Republican convention choice vs. Bush, 157, 216
Domenici, Pete
have heard of, 89, 156, 240
as nominee for Republican presidential candidate, 90
Drinking age
law to raise in all states to 21, 19, 120-21
national trend, 121
law to withhold federal highway funds from states with minimum age below 21, 121-22
Drug abuse
activities listed, in government's fight against, 192-93
double federal excise taxes on alcoholic beverages to raise revenues to fight alcohol and, 271-72
marijuana, alcohol, heroin, crack, other cocaine, or other drug is most serious, 191-92
money and effort spent by government in fighting, 193
as most important problem, 179, 237
possession of marijuana treated as criminal offense, 191
national trend, 191
use of drugs, as biggest problem with which public schools must deal, 29, 222
use of drugs, as biggest problem with which school your oldest child attends must deal, 222
see also Public schools

Dukakis, Michael
have heard of, 242
as nominee for Democratic presidential candidate, 242
national trend, 242
Du Pont, Pierre
have heard of, 89, 156, 240
as nominee for Republican presidential candidate, 90

E

Economic conditions
handled by Reagan, 33-34, 153, 256-57
national trend, 35, 257
Economy
how long recovery will last, 82-83, 194-96
as most important problem, 48, 179, 237
national trend, 48
new tax reform bill will have positive effect on, 198
Education
advantages of, listed, 225-26
advantages of college, listed, 32
developing best system, 252-53
national trend, 253
see also Public schools
Eisenhower, Dwight
approval rating vs. Reagan and other presidents, 6, 113, 186
Elderly people
Catholic Church serving the needs of, 187
involved yourself in helping, 99
national trend, 99
problems of, as most important problem, 48
national trend, 48
Elderly people, views of 65-and-older age group
on death penalty, 14
on increasing chances of nuclear war, 14
on Reagan, 14
on Star Wars, 14
"Entitlement" programs
make cuts in, to reduce federal budget deficit, 45-47
national trend, 47
Episcopalians
religious preference, by national trend, 15
Evangelicals ("born-again" Christians)
and most important problem, 237
political affiliation of, by party, 237
satisfied with way things are going in the United States, 237
satisfied with way things are going in your personal life, 237
and trial heats between Bush and Cuomo, 237
and trial heats between Bush and Hart, 237
yourself a "born-again" or evangelical Christian, 236

F

Families
    Catholic Church serving the needs of, 187
Family life
    has religion in your home strengthened family rela-
        tionships, 279
    of most people you know, has gotten better, 279
    satisfied with your own, 279
    traditional or liberal values about, 110-12
Family size
    ideal number of children, 101-02
        national trend, 103
Farmers, problems of
    as most important problem, 48
        national trend, 48
Feinstein, Dianne
    have heard of, 41, 91, 154, 241
    as nominee for Democratic presidential candidate,
        41, 91, 155
        national trend, 155
Finances. *See* Personal finances
Finland, questions asked in
    arms control talks between United States and Soviet
        Union have increased chance of nuclear war,
        130
    chances of world war breaking out, 3
    heard about resumption of arms control talks between
        Soviet Union and United States, 130
    how often do you talk about chances of nuclear war,
        131
    important for United States and Soviet Union to sign
        arms control treaty, 129
    most people feel that chance of nuclear war has
        increased as consequence of arms control talks,
        130
    1986 as peaceful or troubled year, 3
    predictions for 1986, 2
    strikes will increase in 1986, 4
    your sources of information about problems of rear-
        mament and disarmament, 131
Fishing
    participated in, 249
        by men and women, 249
        national trend, 249
Flag
    display American, outside your home, 125-26
Football
    boys and girls allowed on same school teams, 28
Ford, Gerald
    as outstanding president, 71
Foreign policy
    handled by Reagan, 35-36, 153, 257-59
        national trend, 36, 259
    Reagan makes wise use of military forces to solve
        problems of, 86
France, questions asked in
    approval rating of U.S. raid on Libya, 87

arms control talks between United States and Soviet
    Union have increased chance of nuclear war,
    130
chances for world war breaking out, 2
heard about resumption of arms control talks between
    Soviet Union and United States, 130
how often do you talk about chances of nuclear war,
    131
important for United States and Soviet Union to sign
    arms control treaty, 129
most people feel that chance of nuclear war has
    increased as consequence of arms control talks,
    130
1986 as peaceful or troubled year, 3
predictions for 1986, 2
strikes will increase in 1986, 4
your sources of information about problems of rear-
    mament and disarmament, 131
Frisbee
    participated in, 249

G

Gasoline
    increase taxes on, to raise money for public schools,
        227
Gephardt, Richard
    have heard of, 41, 91, 155, 242
    as nominee for Democratic presidential candidate,
        41, 91
Gingrich, Newt
    have heard of, 89
    as nominee for Republican presidential candidate, 90
Golf
    participated in, 249
        national trend, 249
Government (local)
    quality of service received from, 61
Gramm-Rudman-Hollings Act
    to cut federal deficit, 47
Great Britain, questions asked in
    approval rating of U.S. raid on Libya, 87
    arms control talks between United States and Soviet
        Union have increased chance of nuclear war,
        130
    chances of world war breaking out, 3
    heard about resumption of arms control talks between
        Soviet Union and United States, 130
    how often do you talk about chances of nuclear war,
        131
    important for United States and Soviet Union to sign
        arms control treaty, 129
    most people feel that chance of nuclear war has
        increased as consequence of arms control talks,
        130
    1986 as peaceful or trouble year, 3
    predictions for 1986, 1

strikes will increase in 1986, 4
your sources of information about problems of rearmament and disarmament, 131
Greece, questions asked in
chances of world war breaking out, 3
1986 as peaceful or troubled year, 3
predictions for 1986, 2
strikes will increase in 1986, 4
Greek Orthodox
religious preference, 15

H

Haig, Alexander
have heard of, 89, 156, 240
as nominee for Republican presidential candidate, 89,
90, 157, 240
national trend, 157, 241
Halley's Comet
heard or read about, 54
seen, 54-55
Handguns
federal ban on interstate sales of, 96-97
heard about debate in Congress over interstate sale
of, 96
laws banning sale and possession of, 94-96
national trend, 96
laws covering sale of, 93-94
national trend, 94
Hart, Gary
as Democratic convention choice vs. Cuomo, 155,
212
as Democratic convention choice vs. Iacocca, 155-
56, 212
as Democratic convention choice vs. Jackson, 155,
212
have heard of, 40, 91, 154, 241
as nominee for Democratic presidential candidate,
41, 91, 92, 155, 189-90, 242
national trend, 155, 190, 242
in trial heats vs. Bush, 41-42, 92, 177, 210, 237,
247
national trend, 92, 177, 210, 248
viewed by Evangelicals, 237
Helms, Jesse
have heard of, 89, 156, 240
as nominee for Republican presidential candidate, 90,
157, 240
national trend, 157, 241
Hiking
participated in, 249
Home schools
movement toward, 32
required to meet same standards as public schools, 32
Homosexuality
in instructional program in elementary school, 28
in instructional program in high school, 28

relations legal between consenting adults, 213-14
national trend, 214
ruling that Constitution does not give consenting
adults right to private homosexual relations,
214-15
Honesty
how many running government of state are dishonest,
246
how many running local government are dishonest,
246-47
overall level of ethics and honesty in politics, 246
satisfied with honesty and standards of behavior of
people today, 105-06
national trend, 106
Hospitals
quality of service received in, 60
Hotels
quality of service received in, 60
Hunger
as most important problem, 48, 179, 237
national trend, 48
Hunting
participated in, 249

I

Iacocca, Lee
as Democratic convention choice vs. Hart, 155-56,
212
have heard of, 40, 91, 154, 241
as nominee for Democratic presidential candidate,
41, 91, 92, 155, 189-90, 242
national trend, 155, 190, 242
in trial heats vs. Bush, 178, 211, 248
national trend, 211, 248
Iceland, questions asked in
chances of world war breaking out, 3
1986 as peaceful or troubled year, 3
predictions for 1986, 1
strikes will increase in 1986, 5
Immigrants
Catholic Church serving the needs of new, 187
Independents
affiliation with, 16-18, 145-47, 237
by Evangelicals, 237
national trend, 18, 147
degree of liberals, moderates, and conservatives, 117
India, questions asked in
arms control talks between United States and Soviet
Union have increased chance of nuclear war,
130
chances of world war breaking out, 3
heard about resumption of arms control talks between
Soviet Union and United States, 130
how often do you talk about chances of nuclear war,
131

India (*continued*)
  important for United States and Soviet Union to sign
    arms control treaty, 129
  most people feel that chance of nuclear war has
    increased as consequence of arms control talks,
    130
  1986 as peaceful or troubled year, 3
  predictions for 1986, 1
  strikes will increase in 1986, 5
  your sources of information about problems of rear-
    mament and disarmament, 131
Industrial production
  developing the most efficient system, 250-51
    national trend, 251
Insurance companies
  quality of service received from, 60-61
Intercourse, nature of
  in instructional program in elementary school, 28
  in instructional program in high school, 28
Interest payments. *See* Tax reform
International tensions
  as most important problem, 48, 179, 237
    national trend, 48
Iran
  United States should conduct bombing raids against,
    if Iran commits terrorist acts, 85
Iran-*contra* affair
  handled by Reagan better than Nixon handled Water-
    gate, 266-67
  has damaged America's influence in world affairs,
    264-66
IRAs (Individual Retirement Accounts)
  no longer able to deduct cost of, under Senate plan,
    136
Ireland, Republic of, questions asked in
  arms control talks between United States and Soviet
    Union have increased chance of nuclear war,
    130
  chances of world war breaking out, 2
  heard about resumption of arms control talks between
    Soviet Union and United States, 130
  how often do you talk about chances of nuclear war,
    131
  important for United States and Soviet Union to sign
    arms control treaty, 129
  most people feel that chance of nuclear war has
    increased as consequence of arms control talks,
    130
  1986 as peaceful or troubled year, 3
  predictions for 1986, 1
  strikes will increase in 1986, 4
  your sources of information about problems of rear-
    mament and disarmament, 131
Israel
  military action against Libya, and peace between
    Arab neighbors and, 86
Italy, questions asked in
  chances of world war breaking out, 3

  1986 as peaceful or troubled year, 3
  predictions for 1986, 1
  strikes will increase in 1986, 4

J

Jackson, Jesse
  as Democratic convention choice vs. Hart, 155, 212
  have heard of, 40, 91, 154, 241
  as nominee for Democratic presidential candidate,
    41, 91, 92, 155, 189-90, 242
    national trend, 155, 190, 242
Japan, questions asked in
  arms control talks between United States and Soviet
    Union have increased chance of nuclear war,
    130
  chances of world war breaking out, 3
  heard about resumption of arms control talks between
    Soviet Union and United States, 130
  how often do you talk about chances of nuclear war,
    131
  important for United States and Soviet Union to sign
    arms control treaty, 129
  most people feel that chance of nuclear war has
    increased as consequence of arms control talks,
    130
  1986 as peaceful or troubled year, 3
  predictions for 1986, 2
  strikes will increase in 1986, 5
  your sources of information about problems of rear-
    mament and disarmament, 131
Jews
  religious preference, 15
    decrease in, 16
    national trend, 15
  see also Synagogue
Jogging
  do you happen to jog, 180-81
    national trend, 181
  how far do you usually jog, 181
    national trend, 181
  how often do you jog, 181
    national trend, 181
  participated in, 249
    by men and women, 249
Johnson, Lyndon
  approval rating vs. Reagan and other presidents, 6,
    113, 186
Journalists
  should participate in future space shuttle flights as
    civilian astronauts, 69

K

Kaddafi, Muammar
  what role does he play in international terrorism, 86

Movies (*continued*)
  standard in determining whether movie is obscene,
    176
    national trend, 176
  that depict sexual violence, 160-63
  theaters showing X-rated, and sexual violence, 169-
    72

N

NASA (National Aeronautics and Space Administration)
  will be able to prevent accidents in the future, 68
  see also Space shuttle
Netherlands, questions asked in
  arms control talks between United States and Soviet
    Union have increased chance of nuclear war,
    130
  chances of world war breaking out, 3
  heard about resumption of arms control talks between
    Soviet Union and United States, 130
  how often do you talk about chances of nuclear war,
    131
  important for United States and Soviet Union to sign
    arms control treaty, 129
  most people feel that chance of nuclear war has
    increased as consequence of arms control talks,
    130
  1986 as peaceful or troubled year, 3
  predictions for 1986, 1
  strikes will increase in 1986, 4
  your sources of information about problems of rearma-
    ment and disarmament, 131
Newspapers
  confidence in, 275-76
    national trend, 276
  as source of information about problems of rearma-
    ment and disarmament, 131
Nicaragua
  situation in, handled by Reagan, 154, 261-62
    national trend, 262
  U.S. assistance to guerrilla forces opposing Marxist
    government in, 267-68
  U.S. military and nonmilitary aid to rebels, 65-66
  see also Iran-*contra* affair
Nigeria, questions asked in
  arms control talks between United States and Soviet
    Union have increased chance of nuclear war,
    130
  heard about resumption of arms control talks between
    Soviet Union and United States, 130
  how often do you talk about chances of nuclear war,
    131
  important for United States and Soviet Union to sign
    arms control treaty, 129
  most people feel that chance of nuclear war has
    increased as consequence of arms control talks,
    130

your sources of information about problems of rearmament and disarmament, 131
Nixon, Richard
  approval rating vs. Reagan and other presidents, 6,
    113, 186
  Reagan handling Iran-*contra* affair better than Nixon
    handled Watergate, 266-67
Norway, questions asked in
  arms control talks between United States and Soviet
    Union have increased chance of nuclear war,
    130
  chances of world war breaking out, 2
  heard about resumption of arms control talks between
    Soviet Union and United States, 130
  how often do you talk about chances of nuclear war,
    131
  important for United States and Soviet Union to sign
    arms control treaty, 129
  most people feel that chance of nuclear war has jin-
    creased as consequence of arms control talks,
    130
  1986 as peaceful or troubled year, 3
  predictions for 1986, 1
  strikes will increase in 1986, 4
  your sources of information about problems of rear-
    mament and disarmament, 131
Nuclear disarmament
  negotiations handled by Reagan, 39-40, 154
    national trend, 40
Nuclear power plants
  how about construction of, in this area, 142-44
    national trend, 144
  important to have more, 139-41
    national trend, 141
  safe enough with present regulations, 141-42
    national trend, 142
Nuclear war
  arms control talks between United States and Soviet
    Union have increased chance of, in opinion of
    twenty-one nations, 130
  how often do you talk about chances of, in opinion
    of twenty-one nations, 130-31
  most people feel that chance of nuclear war has
    increased as consequence of arms control talks,
    in opinion of twenty-one nations, 130
Nuclear weapons
  arms buildup here and in Soviet Union increases
    chances of war, 14, 107-08
    national trend, 108
  United States or Soviet Union stronger in, 78, 79,
    120
    national trend, 78
  U.S. ban on nuclear testing if Soviet Union continues
    their ban, 108-09
  see also SALT II; "Star Wars"
Nudity
  magazines that show, and sexual violence, 165-
    67

Nunn, Sam
    have heard of, 41, 91, 155, 241
    as nominee for Democratic presidential candidate,
        41, 91

O

Obscenity
    nationwide or community standard in determining
        whether book, magazine, or movie is obscene,
        176
    national trend, 176
    see also Sexual violence
Orthodox churches
    religious preference, 15

P

Packwood, Robert
    have heard of, 89, 156, 240
    as nominee for Republican presidential candidate, 90
Parochial (church-related) schools
    giving government tax money to help, 231
    have you any children in, 221-22
    increase in number of, 31-32
    send your children to private or, 231
    support for voucher system, 32, 231
        national trend, 32
    use voucher to enroll your oldest child in another
        public, private, or church-related school, 232
Pastimes
    your favorite way of spending an evening, 104
Peace
    chances of world war breaking out, in opinion of
        thirty-five nations, 2-3
    1986 as peaceful or troubled year, in opinion of
        thirty-five nations, 3
Peace (keeping out of war)
    Republican or Democratic party more likely to keep
        United States out of war, 100, 238
        national trend, 100, 239
Personal finances
    better off next year than now, 53, 73, 150-51
        national trend, 53, 73
        national trend in "super optimists," 73, 151
    better off now than a year ago, 52-53, 72, 148-50
        national trend, 53, 72-73, 150
Peru, questions asked in
    chances of world war breaking out, 2
    1986 as peaceful or troubled year, 3
    predictions for 1986, 1
    strikes will increase in 1986, 5
Philippines
    Aquino government has better chance of preventing
        Communist takeover than Marcos, 71

change in government in best interests of United
        States, 71
    tie American aid to agreement that United States can
        maintain its military bases, 72
    United States should increase economic aid to, 72
Philippines, questions asked in
    chances of world war breaking out, 2
    1986 as peaceful or troubled year, 3
    predictions for 1986, 1
    strikes will increase in 1986, 5
Physical fitness
    do anything regularly that helps keep you fit, 187-88
        national trend, 188
    membership in health club, 188
Political affiliation
    by ideology, 117
    by party, 16-18, 117, 145-47, 237
        of Evangelicals, 237
        national trend, 18, 147
Political ideology
    from conservative to liberal, 114-16
        national trend, 116
    by party affiliation, 117
Politicians
    should participate in future space shuttle flights as
        civilian astronauts, 69
Pool
    participated in, 249
        by men and women, 249
Poor people
    involved yourself in helping, 99
        national trend, 99
Portugal, questions asked in
    arms control talks between United States and Soviet
        Union have increased chance of nuclear war, 130
    chances of world war breaking out, 2
    heard about resumption of arms control talks between
        Soviet Union and United States, 130
    how often do you talk about chances of nuclear war,
        131
    important for United States and Soviet Union to sign
        arms control treaty, 129
    most people feel that chance of nuclear war has
        increased as consequence of arms control talks,
        130
    1986 as peaceful or troubled year, 3
    predictions for 1986, 2
    strikes will increase in 1986, 4
    your sources of information about problems of rear-
        mament and disarmament, 131
Poverty
    as most important problem, 48, 179, 237
        national trend, 48
Predictions for 1986
    in developing nations, 1
    in industrial nations, 1-2
    in United States, 1
        national trend, 1

R

S

Schroeder, Patricia
  have heard of, 41, 91, 155, 241
  as nominee for Democratic presidential candidate,
    41, 91
Science and math. *See* Public schools, teacher
    shortage
Seat belts
  your use of, 98
  national trend, 98
Senate Finance Committee
  amount of taxes you now pay if Senate plan were put
    into effect, 134-35
  national trend, 135
  approval rating of tax reform program, 137-38
  capital gains would be taxed as ordinary income,
    under Senate plan, 137
  interest on car loans or credit card bills no longer
    deductible, under Senate plan, 137
  no longer able to deduct cost of IRAs, under Senate
    plan, 136
  Senate plan would make for fairer distribution of tax
    load, 135-36
  national trend, 136
  tax shelters would no longer qualify for favorable
    treatment, 137
Services received
  quality of, 59-61
Sewing and needlework
  as favorite pastime, 104
Sex
  traditional or liberal values about, 110-12
Sex education. *See* Public schools
Sexual morality
  official view of Catholic Church on, should be
    changed or not, 232
  priest/professor forbidden by Vatican to teach on,
    232
Sexual violence
  and community standards regarding sale of sexually
    explicit material, 174-76
  magazines that show, 163-65
  and magazines that show adults having intercourse,
    167-69
  and magazines that show nudity, 165-67
  nationwide or community standard in determining
    whether book, magazine, or movie is obscene,
    176
    national trend, 176
  sale or rental of video cassettes featuring, 158-60
  and sale or rental of video cassettes featuring sexual
    acts involving children, 174
  and sale or rental of X-rated video cassettes for home
    viewing, 172-74
  theaters showing movies that depict, 160-63
  and theaters showing X-rated movies, 169-72
Sick people
  involved yourself in helping, 99
  national trend, 99

Social programs
  make cuts in, to reduce federal budget deficit, 43-45
  national trend, 45
Social Security
  makes cuts in, to reduce federal budget deficit, 45-
    47
  national trend, 47
Social service
  yourself involved in, 99
Softball
  participated in, 249
  by men and women, 249
  national trend, 249
South Africa
  absence of television coverage has caused number of
    racial protests to increase, 76
  followed recent events in, 74, 200
  government has made significant progress in resolv-
    ing racial problems, 203-04
  government will grant power to black majority by
    peaceful means, or blacks will achieve power by
    violent means, 204-05
  protest activities have increased in, 76
  United States should apply economic sanctions
    against, 202
  United States should put more pressure on, to end
    apartheid, 200-02
  your sympathies more with black population or with
    government, 74-75, 205-07
  national trend, 76, 207
South Africa, questions asked in
  arms control talks between United States and Soviet
    Union have increased chance of nuclear war,
    130
  chances of world war breaking out, 2
  heard about resumption of arms control talks between
    Soviet Union and United States, 130
  how often do you talk about chances of nuclear war,
    131
  important for United States and Soviet Union to sign
    arms control treaty, 129
  most people feel that chance of nuclear war has
    increased as consequence of arms control talks,
    130
  1986 as peaceful or troubled year, 3
  predictions for 1986, 1
  strikes will increase in 1986, 5
  your sources of information about problems of rear-
    mament and disarmament, 131
South Korea, questions asked in
  arms control talks between United States and Soviet
    Union have increased chance of nuclear war,
    130
  chances of world war breaking out, 2
  heard about resumption of arms control talks between
    Soviet Union and United States, 130
  how often do you talk about chances of nuclear war,
    131

South Korea (*continued*)

important for United States and Soviet Union to sign arms control treaty, 129

most people feel that chance of nuclear war has increased as consequence of arms control talks, 130

1986 as peaceful or troubled year, 3

predictions for 1986, 1

strikes will increase in 1986, 5

your sources of information about problems of rearmament and disarmament, 131

Soviet Union

arms buildup in, increases chances of nuclear war, 14, 107-08

national trend, 108

arms control talks with United States have increased chance of nuclear war, in opinion of twenty-one nations, 130

heard about resumption of arms control talks with United States, in opinion of twenty-one nations, 130

important to sign arms control treaty with United States, in opinion of twenty-one nations, 129-30

relations with, handled by Reagan, 36-37, 153, 259-60

national trend, 37, 260

stronger than United States in nuclear weapons, 78, 79, 120

national trend, 78

United States falling behind, increases chances of nuclear war, 14, 107-08

national trend, 108

U.S. ban on nuclear testing if Soviet Union continues their ban, 108-09

see also Nuclear disarmament; SALT II

Space shuttle

civilian astronauts should participate in future flights, 69

continue manned program after January disaster, 67-68

NASA will be able to prevent such accidents in the future, 68

would you like to be a passenger, 69-70

Spain, questions asked in

arms control talks between United States and Soviet Union have increased chance of nuclear war, 130

chances of world war breaking out, 2

heard about resumption of arms control talks between Soviet Union and United States, 130

how often do you talk about chances of nuclear war, 131

important for United States and Soviet Union to sign arms control treaty, 129

most people feel that chance of nuclear war has increased as consequence of arms control talks, 130

1986 as peaceful or troubled year, 3

predictions for 1986, 1

strikes will increase in 1986, 4

your sources of information about problems of rearmament and disarmament, 131

Speed limit

55-mile-per-hour has saved lives, 134

keep present 55-mile-per-hour, 132-33, 199

national trend, 134, 199

most drivers obey 55-mile-per-hour, 134

what new national speed limit should be, 199-200

you obey 55-mile-per-hour, 134

Sports

which have you participated in, 249

by men and women, 249

national trend, 249

"Star Wars" (Strategic Defense Initiative)

approval rating by 65-and-older age group, 14

develop a space-based system, 268-70

national trend, 270

Strikes and industrial disputes

will increase or decrease in 1986, in opinion of thirty-six nations, 4-5

national trend, 4

Supermarkets

quality of service received in, 59

Supreme Court

confidence in, 275

national trend, 275

ruling that Constitution does not give consenting adults right to private homosexual relations, 214-15

ruling to end pregnancy during first three months, 49-51

national trend, 51

Sweden, questions asked in

chances of world war breaking out, 3

1986 as peaceful or troubled year, 3

predictions for 1986, 1

strikes will increase in 1986, 4

Swimming

boys and girls allowed on same school teams, 28

participated in, 249

by men and women, 249

national trend, 249

Switzerland, questions asked in

chances of world war breaking out, 2

1986 as peaceful or troubled year, 3

predictions for 1986, 1

strikes will increase in 1986, 4

Synagogue

did you attend, in last seven days, 279-80

national trend, 280

Syria

United States should conduct bombing raids against, if Syria commits terrorist acts, 85

T

Table tennis
  participated in, 249
Target shooting
  participated in, 249
Taxes and taxation
  double federal excise on alcoholic beverages, to raise
    revenues to fight drug and alcohol abuse, 271-72
  finance public schools by local property, state, or
    federal taxes, 182-83, 226
  funds for public schools come from property, state,
    or federal taxes, 227
  giving government money to help parochial schools,
    231
  giving government money to help private schools,
    231
  how many cents are wasted of tax dollar spent for
    defense, 78
  increase alcoholic beverage, for public schools, 227
  increase cigarette and tobacco, for public schools,
    227
  increase gasoline, for public schools, 227
  increase income, for public schools, 228
  increase property, for public schools, 227
  as most important problem, 48, 237
    national trend, 48
  public kindergarten supported by, 230
  raise, for local public schools, 31, 227
    national trend, 31
  raise income, to reduce federal budget deficit, 43
  to support child care centers, 30-31
  to support extension of school day for latchkey chil-
    dren, 31
Tax reform
  amount you now pay if new tax bill is passed, 196-
    97
    national trend, 197
  amount you now pay if Senate plan were put into
    effect, 134-35
    national trend, 135
  approval rating of House and Senate bill, 196
    national trend, 196
  approval rating of Senate Finance Committee's
    reform program, 137-38
  capital gains would be taxed as ordinary income,
    under Senate plan, 137
  interest on car loans or credit card bills no longer
    deductible, under Senate plan, 137
  new bill will have positive effect on economy, 198
  new bill will make for fairer distribution of tax load,
    197
    national trend, 197
  new bill will make it less complicated for you, 197-
    98
  no longer able to deduct cost of IRAs, under Senate
    plan, 136

Senate plan would make for fairer distribution of tax
  load, 135-36
  national trend, 136
tax shelters would no longer qualify for favorable
  treatment, under Senate plan, 137
Teachers
  should participate in future space shuttle flights as
    civilian astronauts, 69
  see also Public schools
Television
  absence of television coverage has caused racial pro-
    tests to increase, in South Africa, 76
  confidence in, 276
    national trend, 276
  place limit on amount of time your child spends
    viewing, 29
  require stations carrying beer and wine commercials
    to provide equal time about drinking, 270-71
  as source of information for problems of rearmament
    and disarmament, 131
  watching, as favorite pastime, 104
Tennis
  boys and girls allowed on same school teams, 28
  participated in, 249
    national trend, 249
Terrorism
  approval rating of U.S. raid on Libya, by France,
    Great Britain, and West Germany, 87
  military action against Libya and peace between
    Israel and its Arab neighbors, 86
  more concerned about threat of, 86
  Reagan administration doing as much as it can to
    bring about peace in Mideast, 86-87
  Reagan makes wise use of military forces to solve
    foreign policy problems, 86
  role of Congress in future military retaliation against,
    86
  take military action again, if Libya conducts terrorist
    acts in the future, 84-85
  travel overseas this summer or not, 86
  United States should conduct bombing raids against
    Syria or Iran, 85
  United States should have conducted bombing raid
    against Libya, 85
  what effect will U.S. action have on international,
    85-86
  what role does Kaddafi play in international, 86
  which U.S. actions as principal means of dealing
    with Libya, 86
Theater
  as favorite pastime, 104
Thompson, James
  have heard of, 89, 156, 240
  as nominee for Republican presidential candidate, 90
Thornburgh, Richard
  have heard of, 89, 156, 240
  as nominee for Republican presidential candidate, 90,
    157

Thornburgh, Richard (*continued*)
national trend, 157
Track
boys and girls allowed on same school teams, 28
Truman, Harry
approval rating vs. Reagan and other presidents, 6,
113, 186
Turkey, questions asked in
arms control talks between United States and Soviet
Union have increased chance of nuclear war,
130
chances of world war breaking out, 3
heard about resumption of arms control talks between
Soviet Union and United States, 130
how often do you talk about chances of nuclear war,
131
important for United States and Soviet Union to sign
arms control treaty, 130
most people feel that chance of nuclear war has
increased as consequence of arms control talks,
130
1986 as peaceful or troubled year, 3
predictions for 1986, 1
strikes will increase in 1986, 5
your sources of information about problems of rearmament and disarmament, 131

U

Unemployment
handled by Reagan, 153
as most important problem, 48, 179, 237
national trend, 48
United Nations
arms trade would be reduced by resolution passed by,
88-89
resolution to request all nations not to sell arms to
other nations, 87-88
United States
factors determining America's future strength, 250-53
Iran-*contra* affair has damaged America's influence,
264-66
party keeping country prosperous, 100, 239
national trend, 100, 239
party likely to keep out of war, 100, 238
national trend, 100, 239
satisfaction with way things are going in, 76-77, 124-
25, 208, 237, 263-64
national trend, 77, 125, 208, 264
and Soviet Union *see* Soviet Union
Uruguay, questions asked in
arms control talks between United States and Soviet
Union have increased chance of nuclear war,
130
chances of world war breaking out, 2
heard about resumption of arms control talks between
Soviet Union and United States, 130

how often do you talk about chances of nuclear war,
131
important for United States and Soviet Union to sign
arms control treaty, 130
most people feel that chance of nuclear war has
increased as consequence of arms control talks,
130
1986 as peaceful or troubled year, 3
predictions for 1986, 1
strikes will increase in 1986, 5
your sources of information about problems of rearmament and disarmament, 131

V

Values
traditional or liberal, about sex, morality, family life,
and religion, 110-12
Venereal disease
in instructional program in elementary school, 28
in instructional program in high school, 27
Video cassettes
sale or rental of, featuring sexual acts involving children, and sexual violence, 174
sale or rental of, featuring sexual violence, 158-60
sale or rental of X-rated, and sexual violence, 172-74
Volleyball
participated in, 249
national trend, 249
by women, 249
Voluntarism
involved yourself in charity or social service activities, 99
national trend, 99

W

War
abandoning SALT II will increase chances of
nuclear, 119
arms buildup here and in Soviet Union increases
chances of nuclear, 57
chances of world war breaking out, in opinion of
thirty-five nations, 2-3
fear of, as most important problem, 48, 179, 237
national trend, 48
1986 as peaceful or troubled year, in opinion of
thirty-six nations, 3
Republican or Democratic party more likely to keep
United States out of, 100, 238
national trend, 100, 239
Watergate
Reagan handling Iran-*contra* affair better than Nixon
handled, 266-67
Weight lifting
participated in, 249

Weight training
    participated in, 249
        by men, 249
West Germany, questions asked in
    approval rating of U.S. raid on Libya, 87
    chances of world war breaking out, 2
    1986 as peaceful or troubled year, 3
    predictions for 1986, 2
    strikes will increase in 1986, 4

White, Mark
    have heard of, 41, 91, 154, 241
    as nominee for Democratic presidential candidate,
        41, 91, 155, 242
    national trend, 155, 242
Women
    role of, in Catholic Church, 187
Wrestling
    boys and girls allowed on same school teams, 28